BECOMING

GREAT

UNIVERSITIES

BECOMING
GREAT
UNIVERSITIES

Small Steps for Sustained Excellence

Richard J. Light and Allison Jegla

PRINCETON UNIVERSITY PRESS

PRINCETON AND OXFORD

Published by Princeton University Press
41 William Street, Princeton, New Jersey 08540
6 Oxford Street, Woodstock, Oxfordshire OX20 1TR

press.princeton.edu

All Rights Reserved

Library of Congress Cataloging-in-Publication Data

Names: Light, Richard J., author. | Jegla, Allison, 1993– author.
Title: Becoming great universities : small steps for sustained excellence /
    Richard J. Light and Allison Jegla.
Description: Princeton : Princeton University Press, 2022. | Includes bibliographical
    references and index.
Identifiers: LCCN 2021034198 (print) | LCCN 2021034199 (ebook) |
    ISBN 9780691212593 (hardback) | ISBN 9780691212609 (ebook)
Subjects: LCSH: Education, Higher—Aims and objectives—United States. |
    Education, Higher—United States—Planning. | College environment—
    United States. | Universities and colleges—United States—Administration. |
    Academic achievement—United States. | Educational change—United States. |
    BISAC: EDUCATION / Higher | EDUCATION / Curricula
Classification: LCC LA227.4 .L55 2022 (print) | LCC LA227.4 (ebook) |
    DDC 378.1/980973—dc23
LC record available at https://lccn.loc.gov/2021034198
LC ebook record available at https://lccn.loc.gov/2021034199

British Library Cataloging-in-Publication Data is available

Editorial: Peter J. Dougherty and Alena Chekanov
Production Editorial: Natalie Baan
Text Design: Pamela L. Schnitter
Cover Design: Lauren Smith
Production: Erin Suydam
Publicity: Alyssa Sanford and Kathryn Stevens
Copyeditor: Dana Henricks

Jacket art: Michael Burrell / Alamy Stock Photo

This book has been composed in Garamond Premier Pro

Printed on acid-free paper. ∞

Printed in the United States of America

10 9 8 7 6 5 4 3 2 1

CONTENTS

BECOMING

GREAT

UNIVERSITIES

Introduction and Overview

A few years ago, author Richard Light attended a conference of nearly one hundred college and university leaders in Aspen, Colorado. The first person to share remarks was the longtime president of a relatively small and highly successful engineering college.

As he stepped up to the podium, the president's opening statement was crisp and powerful. "I have one big idea to share. That idea is this: each college or university represented here is perfectly designed to achieve exactly the results it gets," he began. "Think about it. Is there anyone in this room who can make a compelling argument otherwise? All of us have a large number of policies, requirements, structures, and guidelines in place on our campuses. They have taken years—decades, even—to craft and implement. The results that we get, from graduation rates to our students' academic excellence to student satisfaction metrics, all reflect the impact of these *collective strategies*."

The entire large room, with leaders from many well-known campuses of all kinds, fell silent. Many had heard similar remarks about a variety of other fields. Now the application to higher education hit home hard. The president then, having fully captured the attention of his audience, added several important footnotes to his core statement. "Rather than thinking of campuses as static entities, I encourage all of us to remember they are ever-evolving organizations that shape students' outcomes. Therefore, all progress on any campus involves change in a system. Every university leader and faculty member at any campus should consistently ask themselves and each other, 'What is our strategy for continuous improvement?'"

1

When the president finished his remarks, an audience member raised a hand. "This all sounds admirable of course, but what do each of your faculty members, student leaders on campus, and even you personally as president actually *do* to think in terms of continuous improvement?" The president smiled. "I believe you are not posing quite the right question," he said. "Don't ask what I *do*, ask what I am *part of*."

When Light returned to Harvard and the classes that he teaches on the topic of higher education, he wove this core concept into discussions with graduate students. Light also added the idea of how he thinks about core differences between the many American colleges and universities that are genuinely pretty good, in contrast to the smaller number that are widely considered great. Set aside rankings, admissions rates, or endowment size: those American colleges and universities that are universally considered to be exceptional have at least one fundamental thing in common.

The key differentiator is that the many constituency groups—be that campus administrators, faculty, staff, or students—have achieved, or are frequently working toward, a sense of *collegial collaboration*. By that, we mean that each group feels a sense of *shared responsibility* to tangibly enhance their college or university. They are much more than passive participants, drifting around to collect a degree or paycheck. In short (and to again echo the president who spoke in Aspen), they feel that they are *part of something*.

For some years Light has been developing this philosophy of systemic change, together with various concrete and actionable steps a college or university can take, when he visits campuses across the United States. He has recently been joined by colleague and co-author Allison Jegla, who brings the perspective of a younger person focused on higher education innovation. Light and Jegla graduated from the same undergraduate institution, close to fifty years apart. When they began to talk, he as a professor and she as an experienced graduate student, they found that while some details had of course changed at their alma mater, the core philosophy of driving toward evidence-based and sustained improvement had remained steadfast over some decades.

Jegla's professional expertise also draws upon several years of interacting regularly with large numbers of students to help them to learn to think about their own futures in new and bold ways. She works actively to help them make connections with campuses that inspire them to be change agents rather than passive participants. Both authors believe strongly that when campus culture sends signals to each person at a university that they have a special opportunity to make a positive difference, and to enhance the "common good" at their campus, such a culture is especially productive. The authors' shared belief is one principle that brings together all the chapters in this book that follow.

A Framework for the Book

As a professor and longtime higher education researcher, author Richard Light has visited more than 250 colleges and universities. At each, he interacts with campus community members—including administrators, faculty, and students—to learn about how they view their chosen college or university. He asks about the things that make them feel connected to and proud of their campus, as well as those things that are deemed areas for improvement. Throughout those conversations at campuses *of all types*—public, private, wealthy, struggling, large, small, urban, rural—a surprising number of common challenges emerge, especially with regard to the student experience.

The commonalities identified through those conversations form the framework for this book. Each chapter highlights a different core challenge posed by a large number of the colleges and universities that Light has visited. In each chapter, we provide several suggestions— based both on research and our experiences visiting campuses—for *how constituency groups can come together with a shared sense of responsibility* to address the issues. We have made a special effort to include a variety of examples that we believe are genuinely inclusive of the many types of campus groups.

A recurring theme throughout this book is our view that each member of a campus community—from a president or chancellor to faculty to various staff and even including students—each can play a positive role. For example, we believe the impact that student leaders can have for setting a constructive tone at a university is sometimes underestimated. Therefore some of our actionable and quite specific suggestions throughout this book ask students—especially student leaders—to play a central role for initiating positive change. Other suggestions invite advisors and various key staff members to take the lead by trying a new way of doing something. Certainly, many of our ideas and urgings depend upon faculty enthusiasm for making constant efforts to strengthen their students' experiences. Finally, several of the examples we offer will require leadership from the top, from a president or provost or dean, to work well. We intentionally chose all of our examples to be either no cost or very low cost. Our goal is that any campus should be able to afford to implement them.

Each idea is targeted toward increasing the chances that every student who is willing to do some work can have a successful experience, both inside the classroom and outside of the classroom as well. Considering that most students spend roughly 10 to 15 out of 168 hours per week, or less than 10 percent of their time, inside classrooms, the large amount of their time spent outside the classroom should be given the substantial attention it merits. Our hope is that our actionable suggestions will enable each member of any university community to make a positive difference not just for themselves, but also for their broader college community. We hope this book will introduce ways that any campus's leaders, faculty, and students can begin to create methods of thinking that embed the idea of working collegially toward sustained improvement into the very fabric of that campus. In keeping with the spirit of Light's campus visit conversations, we have written this book using a conversational tone.

A core assumption that we make in the forthcoming pages is that every college and university—from the wealthiest and most selective to the least—wants to create more value for students. We believe the key to strengthening *all* campuses is to identify each campus's key goals, assess current strengths and weaknesses, gather high-quality evidence about how well that university is doing, conceptualize and implement new ways of doing things, and monitor progress to ensure positive momentum. As we wrote this book, we kept in mind the remark in Aspen by that college president: "Each college or university represented here is perfectly designed to achieve exactly the results it gets." We would add a footnote: that every member of the campus community has the potential to affect how a college designs and implements its policies. In that spirit we offer the following chapters.

Chapter 1 explores the idea of campus culture and continuous improvement.

One of our core themes throughout this book is investigating how any university can promote a culture that stimulates and inspires continuous improvement. Just about everyone on any campus can support—in the abstract—the idea of encouraging good-spirited innovation. Yet figuring out effective ways to develop an environment where members of the campus community feel motivated to conceptualize and implement new ideas is not always so straightforward.

In Chapter 1, we highlight four quite different colleges and universities that have enhanced their campus culture in different ways. One did so through the creation of a management credential to complement its traditional liberal arts curriculum. Another conceptualized a bold project that ultimately didn't yield the intended results. Still, we view it as a major success because of the unique way this university approached the implementation and assessment phases. A third example features a professor who—because of her personal, creative spirit and the organization of her college—was able to completely redesign the structure of a course that is notorious for being especially traditional. A final example illustrates what can happen when a university is not so successful in building a sustainable sense of community among its members. We present it as a cautionary tale of what can result when a campus culture fractures.

Of course, the examples we describe did not develop overnight. They exist only because of years of work—building trust within the campus community, establishing a system that rewards trying new things even if they don't immediately bear fruit, and devising guidelines that are supportive but not restrictive.

*Chapter 2 offers concrete suggestions for how a
university can help students from under-resourced
high schools navigate the "hidden curriculum."*

A dean of admissions at an Ivy League university recently told author Richard Light a simple anecdote. He fondly recalled how—coming from a working-class family in Pennsylvania and having attended a small, rural high school—he arrived as an enthusiastic, newly admitted first-year student, full of excitement on move-in day at his new university. Upon entering his room, one of four tiny bedrooms situated around a shared common area, he was warmly greeted with a smile and a handshake by one of his three roommates who had already moved in. "Welcome," the young man began. "I assume you are my new roommate; it is a pleasure to meet you. Where did you summer this year?" It was an honest effort to try to get to know his new roommate. Light's friend now laughs as he remembers this initial greeting—which also marked the first time he had ever heard the word "summer" used as a verb. Then the friend recalls, "I found myself wondering at that minute if 'winter' could also be used as a verb?"

Chapter 2 is written to help students, such as this young, newly arriving first-year student who would become a future dean of admissions, to thrive from their first day on campus at any college or university. Success at any college, and certainly at a demanding one, has two crucial aspects. The first is the inside of the classroom component: pursuing academic excellence and doing well in classes. This is of course especially true at a college that emphasizes rigorous courses with rigorous demands. The second aspect is the rest of the experience—capitalizing on campus opportunities, choosing extracurricular involvements, managing time well, developing friendships, and a vast array of other on-campus experiences.

We focus Chapter 2 on students who specifically come to a college from under-resourced high schools. Those are high schools, whether urban or rural, that, due to financial limitations or organizational weaknesses, are not able to adequately prepare students for the two aspects of a demanding college experience. We highlight especially and emphasize the importance of high-quality advising for helping students navigate what has become known as the "hidden curriculum." These words characterize layers of norms and expectations that underlie much of the college experience. Some are as simple as assisting students with choosing courses in a strategic manner. Others require more sustained effort on the part of both advisors and undergraduates. In this chapter we offer a dozen quite specific suggestions for any college to consider. Each has been tried at demanding campuses. All usually work well. Each of our suggestions requires an investment of exactly zero dollars.

Chapter 3 explores the effects of students' decisions about what activities to engage with while at college.

For many undergraduates, college presents an exciting opportunity to independently manage their own time. Each student must make sometimes-difficult decisions about how to spend their precious hours both in and out of the classroom. Chapter 3 introduces both the concepts and trade-offs of *investing vs. harvesting*. We suggest ways that advisors can help students navigate the decision-making process to make productive trade-offs.

Our definition of *investing* is when students try something completely new. They make a new effort, they invest their time, and they give themselves an opportunity to see if perhaps a new talent or interest will emerge. They may try something they had always wanted to, yet never had the chance before. They might even choose to try something so new they had perhaps never even heard of it until they arrived at their college or university. Because the student doesn't yet know how good they might be or whether they will even like the new activity, *they are taking a risk*. Just like investing in the stock market, it is difficult to bank on a precise outcome in advance.

Our definition of *harvesting* is almost exactly the opposite. Harvesting is when undergraduate students continue to pursue an activity or topic at which they already know they excel: something they already have worked at and know they enjoy. Thus, they are "harvesting" the fruits of a seed that has already been planted. Often students' harvesting efforts can be the payoff of years of hard work. For example, a fantastic cross country runner from high school may well continue to pursue the sport at a college and improve his speed under the tutelage of a college-level coach. In this way, he would be building upon his existing strengths.

On campus after campus, graduating seniors report these choices can matter a lot. Many say that juggling a healthy balance between investing and harvesting is a key to both a substantially successful and also a happy experience. Here is where campus advisors can help students who might not find it easy to make important decisions about how to achieve a constructive balance of investing and harvesting, with the goal of helping each student get the most out of their college-going experience. Chapter 3 offers several brief vignettes of what major successes in investing and harvesting can look like. We also offer a series of recommendations for colleges that may want to revise their extra-curricular policies, and to develop new low-cost advising strategies to help students make wise trade-offs. In each case the goal is for each student to achieve a healthy balance between investing and harvesting.

In Chapter 4 we pose the question, "How can a college attract students who may not even be considering our institution?"

We believe every college and university in America, public and private, large and small, rich or not so rich, selective or not, shares a common goal: to expand its reach. When author Allison Jegla was growing up in rural mid-Michigan, attending college out of state was uncommon. With solid in-state options, her experience was that students from her small, rural high school typically opted to attend familiar schools, all within the state, even if the academic rigor was not on par with the students' abilities. This is a phenomenon defined by Caroline Hoxby from Stanford and Christopher Avery from Harvard as "undermatching." Hoxby and Avery demonstrate how it is striking to consider that students from lower-income households who apply to colleges that match well with their achievement patterns are far more likely to reside in or near urban areas. In Chapter 4, we suggest ways that universities can increase the attention they pay to rural students—and, by extension, others who may not be considering a given school—to try to increase their numbers in the applicant pool.

Chapter 4 offers actionable suggestions to university leaders for attracting these students to campus and ensuring their perspectives are shared once there. Two examples of this are increasing support for pre-college summer program partnerships, as well as engaging current undergraduates from underrepresented areas to help with the recruitment process. Some colleges and universities, both public and private, are already doing exemplary work in this regard. We urge in Chapter 4, together with offering specific examples and a quite detailed case study, that their efforts can and should be extended far more widely.

Chapter 5 investigates how great universities encourage faculty to constantly experiment to improve their teaching effectiveness and their students' learning.

Much of the American public and even many prospective college students may not be fully aware of dramatic changes in faculty emphases at some leading universities. As recently as ten to twenty years ago, many new, young faculty members were told directly by their college's hiring committees they should focus almost entirely on *research*. Spending time interacting with undergraduates and concentrating on teaching brilliantly was hardly valued at all. At best, excellent teaching was valued as a distant second to productive exploration in their fields and producing new academic content, including articles and books. Now, to the benefit of current and future undergraduates, these emphases have changed swiftly and decisively.

The overarching point from Chapter 5 is that outstanding colleges and universities now encourage faculty to do systematic inquiry about how to teach their subjects most effectively. To illustrate briefly, the proportion of classes at most excellent universities that were taught using a traditional lecture format just twenty years ago was more than 70 percent. Now, that proportion has dropped to under 50 percent. We anticipate it will continue to drop. Sustained research led by faculty members has demonstrated that classes using lectures are on average less engaging for students. Lectures rarely encourage students' active learning. They rarely lead to students' participation. They often do not maximize learning outcomes.

Chapter 5 presents data on topics including whether cold-calling (calling on students to speak up in class even when they haven't raised their hand and asked to speak) leads to students coming to classes better prepared. We explore if asking students in a class to post thoughts or responses online before a class session, but after doing a reading or a homework assignment, enhances their actual learning in any measurable way. We examine whether a faculty member's establishing some personal connection with each student in a lecture-based class improves their students' engagement. Each of these experiments requires little, if any, financial investment for a university to undertake. The good news is that building such experimentation into ongoing classroom teaching can really pay dividends for enhancing students' engagement and learning.

Chapter 6 is oriented around how universities can determine how much their students are learning.

Strings of A's and A minuses on a grade transcript convey a picture of a successful student. This is excellent. We salute that student. May they prosper. Yet how can others, whether employers, or graduate schools, or any other organization that sees a grade transcript, actually know what a student knows? How can anyone know what a student actually can do? Many campuses—from the most widely known to the least—are now instituting learning goals for majors, academic departments, and often for individual courses. Professors are increasingly asked to specify how they define student success in their classes: what substantive topics, broad ideas, and ways of thinking they hope students will grasp as a result of participating. Chapter 6 conveys a way to constructively think about answering the question, "How well is each college or university succeeding in genuinely achieving its own goals?"

The word *assessment* emerges as a key idea in Chapter 6. Most people view assessment as a synonym for "standardized testing." Many faculty especially dislike the term assessment, because they believe that much of standardized testing cannot pick up the subtleties and innuendoes of what goes on in their classrooms. That is not at all what we propose in this book. *Our entire discussion is completely devoid of any reference to any standardized testing.* Standardized testing simply never comes up in this book. Instead, we believe that since one of the main goals of a university is to teach students, any strong campus needs to think more broadly about how to develop reliable ways to understand how much its students are actually learning. One possibility is designing a methodology to collect information about some element of interest that university leaders care about (for example, whether students can think analytically about key moments in history or have improved their capacity to write effectively while at college).

These findings then can become the grist for faculty discussions about what curricular changes might over time be helpful or constructive for facilitating students' learning. One kind of assessment asks students *what they know now*. A second type gets at the measure of the *value added for students* while they are at the university. A third kind strives to compare *students' responses to different types of questions about their experiences*—both the good and perhaps the not good— while at college. These responses can help a university to initiate plans for systematic and sustained improvement.

Chapter 7 highlights strategies for asking students about their experiences on campus and acting upon their feedback.

Some campuses are beginning to systematically ask undergraduates about their experiences on campus. This is not meant as any sort of test. Rather, it is done to get a clearer sense from the students' own perspectives about what is working well for them versus not working so well. All campuses routinely tout the importance of treating all students with respect. What better way to treat students with respect than to ask them about their experiences, invite their feedback and suggestions, rigorously analyze and synthesize what they say, *and then to take their observations seriously*?

For some colleges and universities, ideas from students have quickly led to constructive and often simple changes in their campus fabric. To illustrate, one campus routinely asks second-semester first-year students, "What is the best bit of advice you got here on campus this year?" They also ask those same students, "Now that you have been here for nearly a year, what advice do you *wish* someone had given to you when you first arrived, but never did?" Clearly, if large numbers of students point to especially valuable or generalizable bits of advice—for example, that they wish someone had pressed them to take at least one small class per semester so they could get to actually interact with and know a minimum of one faculty person better— this can help many advisors to steer future incoming students in a more productive direction.

A bonus here is that some students actually suggest entirely new and imaginative ideas that go far beyond details of advising. For example, Chapter 7 presents a student initiative at Harvard that aimed to introduce undergraduates to a far wider set of faculty members than they might otherwise meet during their time on campus. To help readers get started, this chapter offers a variety of specific questions that any campus could choose to ask its students.

Chapter 8 explores how to promote positive interactions among students from different backgrounds.

Many of America's strong residential colleges and universities are ideally positioned to make the most of students' diverse backgrounds and to promote constructive interactions across the campus community. When asked, students on leading campuses report that they were happy to observe from the very first day that most of their fellow students share certain basic core values and strengths. Like themselves, many of their fellow students (a) work hard; (b) are very good at something; (c) care deeply about education; (d) come to classes prepared; and (e) are on campus because they have earned it both with past accomplishments and with future promise. Otherwise, regardless of their background, students wouldn't have been accepted to the college. When they focus on these shared values and goals, colleges can help students make the most of their background differences and capitalize on the positive effects these differences can have for learning. Colleges should be, and often in fact are, places where—in the optimal scenario—everyone learns, assumptions are tested, and often even unlikely friendships are formed.

To capitalize on this optimistic perspective, college and university administrators need to make organizational decisions about how to inspire constructive collaboration among different groups on campus. Chapter 8 describes differences—sometimes dramatic differences—among campuses in how they choose to develop their campus culture along this dimension. It also addresses a question that many campus leaders find particularly challenging: How can we acknowledge students' identities while being careful not to pigeonhole them into narrow categories?

For example, labeling *all* first-generation college students as young people who are "at risk" (which some colleges routinely do), or designating them as students who should immediately all be put into some sort of special group with special needs, may indeed fit the needs and wishes of some modest fraction of such individuals. For some students this form of "identity" may be terrific and exactly what they want. Yet for many others, it does not respect how they wish to be perceived at their new home. Their own self-definition has frankly little or nothing to do with being the first generation in their family to attend college. They identify themselves and think of themselves in other ways.

Chapter 8 shares both evidence and illustrations of how various colleges and universities have identified and created ways for students from a variety of backgrounds to thrive on their campuses. This is an area of ongoing exploration for many colleges. One of the main points that we emphasize in Chapter 8 is the importance of everyone bringing lots of goodwill to this enterprise. From the first day. This is not a trivial point. There are so many colleges working hard to get this right.

Chapter 9 suggests ideas for a great university to build a strategy for lifelong learning and lifelong engagement.

Every year, prospective college students pack conference rooms in admissions offices at institutions across the country. They then follow hot on the heels of their campus tour guide as he or she highlights unique elements of that particular college. Many of their questions focus on the experience they will have during their time on campus. Aside from broad inquiries about career prospects of different majors at a college, few of the students' questions revolve around how the college will affect their lives after graduation. Students and most parents, perhaps understandably, focus almost entirely on the next four years and often completely ignore the fifty that come after that. Why? Perhaps it is because lifelong learning and lifelong engagement with an institution has not been most campuses' key value proposition. We think this presents a significant opportunity for colleges to differentiate themselves. It offers each campus a chance to convey an honest, heightened sense of long-term worth to prospective undergraduates.

In Chapter 9, we present ideas about how colleges and universities can extend their value for students through high-quality lifelong learning and extended engagement opportunities. Do we anticipate that *all* alumni will eagerly participate in lifelong engagement opportunities? We do not. Yet even if a modest fraction choose to do so, these activities can be hugely impactful both for the alumni and the institution.

We argue in Chapter 9 that college leaders may very well see positive returns from thoughtful lifelong engagement programs that affect their other institutional priorities as well. The colleges and universities that will become exemplars for lifelong learning for the rest of America's campuses will be those that create rigorous, widespread programming to engage students throughout many phases of their lives—perhaps even beginning before a student even sets foot in his or her first college classroom. We offer in Chapter 9 specific suggestions for how any college or university can begin to plant the seed of a lifelong partnership between each student and their university, beginning even before a student starts their first year. Our impression is that as of now, hardly any universities have implemented this way of thinking.

Chapter 10 looks at how universities can prepare students to become globally minded in an increasingly interconnected world.

It is difficult to find a college or university president of a major campus who does not routinely include "teaching our students to think globally" as a major campus goal. Yet if we ask campus leaders, faculty members, and students how best to do this, their answers vary enormously. Should encouraging undergraduates to participate in a study abroad program be a cornerstone? Many campuses seem to think so. Still, undergraduates should consider that there are many alternatives. For example, a steadily growing number of students—the number is soaring at some universities—are choosing to spend their summers working abroad rather than signing up for a study semester abroad during the normal school year. By living abroad during a time when classes are not in session, they still can experience living in a different culture for three months and possibly even earn some money. A second reason is that increasing numbers of students don't want to miss out on the rigorous and demanding advanced courses on their home campus, which for many are what attracted them to their chosen school in the first place.

For some campuses, another way of looking at global-mindedness may mean different methods of teaching about various world cultures here in the United States. Some campuses create specific, focused classes to expose students to international cultures. Other campuses work hard to tuck in an international component to a broad array of more traditional academic fields and classes. These include disciplines ranging from humanities to social sciences and even to some physical sciences.

We pose the question in Chapter 10 to our readers, "How would you know if your campus is succeeding, in terms of helping undergraduates learn to think globally, beyond the more parochial borders of our nation or even a region of the country?" We offer very specific suggestions and even some sample questions that a university can ask its graduating seniors. The responses from students to these questions will tell university leaders how well they are doing with helping their students learn to "think globally."

Chapter 10 offers actual findings from several universities, where the outcomes for students about learning global thinking turn out to be dramatically different. Whether the news about students' level of global thinking at any campus is good or not so good, the faculty at those campuses then become empowered to decide, based on firm and concrete data, if they want to initiate any curricular changes. It is this critical step, the gathering of reliable evidence, that can help to facilitate constructive faculty discussions about potential curricular and pedagogical changes to lead to steady improvements in student outcomes.

Chapter 11 offers a series of specific suggestions to universities that would like to get started implementing some ideas from this book.

We conclude in Chapter 11 by listing several principles to help any college or university begin implementing new ideas as productively as possible. We know that campuses face many challenges on a daily basis. It can be overwhelming to know which novel projects to start or where to dedicate new or additional effort to innovate. As a result, based on our in-depth experiences with dozens of universities, we offer in Chapter 11 several basic ideas for campus leaders, faculty, staff members, and even for students, to get started.

Since Chapter 11 is our closing chapter, readers will have encountered many suggestions throughout this book. They all are presented in "actionable" format. Nearly all of them are—literally—either no cost or low cost. Many of them have already been successfully implemented across at least several campuses. Those are the reasons we chose to include these recommendations rather than others. The ideas generally require someone on a campus, whether the president or a professor or a student leader, to make an effort and get a useful innovation started, often in a small-scale way, to see how well it works for enhancing students' experiences. In our concluding chapter, we convey that sometimes when initiating a new idea and then gathering preliminary evidence about how well it works, "less can be more."

Put another way, if we want to invite students' feedback and responses to their experiences with first-year advising, and if this project is initiated at a large, public university with eight thousand first-year students, is it really necessary to begin our efforts by asking all eight thousand first-year students the same list of questions? We believe not. In fact, we *strongly* believe not. Perhaps start with a truly small fraction of those eight thousand. For example, choose a random sample of just one hundred first-year students. Even that modest number usually will be enough to identify key ideas or experiences— either positive or negative—that are widespread among students.

Our bottom line for getting started is a simple idea. It is just that: "get started." Implement a pilot project. Earn buy-in from faculty, staff, and students. Treasure the small gains and make adjustments (or even big changes) throughout, over a period of time. The important element is to constantly be striving for improvement. This ongoing process demonstrates to all campus community members that they are part of something that is ever evolving, something that they themselves can help shape. Our experience is that this process results in most every person at a university—whether a campus leader or faculty member or staff or even a student—feeling wonderfully empowered to contribute to their university in the best sense.

A Final Note

In most classes, as with the daily work of many university leaders and certainly most faculty members, the focus often tends to be on various specific details. How do we engage students with physics especially well? What is the best way to pair students into small peer-advising groups? How much time are students spending on their economics or biology homework? These details are important. They certainly matter. We will touch upon many of them frequently throughout this book. Yet often each detail comprises a stand-alone question. We encourage efforts to think more broadly. Every college leader and nearly every faculty member can describe how they are striving for excellence on multiple dimensions. But those definitions of excellence usually are linked to relatively narrow details, as opposed to embedding broader, systemic changes that constitute a constant striving for improvement.

In summary, *an overarching theme that guides this book is that excellence is not about being something. It is about becoming something.* Achieving excellence for any college will always be *ongoing*. It will always be *aspirational*. It will always be a journey. Goals will never fully be reached. The effort for continuous improvement will never fully end. Every campus has the responsibility to strive toward always becoming a better university. If the suggestions and collegial ways of thinking we offer in this book help some universities to push forward on that journey, we will view it as a grand success.

1

Encouraging Continuous
Campus Improvement

Building a Culture of Systemic Innovation

A few years ago, author Richard Light took his two grandchildren to see the finals of the U.S. Open Squash Championship in Philadelphia, Pennsylvania. With some of the world's greatest players slated to participate, it was sure to be a display of elite athletic ability.

Light's grandchildren eagerly scoured the program to see if they recognized any of the competitors' names. None of the four finalists were familiar. So, the grandkids pulled out their phones and did a Google search to learn more about them. A common denominator immediately emerged: all four of the top-ranked men and women in the world were Egyptian. Three hailed from Cairo, and one was from Alexandria.

"Grandpa," asked Light's grandson, upon learning this surprising fact. "What is the population of Egypt?" Richard was unsure yet made his best guess of approximately one hundred million people.

The wheels were turning in the grandson's head as he computed. "Well," he began, "let's assume that Egypt has about 1 percent of the global population. If all else were equal, that means the chance of any of the four players competing here today being Egyptian is maybe about 1 percent."

He continued, becoming increasingly excited about the near impossibility of what they were about to witness. "So, am I right? The chance that all four of the top players would be Egyptian is therefore 1 percent multiplied by itself four times. That is almost zero. Meaning it can't happen. Meaning it never happens. Meaning the probability is near zero. Yet here we are, sitting in Philadelphia at the U.S. Squash Championship, and this is what we are now going to watch. How could this happen, Grandpa? I don't get it. This really does defy all the odds."

Smiling at his inquisitive young grandson, Light responded with an insight that he had witnessed time and again in his professional work. "I'd say that it's all about culture—that is the key idea. Excellence in squash is a core value for Egypt and its culture. It has been a core value for many years. In fact, many American universities that seek to recruit talented players for their teams immediately look to Egypt. Children start to play when they are amazingly young, even entering competitive leagues. Boys and girls both participate and often devote a tremendous amount of energy to practicing. In some ways, the definition of pleasure for the entire country is organized around this sport. A love for the sport of squash permeates Egyptian culture to its very core. Far more so in Egypt than in any other country."

Then his granddaughter spoke up and asked if there were some sort of government person, perhaps a sports minister or an education minister, in charge of setting a national strategy to establish such dominance in the sport.

"No, I don't think so," Light replied. "It simply is embedded in the culture. Remember, culture trumps strategy every time. In fact, to quote the late, distinguished management consultant Peter Drucker, 'culture eats strategy for breakfast.'"

A Culture of Innovation

This simple anecdote about Egypt and squash is intended to illustrate a broader point. It is that excellence does not result from a single strategic decision by a university president or other top administrator.

Rather, building and sustaining a campus culture—particularly, as we will discuss in this chapter, one that hinges on innovation and continuous improvement—requires a university-wide, daily commitment to fostering new ideas. It requires a willingness to embrace and promote change. Every member of a campus community has the capability, and arguably even the responsibility, to contribute to building such a culture.

This chapter shares several examples of intentional culture building. The examples illustrate ways that many variations can exist. Readers can decide for themselves which sorts of campus choices and behaviors they especially like and admire, and which choices they perhaps don't like so much. Our goal here is to share several examples of how universities and colleges that most Americans consider quite good, indeed often excellent, grapple with campus issues quite differently. Our hope for university leaders, faculty leaders, and even student leaders is to promote and advance campus culture purposefully, with clearly defined values.

Duke University: Management
Credentials Fused with Liberal Arts

Throughout his career, author Richard Light has visited over 250 of America's colleges and universities. Many of these are small, often excellent liberal arts colleges that for many years have been especially appealing to students interested in humanities or social sciences. During his visits, Light often enjoys asking leadership—the president, or the provost or a dean—about whether their school offers substantial pre-professional training for humanities majors. His question is not whether they have a full pre-law or undergraduate business curriculum, but rather whether there are any opportunities at all for students to learn about the basics of business, management, social enterprise (starting up various nonprofit entities), or law.

The response to his query is almost always an emphatic no. President after president asserts that even if they wish their campus did have such offerings, they might face a faculty revolution if they tried to expand the undergraduate curriculum to include pre-professional options. "Such a concept would be antithetical to our college's core commitment to the liberal arts," one president told Light. After all, faculty believe that their students clearly chose to attend their college because of its current academic offerings. If they had wanted to study any pre-professional topics, perhaps they should have enrolled elsewhere.

We believe strongly in the value of the liberal arts. Yet the fierce commitment to maintaining traditional liberal arts studies, and not welcoming entire new fields as they develop and grow, risks stifling the spirit of innovation on a campus. We are not for a moment recommending that any campus push out traditional liberal arts. Instead, perhaps some imaginative colleges might seize an opportunity to redefine the way their students interact with the traditional subject matter.

An example brings us to Duke University, where Light was visiting to interview college students for his ongoing research on the undergraduate experience. The highlight of this visit came on the second morning as he sat down with a senior in his final semester at college. The student, Nathaniel, was extraordinarily upbeat and enthusiastic about the quality of his three and a half years on campus. As they sat over a cup of tea, Light asked him to elaborate on why that was the case.

Nathaniel shared that he had chosen to attend Duke because it is "one of those rare universities" that would allow him to focus on his passion for theater history, which he described as "an ultimate traditional liberal arts field," while simultaneously being able to learn something about the management and organizational side of any business. Of all the schools where he had been accepted, Duke was the only one where such interdisciplinary study had not only been permitted but actually *encouraged* by the faculty members in the Theater and Theater History departments. At the other colleges, taking business classes as an undergraduate was generally not allowed because it represented a deviation from their quite strict liberal arts tradition. At Duke, Nathaniel proudly explained, he was encouraged by his professors in a classic, humanities and liberal arts field, and who held him to the highest standards, to also learn something about management because he was enthusiastic to do it.

In contrast to many other great institutions, which Nathaniel saw as rejecting the particular college experience that he hoped to build for himself, Duke had gone above and beyond to signal that its culture is one of innovation, and that dynamic opportunities abound. In conjunction with majoring in theater and theater history, Nathaniel had been warmly encouraged by his traditional humanities professors to pursue the rigorous "Certificate in Management and Organizations." In addition to the full demands of his theater major, the management credential required at least five challenging courses, including a capstone class and honors thesis. For Nathaniel, who sought the liberal arts experience with the added benefit of some basics from a truly rigorous business curriculum, it was a perfect fit.

Upon hearing this, Light inquired about the topic Nathaniel had chosen for his thesis in theater. The enthusiastic senior immediately asked, "Professor, what are you doing this evening? I would like to invite you as my guest to see my senior thesis." Light thought he was joking. "Nathaniel, I must not have asked my question clearly. A thesis is a long, written document. I have read many of them. And you just asked me to come and 'see' your thesis. What do you mean *see*?"

With gusto, Nathaniel explained that his senior thesis was his production of *Ragtime*, the Broadway musical from the 1990s written by Terrence McNally. Nathaniel with great pride announced to Light that he considered it a great piece of theater about the African American experience in the U.S. He continued by pointing out his goal, since *Ragtime* had been produced in New York, London, Toronto, Seattle, and elsewhere, was to now give students at Duke the opportunity to see it, enjoy it, and learn from it. In addition to organizing the actors and overseeing the creative direction of the production, Nathaniel had managed many behind-the-scenes elements related to everything from booking the venue to arranging a student orchestra to renting elaborate costumes to arranging rehearsals. All in all, he oversaw about 120 of his peers, including actors, dancers, the lighting crew, costume designers, and technical specialists. His classroom learning had truly been put to the test, to the tune of eight sold-out shows, each seating five hundred people over eight days, for over four thousand total attendees at Duke's Reynolds Auditorium.

Light did indeed attend the production that evening. He was blown away by the level of professionalism and clear organization that had been achieved by this young man in his early twenties. After the performance, Nathaniel finished their interaction by remarking on his gratitude for Duke's organizational culture:

> To accomplish my goals here, I didn't have to fight the culture. I didn't need to argue with any deans or department chairs. In fact, it has been quite the opposite. The culture here encourages learning combinations of skills, which probably is why the four dozen undergraduates who are choosing to study for the Certificate in Management and Organizations just might be the happiest people on this entire campus. They are getting the very best of a classic liberal arts education, while simultaneously learning how to manage, how to organize, and how to lead a group to accomplish a complex set of tasks. My main point is that here at Duke, I am so happy the culture was to encourage my sort of initiative, rather than saying, "Producing a musical show is not what we do here at Duke, because it would not be in the long-term tradition of the classic liberal arts." Duke's innovative spirit and broad way of thinking changed my life and my dreams by encouraging something that few other top-rated liberal arts colleges would have even allowed me to do.

This example clearly illustrates the messaging that different colleges convey to students by making clear what they encourage, what they discourage, and often even what fields for which the faculty might feel some disdain. For Nathaniel, it had made all the difference in his college decision. As a result of Duke's world-class instruction paired with a creative structure, he had been able to gain both vast knowledge and also have the experience of applying it in a real-world scenario and being innovative himself.

University of Texas at Austin: Innovating, Assessing, and Acting on Evidence

Sometimes a campus will try to implement what it believes is a great, creative new idea. Occasionally, things will work out beautifully. Intended outcomes will be achieved, the time line will be adhered to, and everyone will raise a toast at the end and declare victory. In perhaps the majority of instances, though, the road won't be quite so smooth. The project may extend over time, over budget, or not demonstrate the progress that university leadership had hoped to achieve. It is our experience that even in those instances, great universities relish the opportunity to learn from what didn't work and publicly commit to continued exploration. This constant pursuit of excellence strengthens the campus culture and demonstrates to various constituency groups that innovation is a priority. Acknowledging occasional failures or disappointments, learning from them, and moving forward with good spirit to build something better, surely is a sign of a healthy university culture.

The University of Texas at Austin provides one such example. Several years ago, campus administrators wondered if they could capitalize on technological advances to pursue two specific goals. The first was to develop cost-reduction mechanisms in light of a growing national consensus that college was becoming too expensive. The second goal was to rigorously evaluate every component of the undergraduate academic experience, to better understand whether traditional ways of teaching were still contributing to the best possible learning outcomes. Their bold plan was intended to revolutionize the undergraduate experience and serve as a national model for excellence. The University of Texas at Austin has the distinction of being a top-notch public university that also has an enormous enrollment.

"Project 2021" was officially announced by UT Austin president Gregory Fenves in spring of 2016. Within five years, he hoped, half of UT's forty-thousand-plus students would be able to enroll in a redesigned curriculum. It would be constructed from the ground up and based on what actually worked—based on evidence—to enhance learning. A key component was what UT termed "Synchronous Massive Online Courses" (SMOCs). These online classes, filmed in a production studio by UT faculty, could be streamed live to degree and to nondegree students alike. Other elements included a Faculty Innovation Center, the Texas Extended Campus (including courses for high schoolers and oil and gas workers), and a research team to evaluate learning outcomes. Each component addressed a different target audience and had slightly different goals. Unfortunately, those different goals quickly became fodder for confusion.

Within two years, the university decided to pull the plug on Project 2021. Rather than decreasing costs, SMOCs had actually led to much higher spending—and careful analyses found that the new formats showed no clear advantage over traditional in-person classes. Gaps had also emerged between project leaders' vision and what was actually feasible. For example, an effort to create fractional-credit courses to increase efficiency was met with concerns about the cost of updating recordkeeping systems and potential ramifications for financial aid. From an outsider's perspective, it seemed like maybe UT Austin had tried to do too much, too fast, with too little unified planning. Campus leaders understandably were disappointed.

When this sort of "failure" happens in the world of business, it is often no big surprise nor cause for major concern. In fact, studies show that 93 percent of all companies that ultimately become successful have to cede their original strategy after determining that it won't lead to desired outcomes. Importantly, they *still become successful.* By allowing themselves to fail quickly, they bite the bullet and rapidly recover and learn from their original misstep. This plan enables an organization to prevent possibly years of squandered time and money and to move authoritatively toward a more appropriate strategy.

This is exactly what UT Austin did. Their commitment to the ultimate goal of improving student learning outcomes hadn't waned. But they quickly learned that the original plan wasn't what was going to get them there. They had to try a different strategy.

So, in fall 2020, the University of Texas system announced a partnership with the Association of College and University Educators. Working across *eight* University of Texas campuses, efforts would be made to deepen and expand experimentation in classroom teaching and try new ways of maximizing students' engagement and learning. The university's board of regents wanted to try a new innovation to enhance their students' success. And now they are working to accomplish this across the full set of eight Texas campuses, rather than solely at the flagship Austin campus. Will they succeed? We don't know—the results aren't in yet. But we are confident that UT Austin will carry forth its lessons learned from Project 2021 to this new endeavor.

Though they did not achieve desired metrics, Project 2021 and their experiments with designing SMOCs did not dim the university leadership's enthusiasm to continue to try new ideas, to innovate, and to work in a sustained way toward increasing student success. We chose this example purposefully, to *illustrate that a culture of innovation does not arise simply from implementing new ideas.* There also must be an acknowledgment from the very beginning that some new ideas will succeed, while others will not. UT Austin did this from the start. They baked systems of rigorous internal assessment into the very fabric of the project; one of the leaders' doctoral advisees even wrote his dissertation about the SMOCs. Their constant pulse on progress allowed them to determine as quickly as possible that their specific approach was not working. It allowed them to adjust and to shift course with the smallest loss of time and money. Each campus should embed its own plan for assessing and evaluating the impact of each innovation and be fully prepared to alter direction if necessary—and then try again.

As a final note on this example, while university rankings are often criticized for a variety of reasons, we note that UT Austin actually moved *up* significantly in the rankings of major American public universities during implementation and shortly after Project 2021 was terminated due to its lack of demonstrable success. A key component of such rankings is an expert peer review. A series of interviews reveal that this particular example of the University of Texas Austin and its SMOC initiative in particular is widely known and it is admired. Not because of its ultimate success, but because the entire effort conveys that the university promotes an innovative culture that permeates the campus from administration to students. It is the *process*—the practice of trying new ideas, imagining new ways to help students to succeed and prosper, and then evaluating each idea's true effectiveness—that illustrates a culture of creative yet rigorous and demanding innovation for all universities to admire.

Swarthmore College: Harnessing Students' Skills to Solve Real-World Challenges

For many years one prominent feature of the Swarthmore College culture has been its devotion to classic liberal arts. Some students loved it, and some felt the college should do more to connect Swarthmore undergraduates to real-world events and opportunities outside of the classroom. Most students felt that even though such opportunities need not be required, they should at least be offered to those students who wished to partake.

When Lynne Schofield—a Swarthmore graduate herself—arrived to join the faculty, she began teaching several classes in statistics and data analysis. Over the last several years, she has changed the way the college works with the outside world to solve real problems. Specifically, Schofield created statistics classes where the students learn all the principles of statistics—studying in the classroom as hard as traditional statistics classes require—while applying their work to solve real-world problems.

Professor Schofield identified a Philadelphia food bank that was hoping to use some statistical analyses to determine if it was handing out food with an appropriate nutritional profile to needy recipients. She found a blood bank that wanted to increase efficiency and effectiveness in its operations. Her students then got to work on developing their expertise in statistics by solving the actual problems that these organizations were having. They had not been artificially made to be neat and tidy for the purpose of an in-class problem set; they were messy data that mirrored the complexity of real life outside the classroom.

It would have required far less energy and coordination for Professor Schofield to simply teach statistics the "traditional" way—using in-class instruction, textbook reading, and written problem sets. Instead, she puts in an enormous amount of work before each semester to identify projects that will be mutually beneficial for both the students and for the real-world, external organizations. This sometimes requires attending community meetings, using her own network connections, and partnering with on-campus resource centers.

An impressive feature of Professor Schofield's work is not only how she finds the clients for her students to work with. It is that she simultaneously runs careful data analyses on how well her students are learning their course material compared with a control group of students who are learning statistics the more "traditional" way. In other words, the way it is taught at several hundred other American colleges and universities, as well as how it had historically been taught at Swarthmore.

The campus culture at Swarthmore encourages and even rewards Professor Schofield's natural inclination to be innovative. There are no tightly constrained rules, nor a faculty handbook that limits her ability to develop her own curriculum or disrupt "the way it had always been done." This allows Swarthmore—specifically its students— to reap the benefits of Professor Schofield's passion, dedication, and originality.

Professor Schofield's work could not possibly be more aligned with Swarthmore's defined culture and tradition of "giving students the knowledge, insight, skills, and experience to become leaders for the common good." Undergraduates in her course work directly with nonprofit organizations in the community and help them to enhance their capacity while looking at challenges from a new perspective. The projects also aren't always purely statistical in nature; students must call upon their learning from multiple disciplines to arrive at the best solution. Through Professor Schofield's courses, students are learning how to think across subjects, justify their work, and communicate effectively to clients. We see this work as an exceptional application of a true, *modern* liberal arts education that drives enormous value for students.

University of California System:
Fissures in Community

Colleges and universities across America often make a special point to broadcast their "sense of community." This somewhat nebulous quality informs the way that each member of the campus interacts with colleagues on a daily basis and is a cornerstone of the overall culture. It takes a long time to build a strong, positive, collaborative campus community. Rifts can arise quickly in those that lack stability. When this sense of community does break down, especially if it does so in a public way, it is disheartening for everyone involved. At these occasions, college and university leaders need to do some soul searching to identify what happened to the sense of community that is so central to the campus culture.

In March 2020, the COVID-19 pandemic flared into public consciousness across the United States. After an initially slow start, much of the nation began to suspend regular operations. This was reflected at nearly every college and university in the country, whether urban or rural, large or small. The risks to public health were considered grave. Students were asked to vacate campus housing on short notice and return to their homes or residences. Most universities put into place their best efforts to finish up the academic year with online learning.

These unexpected changes led to valiant efforts by hundreds of thousands of faculty across the nation who had never before taught online, nor used distance learning. While grappling with their own personal response to the pandemic, they also were tasked with navigating new online systems, adapting in-person teaching practices to the screen, and developing creative ways to engage their students from afar. The effects of the pandemic also required millions—literally millions—of undergraduates to leave campus, often with only a few days' notice. Those students then had to learn to connect with their colleges and universities, and the online instruction offered by their faculty members, as best they could. Some students faced extra hardship, either because of severely limited finances, personal heath crises, or impossibly difficult home situations that prevented their safe return. Most universities tried especially hard to accommodate these undergraduates who had special circumstances, sometimes helping financially or ultimately serving as hosts while these students stayed for some extra time on campus.

Amidst so much uncertainty and upheaval, it was a time that showed the true strength of some university communities. There are many widely shared examples of graduate students and alumni who created online forums to help undergraduates secure housing, faculty who helped coordinate department responses—with no thought, nor expectation, of additional pay—and alumni who stepped up to donate their airline and railway miles to students desperately in need of a way home. We also witnessed undergraduates helping each other pack their belongings and seniors tearfully bidding each other farewell with no promise of a graduation celebration. On dozens of campuses, several hundred graduate students spent day and night making calls for undergraduates to arrange trips home. Other graduate students spent days drenched in sweat helping undergraduates to carry their belongings to storage areas nearby. All of this was done in a rush. Unexpected acts of generosity were widespread across hundreds of universities. Many received wide publicity. In the face of so much unease and fear, it was in many ways a demonstration of the very best qualities of higher education. People bonded together by shared experience showed up for each other without hesitation.

Meanwhile, at exactly that same time, dozens of graduate students serving as teaching fellows and teaching assistants at five of the University of California system campuses, led by UC Santa Cruz and UC Berkeley, continued a strike they had begun to demand a cost-of-living adjustment. They refused to grade undergraduate papers. They refused to post grades. They didn't step up to the plate when many of their colleges' undergraduate students were on the verge of panic and the nation itself was reeling from a global emergency. These students claimed that their wages were unsustainable. They complained rents were too high. They complained their teaching fellowships were too low. They complained that their universities were behaving too much like a business, caring only about their bottom line and not about the students. These were claims from students who were receiving full tuition scholarships, plus an additional financial stipend on top of the scholarships. One of their few, specific responsibilities was to help full-time faculty with paper grading, and running teaching sessions for undergraduates.

In some ways, it seemed that the universities had indeed failed them. As the pandemic took hold and graduate students were facing housing insecurity and job prospects that had evaporated overnight, UC Santa Cruz fired some of those who had been on strike, using the justification that the students had violated certain existing collective bargaining agreements. Months, if not years, of tension—probably around many issues—had boiled over and created a situation of ill will and hostility.

Our point with this example is emphatically not to pass judgment on what did happen or speculate about what should have happened across those five schools in the University of California system. We don't live there. We don't work there. Instead, we offer this as an illustration of a different kind of university culture, in sharp contrast to our three enthusiastic examples about innovative culture.

At many universities of similar size and standing, the graduate students wouldn't have dreamed of maintaining a strike during such a dire time. Their institutions make them feel like part of something larger than themselves. Their universities emphasize that their presence on the campus is valued, and important, even if not accompanied by heightened financial compensation. Great universities promote a culture that gives graduate students, including teaching fellows, meaningful chances to interact with both faculty and undergraduates. These students are treated as the future academic leaders that they are. These universities also typically are those that attract students for whom pursuing a graduate degree is viewed as a "calling." Most students work to fulfill that dream by carefully selecting a campus that they genuinely want to join and enhance. These are the colleges and universities that are able to innovate in the face of challenges or disruption—their system of mutual respect within their community allows them to quickly bring everyone on board and work toward common goals.

In the case of the UC schools, the striking graduate students built their own community in a different way. Their "subculture" was divorced from their universities' goals. A crisis then exposed and ultimately exacerbated ruptures in the campus fabric. Unfortunately, it was the current undergraduates, many of whom badly needed grades quickly to apply for graduate school admissions or even for jobs, who ultimately lost. Actions from both the universities' leadership and the graduate students had contributed to a great deal of ill will and fury at the affected campuses, to the point where learning felt like a distant goal. Prospective undergraduates, the very people who will be a critical part of defining the university community in future years, take note of such breakdowns when making their own college decisions.

One final word—a positive one—about this example. The University of California system has ten university campuses. Notice that we said five of them had strikes, which means five others—for example UCLA and UC San Francisco—did not. It would be a terrific topic for a doctoral dissertation to figure out how this sharp cleavage in cultures came about. Five campuses where everyone is angry at everyone, led by Santa Cruz and Santa Barbara and Berkeley and Davis and San Diego. And five other UC campuses where there was little such behavior. Why did these differences occur? Can we figure out why some campuses have a community that others seem to lack?

A Final Note

There is no handbook called "Creating a Strong Campus Culture in Three Easy Steps." Instead, developing a community that everyone can be proud of takes a sustained effort from many constituencies, working collaboratively, over a long time period. Like the Egyptian squash example at the beginning of this chapter, each college and university must decide the qualities and values that it holds at its core. It takes concerted and sustained effort to ensure that those core values permeate the campus at every possible opportunity. When this is successful, campus community members will naturally look for ways to improve the college or university that they have chosen to be part of, ultimately realizing that innovation can come from within.

2

Helping Students from Under-Resourced High Schools to Succeed at a Rigorous College

Both authors Light and Jegla arrived at college (the same college, coincidentally—albeit separated by many years) noticeably underprepared. Our respective public high schools, one in the heart of rough, hardscrabble Bronx, New York City, and the other in rural mid-Michigan, did their best with what they had. But their emphasis for students was not on how to succeed at a demanding college. We didn't get suggestions for how to ask questions at any college during office hours, how to study when a final grade depended purely on three written examinations, nor when to apply for internships and jobs. Author Light didn't even know what an "internship" meant when he began college. It became quite obvious to each of us, despite almost diametrically opposed backgrounds, that the sheer rigor of our academic preparation as well had lagged far behind most peers at our shared Ivy League alma mater.

Jegla recalls an introductory chemistry class that quickly became so overwhelming she didn't even know the right questions to ask in order to better understand the material. Despite that, both Light and Jegla worked hard from day one and were highly motivated. We each knew we were every bit as talented as our fellow students who had completed more rigorous high school curricula. The difference was that our learning curve felt much steeper than theirs, because of all the *other* elements that students somehow seemed expected to inherently know when they arrived at college. Each of us eventually prospered in our own way—again many years apart. Along the way, we each became extra sensitized to the challenges some other students who show up at a great university run into at the outset.

College admissions offices across the country are becoming increasingly adept at reaching out to specific new subgroups of students they weren't searching for ten or twenty years ago. One reason is the rise of technology; it is simply *easier* to connect with students in rural areas or to target online marketing efforts specifically to prospective students from certain backgrounds who traditionally rarely even considered coming to certain colleges. Add to this a dramatically increased emphasis on attracting a heterogeneous cohort of students to make up each year's graduating class. Study after study extols the virtues of people from different backgrounds working together, everywhere from the classroom to Wall Street. The data are clear: different perspectives that each student brings to a college from her or his life experiences enhance the richness of a larger group's discussion. These differences, if thoughtfully curated, can lead to new and innovative ways of thinking for an entire group that works together. The result of these shifts is that the student body demographics of just about any college and university in the United States are changing in a sustained way.

It seems quite logical, then, that a growing number of students arriving at college will feel just like Light and Jegla did during their first months on campus. Many are stunningly unprepared for the university experience—usually through no fault of their own—in two main ways. One is a lack of emphasis on sheer, narrowly defined academic excellence. Students in far too many high schools are asked to do far too little. If a high school does not ask its students to write a single ten- or fifteen-page research paper, complete with revisions based on instructor feedback, during their entire four high school years, it is no surprise that a student who is asked to do so for the first time in college may struggle. This is not a commentary about any student but rather a critique of many high schools.

Another difficult component for other new arrivals to campus is the outside-the-classroom experience. Many students from under-resourced high schools emphasize their struggle with navigating their new environment. One student from a particularly weak high school in southern Texas described the five most important words she had learned to utter, from her academic advisor after she arrived at the University of Texas: "I could use some help. . . ." She hadn't been taught during high school how or where to seek assistance when she needed it. Actually, this student reports she never really needed any significant help before arriving at college, because hardly any challenge was given to her by her weak high school.

This second factor—how students approach the unspoken norms of a college environment—is known as the "hidden curriculum." The concept is especially relevant for students who arrive at college from under-resourced high schools. These undergraduates are the focus of this chapter. A quick note: under-resourced high schools can be found anywhere. While many such schools generally are pictured as concentrated in large cities, many under-resourced high schools can be found in suburbs and exurbs. Certainly, there are also many in rural areas. The universality of these types of high schools means that students arriving to college with strong preparation may increasingly be sitting next to students who are wonderfully talented, yet who were unchallenged at their under-resourced high schools.

We have taken great care not to conflate our discussion of poor college-level preparation with any element of a student's identity, whether that might be first-generation status, racial or ethnic background, or parents' income level. There is of course often a great deal of correlation. But we would like to put the power in students' hands to say, "Yes, I attended a high school that didn't prepare me for college nearly as well as some of my classmates. But that weak academic preparation is not at all reflective of what I can accomplish. Now I am here. I am privileged to attend a strong college. I can actually do something about my weak preparation, I am confident I can succeed, and I am eager to capitalize fully on what this college can offer."

Any college wishing to be outstanding owes it to such students to offer useful help. We choose the words "owes to its students" carefully.

Offering such support, in an unawkward way, should be part of any college's core culture. It seems to us unconscionable for a great college to admit talented and motivated students who happened to attend high schools that lacked funding or staff support, and then to basically ignore them. Each college or university needs to figure out how to best advise this subgroup of students who are talented, eager, and willing to work hard, yet also often insufficiently prepared through no fault of their own.

Tying Great Advising to a Campus Culture of Helping All Students to Succeed

When students first arrive on campus, one of the first people they encounter is likely to be some sort of advisor. The presence of someone who has given serious thought to how to help students, particularly those from under-resourced high schools, to succeed is paramount to welcoming them into the campus and its culture. For any campus then, surely it is worth working hard to figure out what the spirit of its student advising experiences should be. Is the overarching goal for an advisor to be universally supportive, no matter what a student says or does? Is it instead to be helpful by suggesting possible courses of action for a student who has a clear goal? Perhaps a more challenging question for many colleges is how to be simultaneously honest with *and* supportive to a student, especially in circumstances where a formal academic advisor may have so many assigned advisees that it is challenging to get to know each one in depth. In this chapter we offer several concrete, near-zero-cost suggestions for advisors at any college to at least consider.

A Student's Account of a Subpar High School Preparation

To drive home how complex and vexing this challenge is, even for well-endowed campuses, we include below an excerpt from a *Washington Post* article in which a student conveys his frustration with an especially disastrous lack of high school preparation.

An undergraduate at Georgetown University, Darryl Robinson writes about his experiences when he first arrived there. He describes his realization about how badly his Washington, D.C., public charter high school had let him down. His words ring true for millions of students in weak high schools across the nation. This article provides an excellent lead-in to an obvious question: Short of somehow "fixing" thousands of weak K-12 schools in America attended by many of America's 52 million children, which no single college is going to do next week nor next month, what specific steps can any college or university take to help less well-prepared students succeed on their campus? We offer *five actionable suggestions* after this brief *Washington Post* article:

I went to some of D.C.'s best schools. I was still unprepared for college.

Entering my freshman year at Georgetown University, I should have felt as if I'd made it. The students I once put on a pedestal, kids who were fortunate enough to attend some of the nation's top private and public schools, were now my classmates. Having come from D.C. public charter schools, I worked extremely hard to get here.

But after arriving on campus before the school year, with a full scholarship, I quickly felt unprepared and outmatched—and it's taken an entire year of playing catch-up in the classroom to feel like I belong. I know that ultimately I'm responsible for my education, but I can't help blaming the schools and teachers I had in my early years for my struggles today.

Even though I attended some of the District's better schools—including my high school, the Cesar Chavez Public Charter School for Public Policy, at the Parkside campus near Kenilworth—the gap between what I can do and what my college classmates are capable of is enormous. This goes beyond knowing calculus or world history, subjects that I didn't learn in high school but that my peers here mastered long ago. My former teachers simply did not push me to think past a basic level, to apply concepts, to move beyond memorizing facts and figures.

Since the third grade, my teachers told me I was exceptional, but they never pushed me to think for myself. And when I did excel, they didn't trust that I'd done the hard work. They assumed I was cheating. Now, only 10 miles from those teachers and schools where I was considered a standout, I've had to work double-time just to keep up. . . .

I ended up at the Cesar Chavez Parkside campus. Cesar Chavez is a prep school where getting accepted to a college or university is a prerequisite for graduation. This is a great goal, but unfortunately, because students are often coming from low-performing D.C. elementary schools, teachers at Cesar Chavez spend a lot of time helping them catch up to the high school level, let alone preparing them for college.

It wasn't until my junior year at Cesar Chavez that I first opened a textbook to learn material that a teacher had not given to me verbally. It was for Advanced Placement Human Geography, my first AP course. (I had to persuade the administration to let me in.) The class was by far one of the hardest I had in high school, along with AP English and thesis, a class in which we did independent research on a public policy issue. Suddenly, I was expected to think about concepts, such as public policy's cause and effect, and apply these ideas to real-life situations. There was no one correct answer; if I could explain my position, I could be correct.

It dawned on me that this was what college would be like. But with less than two years left in high school, would I be ready? Before that class, all the papers I had written were hardly analytical, simply retelling the plot of a book. I felt cheated.

I stay in contact with most of my graduating class through Facebook. Many of my friends are at four-year schools on the East Coast, and they've been through similar struggles in their freshman year. Generally, we agree that our schools did not prepare us, even though they tried. My high school was one of the best I had the choice of attending; compared with other public schools in the District, it made an excellent attempt at getting me ready for college. But any high school administrator in Washington faces a problem similar to my professors at Georgetown: They're stuck correcting the damage done before we got there. . . .

I can now lead discussions in class and have led calculus and biology study groups. I'm getting mostly A's and B's. This dedication leaves me little free time to go out on the weekend or visit home. My grandmother calls me daily to check up on me and offers moral support. My social life isn't as exciting as I hoped it would be because I'm spending so much time studying. But all my extra effort has paid off: I've gone from floundering to finally making it at Georgetown.

DARRYL ROBINSON IS A FRESHMAN AT GEORGETOWN UNIVERSITY
STUDYING HEALTH-CARE MANAGEMENT AND POLICY.

How Can a University Help Shape Students' Experiences?

Colleges and universities need not sit back and cross their fingers that students like Darryl will eventually figure out how to succeed in college. We know most colleges are increasingly aware of this. There are tangible actions that staff and faculty can take to help soften the transition between a weak high school environment and the demands of a strong college. We can offer five concrete suggestions that have been tried at one or more colleges, including some of the most demanding.

Suggestion 1: Offer Incoming Students a Voluntary Session on What Exams Are Like at College

It is not surprising that students newly arriving at college sometimes have little idea both about what to expect, and maybe even more importantly, what will be expected of them—especially in terms of academic performance. The majority have never set foot in a college classroom, completed college-level coursework, or been evaluated by professors during a final exam. For those students, we urge a simple, essentially no-cost, ninety-minute voluntary program that any college could implement for large numbers of incoming students. What we describe is a representation of what Light has witnessed at colleges that have utilized such a strategy.

Before classes begin—for example during most colleges' orientation periods or even during the summer—invite all new students who wish to come, to a voluntary session. A professor arrives (let's say from the History Department), toting a stack of papers. She distributes the previous year's history final exam to every student in the room. It is comprised of five questions, each inviting a short essay response. This is the actual, final exam the professor in front of the room gave to her history class last year. The content will be completely unfamiliar to many of the new students who haven't even attended their first college class yet.

The professor invites all students to look over her final exam from last year. After the freshmen have a chance to skim through the sections, the history professor then hands out copies of a former student's actual short essay responses, which she has received permission to share. The professor's own feedback has been whited out, so the students are not able to see the professor's comments and ultimate grade that she had assigned to last year's test taker.

"I will now be quiet for fifteen minutes," the professor says. "As you read this student's five brief essay responses, imagine that you are in my role. Pretend you are the professor for this class. Please give each response a letter grade and write a brief comment or two about why you assigned that mark. I fully understand you haven't taken the actual course yet. I know you won't yet have studied the coursework for this test. But just do the best you can. We are here today to look at the big picture topic of how you might want to think about responding well to exams."

The students Light witnessed at one college where this took place engaged fully. Almost all began scribbling furiously. When finished, the professor gave each of the students in the room a piece of paper with the actual grades and written feedback that she had given to her student for each of the student's responses to questions on that exact exam.

This exercise allows students to compare their own responses and expectations about "what constitutes a good response" to those of the professor. Now for the first time in their college career, even before formal classes begin, some students begin to get a flavor of what might be expected of them to write a good exam response. After a few minutes, everyone finishes comparing their own "grading" of last year's student and her five responses with what the professor actually wrote for that student. As a final step of this process that takes well under ninety minutes, the professor asks students to raise their hands if their substantive responses and letter grade evaluations roughly match what she had written for her student the previous year. Typically, about a third to half of the students raise their hands. Then, when the professor invites comments from the other half of the students sitting in the room—those who had judged the responses quite differently—one form of comment comes up over and over.

The most frequent response from students in the room is similar to what Darryl Robinson reported he experienced at Georgetown. Students reflect that in high school, they had simply been asked to *summarize* readings. To show they had done the basic homework. And had done the core readings that were assigned. Little new substantive analysis was invited or required. As a result of this simple exercise of reviewing a history exam, the students were able to see that high-level summary—in other words, simple "regurgitation"—would no longer be enough to succeed in a more rigorous college environment. Instead, the professor makes it clear that in her class and at college more broadly, students would be expected to reach their own conclusions. Students at any good college would need to support their analyses with evidence from readings, homework, and in-class discussions. We believe the best part is that the professor hadn't simply asserted these points as abstractions. She invited students to discover it for themselves using a real example and a memorable exercise.

The point here is that students from weaker high schools—many of whom were routinely only asked to show they could regurgitate what they had read—are now learning about a demanding college's expectations for the first time. For many this is a valuable new insight. We should add that while this can be especially groundbreaking for students from under-resourced high schools, *any* student could reasonably benefit from investing a few minutes with such an exercise. The few minutes with this exercise could productively serve purely as a "refresher" after a summer away from the classroom. This sort of practice is especially powerful because of its potential application for *any* college or university. Grand total time taken: ninety minutes of one professor's time, plus a bit of preparation. Cost to the college for this session: a trivial printing or photocopying fee to make copies of papers, and a bit of planning effort. Nearly zero. Rounding error. Truly any campus could do this.

Suggestion 2: Offer Incoming Students Some Simple, Actionable Suggestions for Meeting Productively with Faculty Members

Some of the most powerful interactions students can have at their college or university are with faculty members. In addition to assisting with comprehension of course material, professors can serve as informal or formal advisors. Ideally, they can provide valuable feedback and guidance to students. Any great college or university should encourage its students to meet with faculty members, either individually or in small groups, as much as is realistic for both sides of those conversations.

We find that despite having been told that they *should* attend office hours when they get to college, most high school students are often given very little instruction about *how* to do so. Asking for further clarification on course content, especially from someone that nervous freshmen often assume is an intimidating figure, can understandably be daunting at first. It is also very different from what most students experience in high school, when they either already know the teacher quite well and are comfortable asking casual questions or don't require additional clarification on top of what they get daily in class.

There are some simple tips that colleges can offer for students who lack clarity on how to productively interact with professors—whether professors from their own classes or sometimes others on the campus (many students may not realize that they can reach out to professors other than those whose classes they are enrolled in, if they have a specific question about those professors' experience or work). These suggestions about "connecting with faculty" can come from advisors or even fellow students.

The first point to convey to students is the importance of making an effort to *define a purpose* before going to see a faculty member. As

Light has experienced firsthand, when a student comes to a professor and states, "I know you work in education—I'd love to hear more about that," is an almost surefire way to make a faculty member's shoulders slump. It certainly can transform a potentially spell binding and wonderful half-hour chat into a rushed, awkward, and empty ten minutes of directionless conversation. Faculty members nearly always can tell within two minutes whether a student who comes to see them has made the slightest effort to prepare for a good discussion. Even the most modest preparation sends a clear signal: that a student really does care about having a productive conversation. It also conveys the student has respect for a faculty member's time. A student's responsibility before seeking a conversation with a professor is to *do just a bit of homework* about what that person does, cares about, or what they might have written recently. It should be clear to every student that meetings should have some purpose. Most students know that. Some don't. All should.

Along the same lines of respecting a faculty member's time, students can be coached on how to *make an appointment* with their professor. Unlike in high school, where it was probably commonplace to "stick around and chat with a teacher for five minutes after the class ended," this is not always feasible in college. Students should not assume that faculty members or advisors are sitting around all day each day in their offices waiting for someone to drop in unexpectedly. In fact, this is hardly ever the case, though many professors are delighted to meet with curious students at a predetermined time. After all, most chose to become faculty members in the first place because they want to help shape the next generation.

A final point is to convey information about *college norms* that may be obvious to some students but have never occurred to others. When, for example, should a student send a thank you note? Many faculty have seen vast discrepancies in the way that undergraduates approach the simple topic. For example, each year Light fields requests from multiple students to write a recommendation for graduate study, or to serve as a reference for employment and often for multiple, potential employers. In almost all cases, he says yes. Here are some numbers. Last year thirteen students asked him. When he had finished and sent the recommendations, four of the students wrote Light a short, simple, pleasant handwritten thank you note within a few days. Two sent gracious emails conveying a thank you. Seven did nothing. Conveying gratitude when someone goes out of their way to assist seems like a simple bit of advice. We wonder how often and how widely this simple suggestion for gracious behavior is conveyed to most undergraduates. Writing a thank you note—in any form—when a professor has done you a big favor and invested some of his time to do it, takes just a minute or two. It conveys a lot. It might even be worth several years of future goodwill.

Discussing these simple suggestions with groups of new incoming students might occasionally be slightly awkward. Nonetheless, we find most students are genuinely grateful when someone takes the time to give them a bit of insight about *how* to specifically interact with faculty. Students are perceptive—they are entirely aware these suggestions are offered with enormous goodwill. Even those students who might feel sheepish for a few moments, as they realize they have never written a thank you note, will appreciate it over time. In the end nearly all students understand that the advisor or staff member is offering these ideas for their benefit.

Suggestion 3: Advise Students to Choose Courses That Enable and Encourage Them to Make Mid-Course Corrections

Feedback is one of the most valuable resources for any student. It is particularly helpful to those newly arriving first-years from under-resourced high schools who may feel in over their heads when they get to college. Getting insight as to whether or not they are meeting faculty expectations allows them to make adjustments and mid-course corrections even if things don't get off to a great start. As students work on crafting their class schedule during the first semester, advisors can guide them to look beyond a class title or meeting time, and encourage them to examine the class syllabus in greater detail to understand a professor's intentions for providing feedback.

A simple example would be choosing between two sociology courses, both of which ultimately require thirty pages of writing over an entire semester. One of the two instructors is choosing to require a single thirty-page final paper, due after the last class. The second instructor assigns eight three-page papers, almost one per week, followed by a six-page final essay. For both courses, the requirements add up to thirty pages of final draft writing. It may be tempting for students to choose the first option, since it requires far less sustained effort throughout the semester. This can be disastrous for students with little experience in a college environment or in preparing serious written content.

Choosing a class where the entire grade and all the professor's feedback is built around a single final paper or examination means that a student who gets a poor grade on that one big assignment or test, together with faculty comments such as "You misunderstood the assignment" or "I wanted far more examples," is out of luck. By the time they receive that feedback, it is too late to do anything. Nothing can be adjusted or improved—the course is over. The student is cooked.

Instead, many students can benefit from taking at least a few courses that require several shorter assignments on a regular basis. This structure enables students who get a C on their first one or two papers to make some adjustments based on feedback from the instructor, to try some mid-course corrections, and to convert that grade into a B-plus or even an A on their last several assignments. Rather than doing poorly all semester, they can actually end up doing well and—most important—actually learning more. With many short assignments, each student is given an opportunity to adjust their work in response to both letter grades and some brief written feedback on each paper. This may require a bit more work on the part of the faculty member, yet it can lead to dramatic improvements in the quality of students' submissions and their actual learning outcomes.

Suggestion 4: Instill in Students the Importance of Learning to Work Collaboratively

Particularly for strong students from weak high schools, the idea of engaging in group work during college is sometimes met with disdain. Many high schools don't help students learn how to work together. Students don't routinely solve problems collaboratively or discuss readings outside of classes. In some cases, collaboration on problem solving outside of classes is defined as flat-out cheating.

New students, especially those from weak high schools who may have never worked in groups or whose only experience has been negative, should know that at college many faculty members will ask them, quite routinely, to work in small groups. Sometimes it will be in the context of preparing for classes. In other cases, it will be for livening up class discussions—maybe utilizing debate teams. Sometimes it will be working collaboratively to solve particularly difficult biology or physics problem sets. Whatever the context, students should know that working in groups is "part of the deal," especially at a great college.

Faculty members should be encouraged, if and when appropriate, to remind students that collaborative work is increasingly becoming one of the most important skills for the modern American workplace. Think of Google, Facebook, Snapchat, and Dropbox. Think about consulting organizations such as McKinsey and Bain and Boston Consulting Group. Consider hospitals, banks, and other organizations right down the street from a great campus. Think about many nonprofits—generally targeting their efforts to "do some good for the world"—that need their staff to work cooperatively to maximize impact. Going into an office and sitting alone in a small, private office to write a paper (which is precisely what so many students have learned to do) is the exact opposite of the direction that many workplace environments are now moving and some have already moved.

Professors can also develop exciting ways for group work to be conducted that offer opportunities for students to showcase and hone unique skills. For example, perhaps each member of a large course is tasked with becoming an expert on a particular subtopic during the first half of the semester. Then in the second half, students are put in small groups and given a challenge that can only be solved collaboratively, with participation from every teammate. Group work doesn't even have to mean that several students in a working group all agree on everything. Often reporting several options from a working group, or sharing several different ways the group has come up with to tackle a challenge, is an ideal skill for students to learn.

Suggestion 5: Encourage Students to Make a Deliberate Effort to Meet Peers from Sharply Different Backgrounds

There are compelling findings about what graduating students from strong universities say when asked, "What is the best piece of advice you would give incoming students to help them make the most of the opportunities at this college?" The single most common response from the happiest graduating students is somewhat surprising and certainly instructive for any student beginning a college journey.

The wisdom and advice from the most satisfied graduating seniors is to seek out others on the campus who come from different backgrounds or who don't share one's views. They strongly advise against *only* befriending students who share core features of one's upbringing or beliefs. "That isn't why you come to a great campus," one student notes. "That isn't taking advantage of the amazing opportunities to have students arguing around a table, where 'steel sharpens steel' in discussions with other students whose values and ideas are different from yours. That can often be the most valuable kind of learning imaginable."

There are myriad ways to do this, but sometimes even just planting the idea is enough to get students started. They may have never thought about the need to be deliberate about putting themselves in situations where they specifically get to interact with students who share opposing political beliefs, or others who attended a strong high school that prepared them for college differently. So many students show up at college simply ready to make friends, hoping that the rest will sort itself out naturally. This is perhaps especially true for students who struggle to navigate the hidden curriculum and who, like Darryl from the *Washington Post* article, find themselves with scant time for social events. Advisors could easily suggest to a student that they follow up independently with a colleague in class who raised a differing opinion during a discussion, or that they attend events held by clubs whose members may hold opposing views. These are quite simple, low-effort activities that any student could do if given the idea and motivation.

Students may not often change their minds during spirited conversations and respectful disagreements with peers. Many report a transformative effect nonetheless. For the first time in their lives, they report, being pushed to justify and explain their views, opinions, and values enabled them to more fully understand *why they believe what they believe*. Especially for students who were not asked to do this in high school, the exercise of being pushed to verbally defend—and internally challenge—their beliefs can be a breakthrough educational experience.

A Final Note

We want to underscore the point that the suggestions we propose do not have to be directed exclusively to those students who graduated from under-resourced high schools. Even a student who holds a diploma from an exceptionally demanding high school doesn't know *everything* about how to be a successful undergraduate. Certainly students from the strongest high schools can benefit from being cordially "pushed" by hearing different arguments from a fellow student who holds different views. College is, after all, a time for students to try new things, to fail sometimes, and then to try again. It also is a time for students to occasionally change their mind about something. That is a core point of the whole experience.

3

Investing vs. Harvesting

Encouraging Students to Balance Risks and Talents

Ask any entering undergraduate first-year student about why they decided to matriculate at their given university, and answers will clearly vary. Some may say they are interested in a particular academic subject and are excited to further hone their knowledge of that field. Others are looking forward to continuing to play the sport that they excelled at in high school but at a higher level of competition. Another group may be completely unsure about what they are hoping to achieve from their college experience. Regardless, all students have to make decisions about how they will spend their time on campus.

In this chapter we present a framework for categorizing the many choices students must make while thinking about their college experience. As with other chapters, we do not pass a value judgment on what is a "right" or "wrong" choice, since of course that will vary by each unique student. We hope nonetheless that thinking about developing a structure will help both undergraduates and their advisors to be maximally intentional about crafting a college experience that allows each student to embrace new ideas while continuing to cultivate existing talents.

Defining Investing and Harvesting

Throughout this chapter, we have created the simple nomenclature *investing vs. harvesting* to help students make sense of their options for using their time on campus. To illustrate the practical use of "investing" and "harvesting" in the college context, let's consider a pair of college juniors: Stephen and Joanne. Both entered college intending to major in chemistry and to do something related to science after graduation.

Stephen's high school only offered classes in core subjects. He earned the best grades in his class, and he had been especially looking forward to college and having a multitude of options for quenching his thirst for broader learning. Stephen took a literature class emphasizing the history of science during freshman year. He loved it so much that he decided to major in the subject. He also tried out for and was admitted to an a cappella group after his roommate suggested that he put his shower singing voice to good use. During the summer between his sophomore and junior year, Stephen interned for an investment banking firm and reflected on how much he had enjoyed the analytical nature of the work. He still intends to work with some aspect of science. Yet now he wonders if perhaps there would be a role that better suits his interests within the financial department of a pharmaceutical company. Stephen's actions illustrate our definition of "investing"—when students try something completely new, *investing* their time and taking the risk that perhaps a new talent or interest will emerge.

Joanne is also an aspiring scientist, but her collegiate path has been quite different from Stephen's. When Joanne was in high school, her AP Chemistry teacher asked her to stay after class one day. "You're incredibly gifted, Joanne," she remarked. "I really hope you continue to pursue chemistry in college. You would be good at it, and it seems clear to me you certainly would enjoy it." Joanne took her words to heart, adopting a mentality of "eat, sleep, breathe chemistry" for the vast majority of her college experience. She became president of the Chemistry Club, earned top grades in her Organic Chemistry class, and spent every summer working for a lab that is housed in the medical school. She developed a close relationship with the Principal Investigator and hopes to publish a paper with her during the first semester of senior year. Joanne exemplifies our definition of "harvesting"—he is continuing to pursue something that she already knows she excels at and has since high school. Thus, she is *harvesting* the fruits of a seed that has already been planted.

On campus after campus, graduating seniors overwhelmingly report that juggling a healthy balance between the two students' strategies is a key both to a substantially successful college career and also to a happy experience. Campus advisors can help students make the important decisions and trade-offs about how to achieve a reasonable balance of investing and harvesting to get the most out of their college-going experience. This skill is not only important for a student's time on campus but also extends far beyond into their postgraduate lives.

The Importance of Creative Thinkers

So why are investing and harvesting so important, anyway? Suppose you are an undergraduate with a novel idea for a new invention. You already have interest from investors and are getting ready to pitch the idea during Startup Night at your college. Your team is just missing one thing: a chief marketing officer to help with publicity and branding. You narrow the applicant pool to two options. Candidate A is a very traditional marketing major who has done all the "right things"—she has taken a vast array of marketing classes, worked her way up as an intern at local and then national agencies, and is currently vice president of the undergraduate Marketing Club. As a textbook harvester, you feel confident that Candidate A has the technical chops to help elevate your invention.

Candidate B is also a marketing major and successfully completed the core requirements, but she also diversified her résumé by blending investing behavior into her college experience. A lifelong urban dweller, she decided to spring forth from her comfort zone and work on a ranch in Colorado during the summer before her junior year. Although her role had initially been solely to help with preparing horses for trail rides, she became adept at capturing content with her cell phone camera. She ended up completely revamping the ranch's website and social media platforms. Candidate B spoke about this experience during her interview, and you were impressed by the results she had achieved as well as how fascinating she was as a person. Since you are developing a new concept with limited funding, your team will need to be nimble and respond to challenges quickly. You feel confident that Candidate B would be adaptable and also would strive to infuse new ideas into your work.

The choice between Candidates A and B, we believe, is not completely obvious. In a situation with the requisite resources, the best course of action might well be to invite both students to join your team so that it has adequate depth and breadth. This, unfortunately, is not always possible for a variety of reasons. In any situation involving team building, the decision maker typically has to make difficult choices about the type of background that will be most helpful in addressing their daily challenges.

One of author Allison Jegla's former colleagues, Maya, presents a compelling example of how *seemingly unrelated courses of study have more in common than one would anticipate.* As an undergraduate at Princeton, Maya majored in art and archaeology. Following graduation, she worked in art galleries in Manhattan, then completed a master's degree in art history at Columbia. Soon after, she realized that a career in the art world was not the best fit. Maya attended Johns Hopkins to complete post-baccalaureate work and then went on to medical school and residency at the University of Michigan. She's now a dermatologist. "Do you regret spending so much time focused on art?" Jegla once asked her. "It just doesn't seem all that related to what you're doing now." Maya laughed and then detailed an experiment in which a group of medical students who took a course on how to examine paintings were more likely to correctly diagnose images of medical ailments than their peers who had not taken the course. "You know, I use my art history background almost every day as a physician," she said. "Dermatologists need to be able to quickly distinguish atypical visual cues and identify patterns. I spent years learning how to do that." The college experiences for "Candidate B" and for Maya underscore the importance of investing as well as creative thinking.

People who have pushed themselves to explore new areas often find that doing so makes them even more effective when pursuing their original passions.

What Are Universities Doing Now to Help Students with Investing and Harvesting?

We find stark differences among colleges and universities, regardless of their size or wealth, in how they encourage their students to both build upon existing passions and strengths while also taking some risks. Some college leaders are vocal about their recommendation for students to try new things. Often they emphasize the unique experience of being in college. For example, while president of Ithaca College, Thomas Rochon posted a blog on the school's website reminding students to take advantage of all the college had to offer:

> One of the most common but nonetheless valuable messages we give our students is: "Get out of your comfort zone." It is especially important for new students to hear this, because the only way to fully take advantage of an Ithaca College education is to sample the enormous breadth of experiences that are available. There are a wide variety of courses to be taken, student clubs and activities to get involved in, friends to meet, perspectives to encounter. The college years are a period of remarkable growth for most young adults, and time spent out of one's comfort zone is a significant factor in producing that growth.

Another especially powerful and positive example comes from Akirah Bradley, dean of students and assistant vice chancellor for student affairs at University of Colorado Boulder. We particularly appreciate the way that she not only tells students they should try new things, but actually gives personal examples of investing and harvesting from her own life. She writes for new students who arrive at Boulder:

> I made a life-changing decision last year that required me to step out of my comfort zone, and I bet many of you can relate to this

experience. Last year, I moved from California to Colorado when I accepted the position of associate vice chancellor of student affairs and dean of students at CU Boulder. Of course, I had some reservations about moving to a new state—what if I didn't fit in? What if the culture wasn't right for me? What if I couldn't handle all the snow in the winter? I was pretty comfortable in California, but I also knew I shouldn't let those reservations hold me back from a good opportunity.

I'm happy I made the decision to embrace the unknown, as it has led to a rewarding experience here at CU Boulder. The community could not have been more welcoming, and I'm still able to hike and enjoy hobbies I had in California. I'm actually stepping outside of my comfort zone again this winter: I've signed up for skiing lessons, which will be completely new for me. I'm nervous but excited!

I strongly encourage all of you to go out and try new things. I know how easy it is to stay in your room and text your friends from home, but you end up missing out on so many experiences by staying comfortable with what you already know. You might be happily surprised by what you find you enjoy and who you meet.

Many offices in the division of student affairs, including the Center for Student Involvement, the Cultural Unity and Engagement Center, the Volunteer Resource Center, the Gender & Sexuality Center, Women's Resource Center, and the Rec Center are great resources to start figuring out how you can get involved.

While many colleges make public statements about the importance of trying new things—in our parlance, doing some "investing"— some campuses are in fact organized and structured to almost guarantee that many students become quickly discouraged. Undergraduates are sometimes turned away when they make an effort to try something different for the first time. Some are turned away from *multiple* efforts to join new activities, student groups, teams, or clubs. There are more than a few examples of students who arrive at college, try out to join four new activities, and they are turned away from all four because "they aren't good enough yet."

The Process of Trying Out for Extracurriculars

At times, curricular risks aren't comfortable or even desirable for certain students. New arrivals to campus may prefer to achieve depth rather than breadth, diving headlong into their chosen academic pathway and becoming as close to an expert as is possible between the ages of eighteen and twenty-two. This is perhaps particularly true for students on a pre-professional track who have been told that graduate schools will only accept their candidacy if their résumé looks a certain way. Especially for these focused students—many of whom are hesitant to deviate from the academic profile they had anticipated when entering college—extracurricular activities can be a low-risk way to elevate creativity and to develop valuable soft skills.

Yet earning a spot in a new extracurricular activity is not always as straightforward as some may imagine. Author Richard Light, working with a team of graduate students, found that more than 60 percent of newly entering first-year students at several selective colleges did not know before arriving that they would be required to try out competitively for at least some of the activities they wished to join. They had expected that when they arrived on campus as new students, they could pretty much join any organization or activity group they wished. This does not seem like an outrageous assumption for a student to make. After all, most extracurriculars are an "extra thing." There is no academic credit. They require a great deal of time input, and many ask for a serious commitment from students. So, one might think that pretty much all students who want to join would be welcomed with open arms.

Unfortunately, not all groups at a college can possibly accept every student who applies or tries out—even if they want to. For example, a typical college debate team might only be able to accommodate twelve members. Suppose fifty new students show up the first day. Think of who will probably be accepted. We just shared our view about the importance of each student trying new things and trying to do some investing as well as harvesting. But of those fifty students, maybe four or five were the captain of their high school debate team. Perhaps half a dozen others were not the captain but were still solid members in high school. Meanwhile, the remaining students—though eager to learn—may never have debated in their lives. They might not even fully know the rules of debate yet. Surely one can't fault the leaders of the debate team for choosing the twelve students who seem to be the strongest debaters. After all, debating is a competitive enterprise. Everyone on the debate team wants to perform well in "matches" against other schools. So a new student who simply shows up and wants to learn how to debate, in the good-hearted spirit of trying something new, clearly is at an enormous disadvantage.

Other groups may have constraints on their numbers, based on other factors. For example, many colleges have a small group of students who participate in a student crisis helpline. These volunteers receive phone calls from other students on campus who are experiencing mental health challenges, have just heard very bad news, might be severely depressed, or are even potentially considering self-harm. This is truly serious business. Most colleges indeed do take it seriously. Becoming a student staff member of such a group requires both thorough training and excellent judgment. Clearly these students cannot just be random volunteers. To act responsibly, the organizing group's leaders need to select students who already have certain skills or certifications, or who are willing to go through a great deal of training. To do otherwise would be irresponsible to many fellow students. This is a slightly unusual example, yet it makes the main point that not all students who want to invest in a new extracurricular activity during college can—or should—immediately be accepted into a voluntary, extracurricular group.

So what happens when students try out for an extracurricular activity on campus and are rejected? One Harvard student reflected on the frustration that can arise: "Harvard always says that we have a million clubs, so there's so much that you can do. But in reality, the number of clubs that are completely open to everyone is somewhat limited," she noted in the student newspaper. "College is a chance to experiment and try new things, and [the competitive process] here just makes that profoundly challenging."

Katherine O'Dair, the Harvard College dean of students, invited Light and a team of fourteen graduate students to explore this very topic. They interviewed Harvard students and compared practices with those at many other institutions, including Pomona College, Brown University, Pitzer College, the University of Virginia, Princeton, Georgetown, and Cornell.

The key takeaway from this research was that many students come to campus anticipating their biggest challenges will arise in their formal classes and with their academic work. Of course, that is indeed sometimes correct. Yet to the research team's surprise, a majority of challenges and rejections came not from regular classes, but rather from the "other part"—the many voluntary, not-for-academic-credit extracurricular activities. A simple benchmarking effort with other colleges and universities found that students arriving at those campuses face roughly similar challenges.

How Can Universities Improve Their Efforts to Help Students with Investing and Harvesting?

What can a college or university do, then, to welcome students into extracurricular pursuits, to facilitate the balancing of investing and harvesting? While some campus leaders now encourage students to achieve a balance between building on existing strengths while also trying new things, often this idea is presented in broad terms. For some students, more specific and focused advice about how to actually do this could be helpful. Here are several ideas and suggestions.

Suggestion 1: Think about How Students Can Interact with Extracurriculars; Make Adjustments When Necessary

Light's graduate student team identified five recommendations to improve the process of students' extracurricular participation. None are expensive to implement. We anticipate other colleges may well find some of these suggestions helpful.

1. Encourage student organizations at a college to *develop tiered membership levels* rather than simply using a "you are in or you are out" joining process. For example, a prospective writer

for the student newspaper may not have the time nor the inclination to write the three articles per week all year that are required of a full-time staff member. Instead, they may be more than delighted when invited to contribute one article per week as an associate op-ed editor.

2. On each of the campuses that Light's team contacted, approximately half of the student organizations have open participation (no competitive tryout involved), while the other half have requisite application or audition processes that can involve rejections. Across campuses, examples of open clubs include those such as the College Chorus for singers, the Mountain Climbing Club for those who enjoy mountain climbing, and dozens of religious organizations, political groups, and clubs based on academic or professional interest.

    The recommendation then is *to encourage each new student to select, join, and engage with at least one or two organizations that warmly welcome everyone.* And then that same student should of course feel free to try to join a different one or two competitive groups they find appealing. If they are accepted to one or some limited-admission groups, they are free to leave the open group. If not accepted, they know for sure they have a slot in an organization they themselves chose and are enthusiastic to join. This way each student at college can invest in and try at least one or two new activities, even if other, competitive groups may turn them down for some reason.

3. Student organizations that have full-time members who are fully committed to that organization (such as the student newspaper on campus) should find ways for nonmembers to participate. It is understandable that students who are "all in," meaning they are committed to doing the work and building events and outputs, should become the leaders of campus organizations. Yet surely— staying with the campus newspaper as a concrete example— there can be room for an occasional contribution from a student guest writer, one who contributes an occasional op-ed, or someone who volunteers to cover a specific event, like a campus

speaker or basketball tournament. If the *New York Times* and the *Washington Post* and the *Wall Street Journal* can figure out how do it, perhaps many colleges can too.

It should not be hard to structure such opportunities, thereby creating a tone of both inclusion and welcome that extends beyond the limited membership of any student club. Meanwhile, that new student who writes just three or four guest op-ed articles over her entire first year at college might decide she really loves doing it. In fact, she might even go on to write for the *Washington Post*. This could be "investing" at its best.

4. We recommend *enhanced and thorough communications with incoming students to share more details in advance about the amazing opportunities available to them outside of classes.* This information can include details about a typical level of engagement with each organization, how much time is required each semester since that varies enormously among organizations, and what skills are especially helpful or needed. Finally, each organization should convey whether or not they require a tryout or application process. For example, if the college student newspaper in fact asks every prospective member to write four short articles and one longer, feature-length editorial in the first two months of fall semester, that is their choice. Such a requirement may help the leaders of the student newspaper to see how well new applicants write. Plus, the level of follow-up from applicants can convey how eager each new applicant actually is to do the real work. Our point is—just tell and convey this simple fact to incoming students. There should be no reason for secrets.

5. Student organizations can be encouraged, if they find it a useful idea, to *incorporate a modest level of a "teaching function" for newcomers who want to "invest" and learn a new skill, yet clearly have no experience in an outside-of-classroom activity.* A drama group can have a small number of their more experienced, full-time members devote a fraction of their time and energy to teaching students who are excited to learn how to

act and have literally never tried it before. Same for singing groups. Same for the debate team, where the dozen debaters who all participated in high school debate can "harvest" their own skills by teaching new students who don't even know the precise rules of debating, yet who express a strong interest in learning the rules and getting some experience. While doing this, the new students who are "investing" may decide they want to try out for the college debate team next year, after they have learned the ropes far better.

This fifth recommendation has an upbeat takeaway. It is that if a campus organization has a few members who are willing to harvest their expertise and to devote modest time and energy to teaching, to working with new students who are investing to try to learn new skills, both groups win an enormous amount. The experienced student harvesters are making a major contribution to their college community. The new student investors are learning an entirely new skill that can enrich their lives for years to come. And the bonus comes when both groups of students—those investing and those harvesting—form new and perhaps lasting friendships and bonds with one another around a shared interest. Both the tutor and the tutee have put some effort into working together.

At most colleges, these changes won't happen by themselves even with many students having the best intentions. It might require the office of the Dean of Students, or the Office of Student Affairs, or the Dean of a College to take a lead role in encouraging student organizations to consider these recommendations.

Suggestion 2: Help Students Build a Diversified Portfolio

A diversified portfolio of investments exists ideally to protect one's money against excessive losses. When equities dip in the stock market, having funds allocated elsewhere allows for the possibility of more stability and even alternative gains in a full portfolio. A person with all their eggs in one basket is susceptible to significant loss if their sole area of investment tanks.

In this case, investment strategy is an analogy for students' experiences on campus. The risky approach is when a student focuses the vast majority of their time and energy on a single, narrow academic subject—supplemented by extracurriculars on that same topic. It may pay off if the subject does remain their primary passion throughout college and beyond. But it could also land the student with an inability to easily pivot if their engagement wanes, or if exciting new interests emerge.

To illustrate, one of author Richard Light's undergraduate advisees strode into his office years ago, gung-ho about studying math at Harvard. After spending some time with the student, Light asked what courses he was planning to take for his first semester in college. The student's response? A variation of "Calculus 1, Calculus 2, Calculus 3, Calculus 4." As a seasoned advisor, Light recognized a red flag. Too much of a good thing is, after all, not always such a good thing. He encouraged the student to think outside the box, asking him what else he was interested in, and inquiring about his high school and upbringing. "Think about the classes you've taken for the past four years," Light suggested. "What is something you might enjoy studying that wasn't offered in your high school curriculum?" The student thought for a moment and then recalled how he had spent a lot of time studying water pollution off the California coast with his family while growing up. The student sifted through an enormous number of course choices and ultimately decided on one called "The History of Fish." In that class, he got to study alongside classmates whose perspectives on many topics differed significantly from those of his math colleagues. He got to exercise his brain in entirely new ways. Infusing a bit of investing into his original total emphasis on a strategy of harvesting could potentially make this student a more creative thinker. It also makes him a more interesting person. Who wouldn't want to hear that story during an interview?

Though advising conversations like this one can effectively alter the course of a student's experience, many academic advisors are already balancing massive caseloads. We're not suggesting a blanket solution of "hire more advisors" nor "spend more time with each student." We know doing this is simply not realistic for the majority of college campuses in the U.S.

We have several recommendations for how this idea of investing versus harvesting can be conveyed to students so that they can ultimately find a balance that works best for them and for their unique goals.

Enlist the Help of Alumni for Advising

Students interact with different types of advisors, both formal and informal, as they progress through their undergraduate journey. The formal team may include individuals such as a pre-major advisor, who helps select courses and recommends campus resources, peer (upperclassman) advisor, who helps navigate campus and gives suggestions based on their own undergraduate experience, and a residential advisor, who assists with living arrangements and gives general advice on a more familiar basis. The degree to which these people interact with each other varies by campus, as does the duration that they stay with a student (for example, a student may switch to an advisor in a new department after declaring his or her major).

As she progresses through her time at the college or university, the student may also identify informal advisors or mentors, such as professors, teaching assistants, or other campus staff. These are typically people that the student forms relationships with somewhat organically based on personality fit, common background, or shared interests.

Both formal and informal advisors can provide valuable guidance to students. Yet we find that one piece seems missing from many campuses' strategies. There are not many institutions—though certainly they may exist—that loop *alumni* into the equation as a valued part of undergraduates' formal advising team. These are the people who "have been through it before," and indeed at that same college—they are equipped to speak to the unique context of that particular institution and help students sort through what feels like a whole world of untapped possibilities. This seems a major missed opportunity.

Indeed, who is more equipped to help a student navigate their freshman year than someone who has not only gone through it, at the same college, and who also has the ability to reflect after having spent some time in the "real world"? An alumni presence on any undergraduate's advising team would complement the upperclassman peer advisor's more immediate experience.

An alumnus will be able to expand on the investing versus harvesting conversation, helping to remind the student of how their choices during college can affect the years that lie ahead. They may be able to shed light on certain choices they would have made differently during their own college experience, perhaps encouraging the student to try new things or sometimes to stay grounded by honing a lifelong interest. This alumni perspective is unique. Clearly it has the potential to be extremely valuable for any student. Although every college or university should design programming to fit its unique alumni base, we recommend a fairly structured curriculum for effective advising to make sure that alumni feel like an equal part of the team. This might include an in-person meeting before the undergraduate arrives to college, if the alumnus is from the same geographic region. It could take the form of a get-acquainted video chat meeting with an initial agenda sent out by the university. Video chats are no-cost and easy. Schools should attempt to target alumni advisors who are not that far removed from their own undergraduate experience—likely those between the ages of twenty and thirty if possible.

The question mark that exists for this suggestion—and the one for which an appropriate answer will vary based on the campus context—is about who can best manage the logistics of identifying, assigning, and training alumni volunteers. Possibilities will vary based on the size of the alumni community interested in participating, as well as the number of students in the incoming freshman class.

If the college or university is on the larger side and there is the possibility of the assignment process becoming unwieldy, it may be best to fold alumni mentoring in as a function of the existing Alumni Relations Office. In some cases, this may require hiring an additional administrator or small team to manage the program—so we acknowledge this is not always a no-cost suggestion. These staff members should be able to take advantage of existing alumni listservs and regional interview teams to market the opportunity and secure an adequate number of alumni volunteers. For a college where the first-year class is relatively small, such an alumni advising program could be overseen by regional alumni clubs, often on a volunteer basis.

Engaging with alumni as part of the advising structure serves not only to provide a valuable perspective to the first-year college student; it also enhances the bond that alumni feel with their alma mater (see Chapter 9 for additional thoughts about lifelong learning). Many alumni already appreciate and enjoy the opportunity to interview students for admission. Right now, that is one of the only touchpoints they have with undergraduates. Many alumni hunger for more contact with their beloved alma mater. Including them as part of the advising team allows them to hear about exciting changes at their university and to learn about evolving challenges that current students face. These connections may further catalyze their motivation to give back with their time or even their financial resources. Interacting one-on-one with alumni also primes undergraduates to think about how they will give back to the university after graduating.

Teach Students Intentional Calendar Use

In many cases, students probably won't have thought much about how to balance their time when they arrive on campus. They may assume the methods they used in high school will enable them to complete assignments on time, be adequately prepared for tests and assessments, stay healthy, and have a thriving social life. But what happens when suddenly their entire final grade rests upon one or two tests? How can they capitalize on faculty office hours? Are visits mandatory? How do they still stay in shape without a daily after-school track practice? How does one make new friends when everyone from high school has dispersed to universities all over the country?

In addition to all of these questions, many students arrive on campus wanting to take advantage of the "college experience" by trying new things, meeting new people, and reshaping their identity—

sometimes while trying to reinvent themselves to suit the new setting. It can be overwhelming to balance an onslaught of so much new information with each student's passions and interests.

Most successful students use some sort of system to keep track of appointments, assignments, and class meeting times. Organizational strategies may differ, but let's assume that the most common tool is a simple weekly calendar or planner—either hard copy or electronic. A peer advisor or upperclassman friend can sit down with the student and analyze what is currently on their calendar, marking activities that fall into the category of "investing" in one color and "harvesting" in another. This may sound overly simplistic, yet it can be valuable. If the student's entire calendar is one hue, it signals to a student that it might be time to make some adjustments about how they are allocating their time.

For example, consider a student who was on her high school's cross country and track teams, but considered those activities secondary to academics. Upon arrival at her college campus, she dives headlong into new opportunities—loading up her course schedule and joining as many extracurricular groups as possible. The advisor realizes this when the student reviews and shares her calendar. "I see that you don't have a lot of harvesting on here—is there anything you really loved in high school that you find is missing from your life now?" the advisor queries. The student ponders momentarily and then says, "You know, I used to exercise a lot. That was during high school when the academic work was far less demanding, though. Now, I don't have time to make it to the gym because my schedule is so hectic. These classes are difficult; studying has to be my top priority."

Being "too busy" is a common refrain. We all know it. Many students see the activities for which they get grades or recognition, or for which others are relying on them, as being disproportionately more important. Because the number of hours in a day and a week are finite, students then sacrifice those activities they see as "nonessential": going to the gym, catching up with friends, reading a book just for sheer pleasure. This may be fine on a temporary basis, but eventually it starts contributing to burnout and can even affect the quality of the activities that they had originally prioritized.

This is specifically why doing at least some harvesting is important. Similar to the way reading a familiar book or watching a well-loved movie can bring a sense of security during a stressful time, reverting to an activity that *isn't* new can help to *center and ground a student*. In our example, the student's advisor suggests reintroducing physical activity into her life. The student and advisor consider the calendar together, first identifying a single hour per week that the student will dedicate to running. Just one hour. The student schedules this ahead of time on her calendar, just as she would for lunch plans or a class meeting. The advisor encourages her to maintain the same discipline as she would with plans that she deems more important. She would never fail to show up to class or come to a meeting with a professor; now, similarly, the student cannot be late or cancel these plans with herself.

The student quickly begins to see the positive results of her harvesting. She feels more energized. She realizes that her long runs actually allow her brain to work through some class problems without the pressure of staring at a computer screen. She ramps her exercise up to two hours per week, then three, then five—adding each activity to her calendar in advance and listing it as a firm commitment.

Working through a calendar with a peer advisor may seem like a relatively benign and insignificant activity, but it could have huge positive benefits—particularly for first-year students who are not yet acclimated to the different demands of college. We also find this to be a particularly appealing intervention because it doesn't require a massive investment of time on the part of the student's advisor. The purpose of the calendaring exercise can be easily explained—and the student's current schedule analyzed—within a matter of minutes. Once any student learns a systematic method for tracking their time, she can always choose to either maintain the same structure or make small adjustments based on her personal preferences.

Suggestion 3: Make Advising Appointments More Efficient

At some large colleges and universities, full-time staff advisors can be responsible for large numbers of students per year. With caseloads this large, efficiency is of the essence; the faster an advisor can get to the heart of a question or issue, the more time they can spend actually addressing the issue that matters with a student.

Because the concept of investing and harvesting is not something that is difficult to understand, advisors can ask students to complete a simple exercise in advance of their appointment in order to maximize their discussion time. This could take the form of a template worksheet that can be used, with very little—if any—modification, year after year. A single sheet of paper could be split into two sections: activities or subjects the student has always excelled at or enjoyed, as well as those that they have always wanted to try but haven't yet had the chance. Each header could have three to five bullet points that students are instructed to fill out before the advising appointment. By the time they arrive at their advisor's desk, the student will have already been primed to think about their investing and harvesting goals. The advisor's time and knowledge can then be applied to helping the student find those activities that allow them to strike a healthy balance between continuing to nurture their talents, as well as trying new things.

Time spent interacting with peers can also help students prepare for sessions with their formal advisors. By the time students arrive at college, their only experience in an academic setting—save for any dual-enrollment or pre-college summer classes—will have been at their high schools. We believe this context, which can vary significantly from student to student, plays a significant role in the way that many undergraduates approach their college choices. However, it can often be difficult for students to appraise the opportunities that they had. For those who never transferred high schools, they have a singular reference point. One way to address this may be to create student advising groups comprised of new first-year students. At a freshmen meeting, students can be asked to discuss their high schools and also their plan for college: to share which classes they intend to take and which groups they seek to join. This allows students to hear their new classmates' ideas, make comparisons between everyone's interests, and gain ideas about new classes and new clubs they may not have actively sought out on their own. It also frees up time for the advisor, who can then help guide students after they have already been primed to think about what they seek to maintain—or add or subtract—during college.

We believe that thinking seriously about investing and harvesting is a useful activity for *all* students. It emphatically is not just for those who may be identified as potentially needing extra help academically or those who may not have had role models in their lives to help guide them. This simple exercise may or may not change the course of a student's entire academic trajectory; in fact, we hope it doesn't. Instead, our goal is to help students be just a little more intentional about achieving a balance between nurturing their strengths and trying to find new ones. We hope that it helps both ground students in what is comfortable, while also inspiring them to take a few sensible risks. We do not believe there exists some single "correct" blend of the quantity of investing- and harvesting-type activities. Ultimately, each student needs to listen to their own heart and head to make the decision that works best for them.

Suggestion 4: Connect Learning across Disciplines

Making connections across different ideas and topics can be a big idea for new students at any college. Throughout this chapter, we have described our concepts of investing versus harvesting as though they are separate actions. The ultimate mastery of this idea and—in our opinion—the fulfillment of one's college experience potential, is to learn how to connect ideas or impressions across seemingly unrelated activities or topics.

Imagine a student—we'll call her Elizabeth—who has never in her life played a sport. In fact, she has actively avoided them for the last eighteen years, preferring instead to dedicate her time to academics. Elizabeth has always been rather quiet and fiercely independent. She always felt the results she got on a test were a direct result of the effort that she personally put into studying. She has never had to rely on others because she herself is so capable.

When Elizabeth arrives at college, she decides that she is tired of being labeled as a non-athlete. She wants to embrace the college experience and try something completely new. In other words, she wants to try investing. This seems like the perfect time to do so, because she doesn't know anyone at college yet—failure seems to be of little lasting consequence. Swallowing back her apprehension, Elizabeth walks out tentatively on the field during the first day of women's club rugby practice. "Ten laps—let's go!" hollers the captain, lining the new recruits up at the end of the field. As Elizabeth falls into stride next to her new teammates, she feels the power of a collective. She takes in energy from those around her who push her to persevere through the physical challenge. It doesn't matter if Elizabeth is the fastest or the slowest; the team can only function if everyone puts in the work.

The conversation during the pre-practice warmup and at team social events often shifts away from rugby and more toward academic interests and life experiences. One of the young women on the team is focusing on business. This is a field that Elizabeth never considered because she had not yet been exposed to it as a field of study. The very next semester, Elizabeth enrolls alongside a rugby teammate in a marketing class. She doesn't develop a deep passion for marketing, but she does gain exposure to a new way of thinking that she appreciates. Throughout the rest of college and her life, Elizabeth can call upon pieces of what she learned in that marketing class to give her a unique way to approach new challenges.

Although her intent was initially simply to become a better athlete, Elizabeth has accomplished something very important by choosing to invest: she has now interacted with peers whose perspectives and backgrounds are very different from her own. Elizabeth could easily have arrived at college and surrounded herself with people who share her interests and have similar personalities; she probably would still have learned a lot. Yet now, as a direct result of investing, Elizabeth has become a better and more efficient harvester. She sees what works well in an athletic setting and applies it directly to her academic work. Rather than toil away in the library alone, Elizabeth creates a study group for her math course. In doing so, she ends up making several new friends who expand her understanding of the math subject matter. She also contributes to the rugby team; as someone who has never played before, Elizabeth's fresh set of eyes allow her to ask new questions about strategy that result in making her team more efficient.

A Final Note

At its core, any great college experience should be far more than an instrumental means to an end. Yes, it is a prerequisite for many jobs, but we hope most students do not see that as their sole motivator. College is an opportune time to do just a bit of "fumbling around"—to try new things that seem completely unrelated simply for the pure joy of it all. If a student invests their time trying something new and ends up loving it, count that as a success. In equal measure, we consider it a success if a student invests their time and ends up *not* developing a deep passion for something new. With a constructive mentality, each person can still learn about themselves and about the world from activities they try and decide they dislike. In fact, a reflective student can think deeply about an unfulfilling investing experience and perhaps even incorporate lessons and nuances into their harvesting practice.

Regardless of their personal or family background or high school context, an incoming college student faces a lot of "newness." They are adapting to a novel living situation. Unfamiliar people. New and different pedagogies. Many new students grapple with what can feel like an overwhelming number of options for learning. Formal and informal advisors can help to ease this learning curve by collaboratively providing students with an investing and harvesting framework. Our hope is that students feel supported and emboldened to craft a college experience that builds upon their existing strengths, while also cultivating a genuine love for learning and grappling with new opportunities, that continues for the rest of their lives.

4

How Do We Attract and Support Students Who May Not Be Considering Our Institution?

Rural Americans as a Case Study

Rural areas in the United States have a special place in author Allison Jegla's heart. She vividly remembers one particular meet during a high school track and field season. As she set up her starting blocks for the 100-meter dash, a competitor from a more urban district glanced over at her. "Do you smell that?" she asked, wrinkling her nose. Jegla laughed. "Yeah—it's manure," she explained, gesturing to the dairy farm located right across the street from the high school. "You get used to it."

Cow patties and all, Jegla wouldn't trade her rural Michigan upbringing for anything. At the core, her hometown felt like a truly safe and healthy place to grow up. The members of her eighty-person graduating class had almost all known each other since kindergarten, and bullying felt largely nonexistent (granted, this was also before the days of social media) because the town was simply so intertwined. People showed up for each other, usually without even beginning to fathom that they would receive anything in return. When Jegla decided to self-study for AP tests that weren't offered at the high school, two of her teachers came in an hour early several times per week—with no additional recognition or compensation—to help her prepare. Anytime anyone was sick or a family member passed away, it felt like the whole town rose up in support.

The principal, a 6′4″ former college basketball player who won Michigan's 2020 Principal of the Year Award, greets students each morning with a powerful handshake. "Tell me a story," he prompts— subtly reminding every student that they have something valuable to share. Almost without fail, he can be found pumping iron in the weight room alongside student athletes after school, encouraging every person to give his or her "personal best" both in and out of the classroom. Over time, the school and community built what they now call a "Champion's Culture," and it is—in every sense of those words.

This Champion's Culture comes across perhaps most clearly in athletics, where nearly every single team dominates the conference and wins state championships year after year. The head track and cross country coach—who today remains one of the very best leaders Jegla has ever met—asks his athletes to set expectations, not goals. "Goals are things that we *hope* will happen; expectations are things that we *believe* will happen," he once said. Now, those ideas have become a motto of the program and really of the school. Students are held to a high standard that is engrained in everything they do. It is simply not acceptable to be anything less than respectful, trustworthy, loyal, and hardworking.

Why do we share these details? We do so to illustrate just a handful of the many powerfully positive elements that can define rural schools. This is usually *not* the public perception of these areas—the stereotype is more often that rural schools are underfunded, rundown, and outdated. This is of course true for some, the same as it is true for some urban high schools. But with only 29 percent of rural eighteen- to twenty-four-year-old young adults enrolled in postsecondary education compared to 48 percent of their urban peers, we cannot ignore these areas or simply assert that these students are not ready for a rigorous college curriculum. Students from these schools deserve the same opportunities for education as do students from urban and suburban areas—in some cases it might just take a bit more effort. Higher education prospects should not just be championed for those who can access them most easily.

Throughout this book, we often describe college and university environments that already contain students who hail from all over the United States and even the world. This is the college experience that many high school students dream about: being able to interact with peers from all walks of life who were drawn to that particular campus to pursue their dreams and nourish their love for learning. But how do you achieve such a diverse mix? Especially when many students are never taught to believe that they can or should attend selective schools or those that are located far from home?

This chapter is divided into three sections, all of which focus on rural students as a case study; however, the core principles can be extended far more broadly. The first section outlines suggestions for how colleges and universities can encourage students from rural areas to start to envision themselves at certain types of institutions and sometimes even take the next step to submit an application. The second speaks to rural students' presence on the campus: why their perspective is important and how it can be encouraged. This is also where we respond to a common criticism that introducing young adults to their college options will contribute to brain drain—the phenomenon of the most talented young people leaving and using their resources elsewhere—at great loss to those rural areas. To close, we detail an organization that partners with several outstanding colleges to help prospective students better understand how to navigate the landscape of higher education.

Before diving into this chapter, we want to give a few disclaimers that we think are important:

- First, our goal is absolutely not to suggest that every talented rural high school student should leave their home state and never return. Rather, we believe that giving them the tools to find the college or university that is *right for them* will allow them to begin their path of pursuing personal and professional fulfillment. Then, we hope that they will have the tools and desire to contribute back to their home community in some way. Perhaps they volunteer to help mentor students from their hometown, or maybe they even move back and use their new perspective to effect change in some way.

- Second, we recognize and appreciate that some students simply do not *want* to attend college far from home. They might have deeply personal and compelling reasons for doing so. They may have explored their various options and decided that moving away for college isn't the right move for them at this point in their life. This latter action—informed decision-making and operating from a place of knowledge—is what we want to stress.

- Third, our specific focus is on rural students, but core concepts for rural students can be adjusted—with thoughtful modification—to any presently untapped population.

This chapter has relatively fewer concrete recommendations than the others, largely because the ones we include in other sections in the book—for example, involving alumni interviewers in the application process and encouraging staff to strategically advise students from lower-resourced high schools—can be productively applied when thinking specifically about attracting and supporting rural students.

Section 1: Encouraging Students to Apply

For many students, the choice about where to apply and attend college is driven in large part by geographic proximity. A 2016 American Council on Education report found that at public two-year colleges, the average distance that students are from their permanent homes is 31 miles. At public four-year colleges, the number increases to 82 miles. And at private four-year? 258 miles. Put very simply, location matters.

Students' motivations for remaining near to home, if they choose to do so, are varied. Some feel compelled to stay because of personal family reasons. Others opt to live at home to cut costs and thus need a school within commuting distance. Still others don't buy into the value proposition of attending college far from home or in another state. These choices are personal and should not be minimized, but one thing seems quite clear: the farther you live from a high-quality two- or four-year institution, the less likely you are to attend one. This core fact certainly conflicts with the widely held view that geographic diversity is an important part of the college experience, and it suggests that there is work to be done in helping students to better understand their wide array of options.

To illustrate the point, let's consider two students: Emma and Jacob. Emma lives on a dairy farm in Manhattan, Kansas. Making a list of all the colleges within a fifty-mile radius takes Emma less than thirty seconds. There are four: Manhattan Christian College (four-year private), Kansas State University (four-year public), Bellus Academy (certificate only, for-profit), and Manhattan Area Technical College (two-year public). Compare that to Jacob's experience living in Manhattan, New York. Jacob's wrist starts to cramp as he makes a list of all of the colleges and universities that are geographically proximate to him. Including technical and trade schools, there are over 250 schools within just twenty-five miles of where Jacob lives. Sure, having that many choices within a small area is a bit overwhelming. But, when looking *strictly* at geography and college proximity, Jacob has fewer barriers to entry than does Emma. He can hop on the subway and spend $3 to explore many of the top-notch colleges that surround him. He can then make an informed decision about whether he would like to stay or leave. Emma doesn't have that luxury. She would have to spend much more time and money, neither of which she happens to have in excess, to explore the same number of colleges as Jacob. She also doesn't know anyone else who went out of the state for college, so she has no model for what her own experience could look like. The end result for Emma is that she decides to apply only to the colleges in her area, all of which she gains acceptance to easily due to her stellar grades, strong test scores, and community involvement.

This is a phenomenon known as undermatching: students not attending the caliber of college that their achievements suggest they could.

Suggestion 1: Pre-College Summer Programs— An Answer to Undermatching

Pre-college summer academic programs are opportunities for high school students to spend time on a college campus, taking classes and living in undergraduate residence halls. These programs range in length, typically from as little as one week to as much as the whole summer. Particularly at selective schools, they can be prohibitively expensive or not recognized by the public for what they are—essentially, a tool for students to "practice" the college experience.

In 2013, researchers Caroline Hoxby and Chris Avery published a report with findings that align with this idea. In their work, they examined high-achieving students from various income bands and found significant differences in how students apply to college. They determined that talented low-income students who did *not* apply to highly selective colleges (they call their behavior "income-typical") were much more likely to reside in rural areas or small towns than in urban areas. Somewhat surprisingly, Hoxby and Avery also found that these students were no more economically disadvantaged than those low-income students who did apply (their behavior is considered "achievement-typical"). Rather, the differentiating components are instead

1. whether their high schools are academically challenging;

2. if there is a critical mass of fellow high achievers; and

3. whether students have encountered a high school instructor who attended a selective college.

Those who undermatch tend to be part of high school environments that are lacking in each of those regards. Although these elements may seem like they are intrinsic to a student's high school environment (and thus, hard to change), we believe that Hoxby and Avery's findings are actually quite encouraging. In fact, these three elements convey an almost perfect correlation with the benefits of pre-college summer academic programs.

Academic Challenge

Because pre-college summer programs take place on college campuses, classes can utilize resources that far exceed what is available at the majority of high schools. A course at Cornell Pre-College called "The Fashion Studio: Portfolio Development" invites students to use the school's 3D body scanner and utilize Adobe Photoshop and Illustrator to assemble a portfolio that goes on display in the Jill Stuart Gallery at Cornell's Department of Fiber Science and Apparel Design. Another class, "Brain Basics: Biology to Behavior," at Brown University's Summer@Brown program allows students to get up close and personal with a human brain in the literal sense; they actually get to hold one in their hands. If there are many rural high schools out there that offer those same opportunities, we would love to hear about them.

For students who have cruised through high school earning exceptional grades with relatively low effort, experiencing a rigorous academic environment may serve as a welcome wakeup call. It allows them to understand much more reliably how their current level of preparation may be adequate—or not—for college-level coursework. Importantly, it gives each student a chance to make a "course correction" if they wish. Perhaps a student gets to her pre-college summer engineering course and realizes that her math skills are among the weakest in the whole class, even though she had always received A's in high school math. She returns home and does extra work; she spends the rest of the summer watching videos through Khan Academy and reading ahead in her textbook. Maybe she even signs up for an extra dual-enrollment math class during the academic year. When that student eventually arrives at college, she feels much more confident that her math skills will allow her to dive right into the curriculum.

Critical Mass of High Achievers

Students at selective summer programs hail from all over the world, hold various identities—including racial, ethnic, and religious—and are from backgrounds and socioeconomic conditions that are not always represented within the communities that rural students call home. Hosting students from all backgrounds allows groups to learn from and gain an understanding of each other. Joi-Danelle White-head, associate director for pre-college programs and diversity initiatives at Brown University, notes that their office includes a Student Life team that works to create a residential and co-curricular experience that mirrors the actual undergraduate experience. That way, students are able to get a real sense of what it might be like to attend a college that attracts a diverse undergraduate population.

This was the case for a student named Michelle Zabat, who grew up in Michigan. Before attending a summer program at Brown University in the summer of 2013, Michelle's definition of leadership was antithetical to her own self-perception. "In Michigan, and in the Midwest more generally, I felt that leaders were the loudest in the room who could rally crowds: they were the people standing in the barn with a pitchfork. I've never been like that. My way of moving through the world is that I like to take a moment to internalize and analyze before making a statement." When she arrived at Brown University for her two-week summer program, Michelle suddenly found herself in an environment of peers who were equally excited about learning. "It was the first time I felt like people were really listening to me and that my way of thinking and learning was valued." Michelle later applied and was accepted to Brown for her undergraduate study.

Being around peers who share one's love for learning can be a powerful experience. Even if encouraged by parents, every student at a pre-college program has chosen to take classes rather than a multitude of other things they could be doing over the summer. As one Summer@Brown alumna remembers, attending the pre-college program was the first time that she could sit around a lunch table with people her own age and discuss topics like literature and economics. At her high school, the conversation seemed to focus more on relationships and sports, which was fine in moderation but didn't do much to spark her intellectual drive.

Additionally, providing a venue for students from different high schools, different states, or even different countries to interact and actually live together provides opportunity for vast sharing of social capital and resources. One student remembers complaining about the lack of Advanced Placement course offerings in her rural high school. One of her friends in the program who attended a better resourced high school spoke up and said, "Well, why don't you just self-study and take the test yourself?" Because they were in the same program and actually cared about each other's success, it felt natural for her to share her experience. That idea had never occurred to the rural student. No one in her high school had taken AP tests independently, so teachers hadn't thought to suggest it—or perhaps hadn't even known themselves that it was an option.

Instructor Who Attended a Selective College

Rural high schools are often quite small, with a devoted but fairly standard set of staff members for common subjects. Instructors often teach multiple classes or hold joint appointments as athletic coaches and academic teachers. It's somewhat rare to find someone who has attended college out of state. In fact, research has found that teachers in rural areas are about half as likely to have graduated from top-ranked colleges and universities as their urban peers. Although rural students have the luxury of relatively small class sizes and the opportunity to build deep personal relationships with their teachers, the range of college options that rural high school instructors represent is often quite limited.

In sharp contrast, many of the instructors who teach during pre-college summer programs are also involved with the university during the academic year and have attended a wide range of institutions for their undergraduate and graduate work. Joi-Danelle at Brown speaks to the power of such a diverse and accomplished faculty in terms of what they can provide to high school students. One of her favorite examples involves a high-profile bioinformatics professor who specifically requests to teach high school students during the summer session. His rationale for this is that he wants to introduce the next generation to a field that they may never have heard of before attending the program.

In a pre-college environment where class sizes are often capped and students have vast opportunities to interact with their instructors, exposure to such talented faculty can help give students a wider perspective about their options. For instance, let's say that a student is deeply passionate about political science and has enrolled in a four-week course over the summer. She attends office hours to ask her professor a clarifying question about class the previous day, and they begin engaging in a discussion about the student's longer-term aspirations. The professor gives her insight into how she made her own college choice with political science in mind. She also helps the student understand the colleges and universities that have particularly strong opportunities in the field—including course offerings, networking prospects, and internships. By having the opportunity to speak with someone who has been through her same decision-making process and has emerged as a practitioner and instructor, the high school student is able to make a more informed choice about her own path.

What to Do

We use Brown University as a reference in several pieces of this section because it truly is an exemplar in the pre-college summer program space. In addition to its multitude of course options and deliberate planning efforts around mimicking the college experience, Brown maintains partnerships with community-based organizations and offers generous scholarships to students who meet a certain need-based threshold.

Contrast this to our beloved alma mater, the University of Pennsylvania, which also has robust summer programming. Unlike Brown, Penn offers scholarships only for noncredit options, and only to students who are Philadelphia residents and attend a School District of Philadelphia public or charter high school. At the time of this book's publication, no financial aid is available for the credit-bearing Pre-College Program, where tuition ranges from $11,729 to $17,899 for a six-week program. Students who are able to afford it then have a leg-up when they actually begin college, as they are entering with course credit already on their transcripts. We would love to see more universities, including our beloved Penn, think about how to allocate their resources to include rural students who have financial need.

Whether it takes the specific form of summer programming or not, we encourage colleges to offer funded or partially funded opportunities for new groups of students and for prospective undergraduates to seek out and take advantage of them. Colleges that do this are contributing to a positive systemic change: even if students decide that their summer program institution isn't the right fit for them, they will have learned something valuable about their preferences. This allows them to make a more informed choice about the college that they do end up selecting—which ideally will contribute to it being a better fit and set the student up for success in that environment.

We are not suggesting that pre-college summer programs and scholarships for underrepresented students are a silver bullet solution. Clearly, though, they can be a positive step for expanding opportunities. When we begin to involve groups who historically haven't been part of the campus community—and support them financially—during the summer, it breaks down a piece of the barrier for their future involvement in the full four-year experience.

There are large numbers of students who grow up in small towns, many of whom have never been outside of their home state. Still, they are talented and deeply passionate about learning. How do such students know where to even begin looking at colleges? How can they possibly have a sense of whether they prefer a large or small campus when they have never experienced an environment different from their own rural high school? Similarly, how can the admissions officers at a strong college who read their future application be able to anticipate whether the students will succeed in a rigorous environment? How will the students *themselves* know whether they can succeed, if their only point of comparison is the other students in their small, rural high school? Experimentation during a low-stakes summer program is a great way to develop far better answers to such questions.

At present, perceptions of such programming are not always aligned with the very real benefits. The public often perceive pre-college summer programs as being a cash-cow for the institution. Some see them as catering only to wealthy international students. To be fair, this is how some summer programs actually operate—but those schools have a great deal of potential for involving a blend of students that will enhance the experience for everyone involved.

Suggestion 2: Create Partnerships for Outreach

Rural students are notoriously difficult to reach. An admissions officer conducting a high school visit in an urban area can fly into the most populous city, often for a reasonable ticket price, before driving short distances between densely populated high schools. Over the course of a single day, that representative can realistically interact with hundreds, if not thousands, of students.

But what if his goal had been to reach rural students? That same admissions officer may have opted to fly to a smaller city, which usually costs more, and then spent days traversing the area to give presentations to small groups. The investment of time and effort required per student is significantly higher, perhaps prohibitively so, for many colleges and universities.

Relying on high schools to connect with students is effective in many cases, but they actually might not have the best insight into which students might be great candidates for admission to a particular college. Taking students out of class for information sessions can also be disruptive, particularly for those with smaller class sizes. Many colleges to their credit are already thinking creatively about how they can reach students from rural areas, but we encourage all institutions to push themselves even further. The core questions at play are "Who do students trust for their information?" and "How can we set up a mutually beneficial partnership?"

Community-based organizations are one place to look, as they likely have a deep understanding of their students' interests, as well as their resources. For example, if not every student has access to reliable internet at home, perhaps a live virtual information session is not the best answer. Maybe in that case, the admissions officer could get on a conference call to speak directly with the students by phone. Current students at the college can help colleges to begin to identify what these community-based organizations might be for a given geography. These students, even if just a few, likely have a strong sense of what is available not just in their hometown, but also in the greater region.

Current students headed home for break can be another excellent resource. The admissions office could consider surveying students before spring, summer, and winter break and ask them to self-report if they will be heading home for any duration of time. Those who are interested can then opt-in to schedule a talk in their hometown or a surrounding area and chat with students about their experience. We have seen how a particularly intrepid student even organized a "college night" with several of their friends who also went to an "unusual for this town" type of institution. Other students who wish to pay it forward have hosted informal events at a local store or coffee shop and spoken about their experience to current high school students. Then, when those students return to campus, they meet with the admissions office to show photos and help convey information about the town and high school options that exist. Even if colleges were to give their students a small stipend for completing these talks, it would be far more economical than asking admissions representatives to crisscross the nation trying to find these small, relatively isolated high schools. The admissions officers' time could also then be re-allocated to geographies without *any* undergraduate representation.

Section 2: Suggestions for Engaging Rural Students Once on Campus

One of the most common criticisms of colleges' efforts to attract rural students is the question of brain drain. If small towns are putting all of their finite resources into fueling students' dreams that ultimately pull the "best and brightest" away to college, what happens to the community? Once students get a taste of "what could be," will they ever return the investment that their high schools made? Are colleges actually serving in a predatory capacity if they are trying to lure students from such backgrounds? Although every student is different and will make unique choices, we believe that there are ways that colleges can encourage students to serve as representatives of their hometowns and set expectations for how they give back.

Suggestion 1: Create an Ambassador
Culture for All Students

In their 2009 ethnography, *Hollowing Out the Middle*, sociologists Patrick J. Carr and Maria J. Kefalas arranged students from a rural area in Nebraska into four categories. Their "Achievers" were the students that are typically at the center of the brain drain argument. They were the high-achieving and motivated students who left the state for college and didn't return to their hometown except for the holidays. Carr and Kefalas argued that the town was investing far too many of its resources into teaching and inspiring these students who would never return the favor.

But what if that trope could be shattered? What if we stop seeing these students as deserters who have turned their back on their communities, but rather as ambassadors of all that rural areas have to offer? What would it look like if students stopped feeling embarrassed about where they come from, but instead proud to represent such interesting places and eager to help others understand what life there is like?

How specifically to do this will vary, based on the composition of a college's student body and its overall campus culture. One easy way to foster this spirt of ambassadorship may be to host group orientation sessions where new students are asked to share one thing they are proud of and one challenging thing about their hometown. Once this has been done with a small group of students, session leaders could prompt each participant to carry those ideas with them for the remainder of their college experience. It is a no-cost, subtle, but potentially effective way to signal to students that their stories are worth sharing.

Suggestion 2: Provide Opportunities for All Students to Learn about Rural Areas

We recently read an article in the *Yale Daily News* written by a second-year student, Mckinsey Crozier, who grew up in rural northern Michigan. Two lines in her article have stuck with us in the months since: "I have acquaintances I wouldn't be surprised to see become congressmen, top executives and lobbyists," she writes. "If America's future leaders know nothing about rural areas—which are home to approximately 50 million people, between 15 and 20 percent of the U.S. population—then how will they actually lead this country?" Mckinsey is right.

If you are a professor or college administrator, we encourage you to think about whether the rural voice is included in the majority of the syllabi for which it is relevant (physics, for example, probably doesn't need to include much about rural areas, whereas political science certainly does). Review the student enrollee list and ask students from rural areas if they might be willing to shed light on the topics about which they are familiar. For example, perhaps the topic of a particular class session is a focus on concealed carry laws for firearms. As the debate heats up, a formerly city-dwelling student criticizes the use of such weapons and points to statistics about gun violence in his city. The course leader then prompts for a reaction from students who are from rural areas. One student pipes up to explain how her mother lives alone in a wooded area. The closest neighbor is nearly half a mile away, and the student has experienced how eerie it can be especially at night. While she is at college, it makes her feel at ease to know that her mother—who has taken the requisite gun safety class, routinely does target practice, and keeps a small pistol in a locked box in a safe location—could defend herself in case of an intruder. When this is done well in a college classroom, each student sees and appreciates the other's point and they leave the class with a slightly different lens through which to view a complex issue.

Many colleges and universities provide opportunities for students to engage in hands-on activities both domestically and abroad. These in-depth experiences typically take place during spring, winter, or even summer breaks and allow students to apply what they have learned in the classroom. Some colleges incorporate this experiential learning during the academic year as well; for example, engineering students might learn about product design and then go into their community to work with a local nursing home to learn about resident needs. If an institution doesn't currently have such opportunities in rural areas within the United States, leaders can consider working with students from such areas to establish some. Maybe a student from rural Montana works with the Biology Department and connects administrators with their local wildlife reserve. That student could then serve as the leader for a group of his peers to spend the summer in Montana helping the department classify and study fish species through a paid internship from the college. Many other students would gain valuable biology experience, as well as insight about rural communities. It also empowers the rural students to teach others about their hometowns and simultaneously instills a sense of appreciation from those who may never have experienced something similar. The Urban-Rural Ambassadors Institute at Portland State University and Eastern Oregon University is one such example of a program that has executed on this mission. Each summer, about twenty students from those campuses spend time in both urban Portland and rural La Grange, Oregon. They hear from elected officials and community leaders on issues from gentrification to forest management. The students collaborate with each other and work to bridge the gaps and misconceptions that might exist; ultimately, many report realizing that they face more similar issues in their environments than they might have imagined.

A Final Note

There is one element in particular that will make this work of targeting and supporting students from rural America increasingly important in the years to come. When the COVID-19 pandemic hit the United States, every high school, college, and university in the country had to make very difficult decisions about students' physical presence on campuses. We want to highlight the potential impact on rural students as further kindling for our concern that this population might soon become harder to reach and encourage to attend college than ever before.

A June 2020 report from the Center on Reinventing Public Education examined 477 school districts in the U.S. during coronavirus closures. Fifty-one percent of teachers in cities were expected to provide instruction to all students, compared to only 27 percent of those in rural areas. Many rural school districts found that a major issue was reliable internet access: they simply could not expect students to shift to virtual learning if they didn't have WiFi at home. Though perhaps most pronounced in rural areas, this is a problem that affects more students than some might realize; at least 14 percent of school-age children across the U.S. lived in homes without internet access as of 2017. In addition to not being able to attend classes, this also means that rural students or those who lack connectivity may also be missing out on networking opportunities, advising calls, virtual college sessions, and online campus tours.

If rural students actually become less prepared for college due to lack of instruction or even just *perceive* that they might be compared to suburban or urban peers, that gap may really be felt in the years ahead. Similarly, the pandemic taught us how rural school districts will have to respond to their resource constraints, with evidence that there may be even less support in those areas available to students—particularly in areas like counseling and college advising. This has the potential to be catastrophic for rural students who largely rely on exposure to others when understanding their options and making their college lists. If at least some of those students don't end up making their way to a variety of campuses, where rural students often are already underrepresented, we risk missing out on an entire generation of rural students who would otherwise be able to share their unique perspective. Addressing such inequities should be a priority not in five or ten years, but *now*. Hopefully, rural students—among other groups that often have not been represented on selective college campuses—won't be left behind.

A Powerful Example of Action: The Joyce Ivy Foundation—Equipping and Empowering Students to Make Intentional Choices about Education

The following case study details a nonprofit organization that illustrates what we mean about establishing partnerships to maximize impact and inspire new groups of students to consider particular types of campuses. The Midwest-based Joyce Ivy Foundation has done an admirable job of identifying and supporting students to stretch beyond what they might have deemed possible, all with the goal of achieving personal fulfillment and enhancing both their colleges and home communities.

Overview of the Organization and Original Goals

In the early 2000s, a group of friends came together with an idea. All Michiganders by birth, each had gone on to attend highly selective colleges, including Dartmouth, Brown, Princeton, and Harvard. Their paths to these colleges were defined by a series of fortunate events: a dedicated English teacher, a proactive hockey coach. They deeply appreciated the value of their undergraduate experiences. As one founder remarked, "Princeton opened up the world for me. I remember discovering the *New York Times* at the library. Sure, I could have accessed many of these things from the Midwest, but venturing away and being completely surrounded by peers from all over the world opened my eyes in new ways." They went on to graduate school and successful careers in different industries, but they realized many Midwesterners lacked awareness about the opportunities and financial resources that existed at selective campuses. In their conversations with Midwestern friends, they realized families seemed particularly reluctant to send their daughters farther from home for college, and there was little understanding of financial aid policies that made some of these more selective colleges more affordable for lower- and middle-income families. They also saw that Midwest students were underrepresented on these highly selective college campuses.

They set out to do something about this. How could they inspire Midwest families to consider highly selective colleges? They thought about financing undergraduate scholarships but ultimately decided scholarships were readily available, and also very costly to fund. They needed to figure out how to get young Midwesterners to *apply* for admission and financial aid. If they could get them to see the opportunities at these colleges, they were confident they'd be admitted and receive the financial aid that would make it possible. The friends turned their focus to influencing talented students who *hadn't* yet imagined themselves fitting in at the top tier of colleges and universities.

They identified a slightly unorthodox lever: summer academic programs held at these selective campuses. Students could spend a number of weeks living on campus, studying with peers from around the globe, and taking classes on subjects typically not offered in high school from renowned faculty. In short, it was a taste of the full college experience they had all enjoyed. Scholarship programs existed, but they saw an opportunity to partner with these programs to promote the opportunity to talented young women from the Midwest and contribute to the funding of scholarships for these young scholars.

In 2006, they established a 501(c)(3) called the Joyce Ivy Foundation, named in honor of a founder's sister, with the mission of supporting the academic advancement and leadership development of talented young women. They partnered with a set of college summer academic programs—including Harvard, Brown, and Stanford—and launched the Joyce Ivy Summer Scholars program: a cohort of students, chosen by a competitive application process, who were awarded scholarships to attend one of the partner summer programs. To further target their dollars, the group decided that its Summer Scholars program would focus on young women from lower and middle economic circumstances—since they knew that group was among the least likely to be fully informed about college options but had strong potential for need-based financial aid once they were accepted to a well-resourced institution.

Once the first cohort of scholarship recipients returned later that summer, the founders were struck by feedback about how impactful the experience had been. The students reported that they had learned a great deal about what they wanted for their futures and felt considerably more prepared to make an informed decision about college plans. Fueled by that early success, the Joyce Ivy Foundation grew from providing eleven summer scholarships to students from Michigan and Ohio in 2006 to supporting ninety-two Scholars from seven Midwest states in 2020. The organization now has two paid staff members, a twelve-member board of directors, and two annual in-person college admissions and financial aid events in addition to its scholarship program—which had raised and leveraged over $4.6 million. Scholarship alumnae are over eight hundred strong, and the Foundation's core structure includes a robust alumnae Fellows team and alumnae associate board to provide additional volunteer support to the organization.

Method and Programs

The Joyce Ivy partnership model is based on the principle of cost sharing. The ten partner institutions (as of 2020: Barnard, Brown, Cornell, Emory, Harvard, Johns Hopkins, MIT, Smith, Washington University in St. Louis, and Yale) each contribute approximately half of the tuition and room and board costs for students who have been both accepted to their summer programs and named Joyce Ivy Summer Scholars. The Foundation provides the other portion of funding, which also includes stipends for travel, books, and supplies, totaling approximately $500,000 in 2019. This model allows dollars from both the summer programs and Joyce Ivy to stretch further.

Joyce Ivy–supported summer programs are specifically geared for high school students and feature rigorous, college-level academic coursework as well as social activities, admissions and financial aid presentations, and college preparedness workshops. In many cases, the universities do provide financial aid to some non–Joyce Ivy students, but many participants are paying full tuition. The cost of a two- to ten-week program can range from a few thousand dollars to well over $15,000 depending on the length of the program and whether it is credit bearing.

Summer Program Impact

Each year, Joyce Ivy surveys its scholarship recipients when they return from their summer program as well as when they graduate from high school. In nearly all cases, program alumnae report that their plans for college have been altered as a result of the experience (Figure 4.A; Figures 4.A, 4.B, and 4.C are located in this chapter's Appendix). Most graduating seniors report that participation in a summer program had made them more aggressive in their reach school list (a reach school is one to which a student has a comparatively low expectation of acceptance), confirmed or broadened their interest in applying out of state, clarified academic interests, and increased preparation and confidence for attending college (Table 4.1; see this chapter's Appendix). A quote from a 2019 Summer Scholar illustrates the point:

> I am beyond grateful for my Joyce Ivy experience. Before my summer program, I was mostly planning on staying in state and getting a good scholarship. However, my experience at Brown taught me that I was beyond comfortable

and capable in a more prestigious environment. I loved the diversity of the people, the engaging conversations in and out of class, the opportunity, and the challenge. After my summer program, I was confident enough to apply to many top-tier schools. I was even fortunate enough to get a full scholarship to my dream school—Duke; this is something that I never even would have DREAMED of before Joyce Ivy. I genuinely attribute much of my college application success to the opportunity provided to me by the Joyce Ivy Foundation. Thank you with all of my heart.

Throughout the past five years, only a very small percentage of students (likely merit scholarship recipients) reported that they would have been able to attend their exact program without financial support from Joyce Ivy (Figure 4.B). These data further emphasize the power that Joyce Ivy has in affecting students who may otherwise undermatch during the college application process.

Summer Is Only the Start

After about six years of solely providing pre-college scholarships, the Joyce Ivy Foundation tapped into its deep set of relationships with admissions professionals and launched in-person events for counselors, students, and their parents. These sessions are free of charge and draw hundreds of participants each year. Admissions professionals from a variety of institutions, including Amherst, Barnard, Brown, Dartmouth, Harvard, Johns Hopkins, the University of Pennsylvania, Princeton, and Yale speak with attendees about specific pieces of the application process. Past sessions have included topics like "How to Make Your Application Stand Out," "Generating Your College List: How to Find the Right Fit," and "Understanding the Numbers: A Financial Aid Case

Study." For a set of schools that generally feel out of reach for many students from Joyce Ivy target geographies, meeting the actual people who read applications and learning about admissions and financial aid directly from them goes a long way in demystifying an often-misunderstood process. "When admissions office representatives participate in the Joyce Ivy program, it humanizes the application process," said one higher education partner. "In these events, we are able to reinforce the message that highly selective institutions are a possibility for participants. We appreciate the many opportunities that Joyce Ivy provides in terms of information and experiences that support students making an informed choice about their college education."

A group of the event attendees (though certainly not a majority) are Joyce Ivy scholarship recipients, for whom Joyce Ivy–hosted programming is only one example of what is available to them through their participation in the community. The moment students are named Joyce Ivy Summer Scholars, they are placed into a powerful peer and professional network that supports them with information and connection well into college and beyond. The formalized Fellows program and associate board also provide alumnae the opportunity to hone leadership skills and develop strong friendships with peers while helping the Foundation prosper.

One Scholar's Story

Originally from a small town in Michigan, Anne Gentry (a 2010 Joyce Ivy Summer Scholar) attended Summer@Brown and took a course in art history: a subject that was not offered at her high school. She applied to Brown under its Early Decision policy and graduated with a degree in comparative literature in 2016. Anne currently serves as the executive director of her hometown's Downtown Development Authority, where she works on improving the district through historic preservation, promotional events, marketing, business recruitment, and aesthetic enhancements. We find her story particularly compelling, as she took an opportunity to expand her own perspective before returning to enhance her community in a way that is incredibly unique.

Please describe what your Joyce Ivy summer experience meant to you.

Where to start? My life path would be unbelievably different if Joyce Ivy had not been a part of it. Before I received the scholarship, I never dreamed of even attempting to apply to an Ivy League, East Coast school—let alone had the confidence that I had a shot at getting in. Without Joyce Ivy, I never would have attempted to apply to Brown. Meeting so many friends from vastly different experiences and upbringings than mine, I realized that my experiences from small-town America were equally as valid, and interesting, and meaningful—something that truly I have carried with me as a core value since then. So many people that I meet that live and grew up here believe that "it's just a small town," "there's nothing special here," "I could never be as successful as someone who grew up in the city." That belief—and my work to dispel it and instill in others that this place is valuable—drew me to the career I'm in now (community and downtown development). In my work and personal life, I always try to show that people who grow up in places like Alpena are capable of anything that anyone else is who grew up elsewhere—and that choosing to live here after college isn't a "lesser" form of experience, but just as meaningful if you find purpose in it.

When I attended Summer at Brown, I fell in love with Brown's value for open and liberal learning, their commitment to a diverse student body, and their holistic approach to education and experiences. Because of that, Brown was my first choice, and I attended there and received my bachelor's degree in 2015. Joyce Ivy introduced me to a whole world and approach of education that I never knew existed—and gave me the confidence to go there and thrive. Since college, I have moved back to my hometown and work in a non-profit/local government role devoted to improving the downtown district through historic preservation, promotional events, marketing, business recruitment, and physical/aesthetic improvements. Many people often ask: Don't you wish you lived in a big city? Or, why would you move back here? The core value of Joyce Ivy, that small, rural areas are just as valuable and need to be represented, is something that has informed so much of my career path and decision to move back home. When I think back on pivotal experiences in my life, Joyce Ivy is ALWAYS number one.

Did your peers from high school pursue the same kind of educational/professional opportunities?

Absolutely not. I was the only one out of my graduating class to attend out of state, and the only one in forty years to attend an Ivy League school. Similarly, I wasn't aware of anyone who truly sought a liberal education (broad coursework across disciplines) in the way that I did at Brown.

Many times in high school I was told, from counselors and peers, "Well, you're smart, why don't you become a doctor? or a pharmacist?" There is a huge focus here on technical training and STEM fields—never are students encouraged to attend college because of the love of learning or to gain a well-rounded education; instead, most are pushed to get a degree that will "lead to a direct career outcome." The fact that I went into college undecided, studied across disciplines, and graduated with a liberal arts degree (comparative literature), truly made me an outlier from what the norm is here.

I have always been interested in how places develop, how places develop culture, and how places shape identity—but I didn't know a field like what I work in now existed as a valid career path when I was in high school.

A Final Note

At its core, the Joyce Ivy Foundation strives to expose students to their various undergraduate options. It does not prescribe highly selective institutions as the best or only path for all students; rather, it encourages them to investigate and make an informed choice when applying and matriculating to college. Outcomes from the past fifteen years have been overwhelmingly positive toward this aim, and it is encouraging that pre-college scholarships can serve as a relatively low-cost intervention for those who may otherwise undermatch in their college application decisions. The Joyce Ivy Foundation hopes that the exposure generated by this experience will allow students to confidently select an institution that will provide a supportive and motivating experience.

Appendix

Figures 4.A–B and Table 4.1 include unpublished data from Joyce Ivy Summer Scholar surveys. Participants are surveyed immediately after their summer experience (Post-Summer Survey) as well as during their final month of high school (Senior Survey). Figure 4.C shows the importance of engaging students who are not as geographically proximate to strong colleges and universities, as high-achieving seventeen-year-olds are found in all areas of the country.

Did your college plans change as a result of your participation?

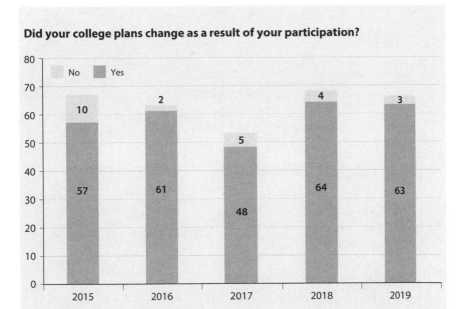

Figure 4.A. Effect of a Summer Program on College Plans
(Post-Summer Survey)

Influence of scholarship in decision to attend

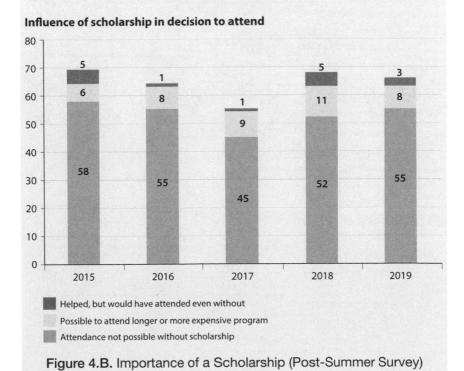

Figure 4.B. Importance of a Scholarship (Post-Summer Survey)

Table 4.1. Effects of summer program participation

	2015	2016	2017	2018	2019
College List					
More aggressive in reach schools	41%	43%	59%	53%	49%
Completely rethought target and reach schools	22%	18%	10%	18%	22%
No change to target or reach schools	19%	19%	23%	16%	18%
More aggressive in target schools	17%	19%	8%	13%	11%
Geographic Preference					
Convinced student to apply out of state	38%	43%	37%	50%	35%
No impact on geographic preference	24%	27%	23%	29%	15%
Broadened interest in applying out of state	36%	27%	37%	21%	42%
Reaffirmed commitment to stay in-state	2%	3%	3%	0%	8%
Academic Interests					
Clarified academic subject interests	55%	52%	64%	66%	55%
Significant effect on intended college major	31%	27%	26%	26%	31%
No effect on long-term academic interests	14%	21%	10%	8%	12%
Preparation and Confidence					
Increased confidence in social fit for college	77%	80%	84%	79%	74%
Increased confidence in academic ability	88%	88%	78%	89%	80%
Better prepared for college application process	68%	69%	66%	66%	63%
Increased knowledge about financial aid	43%	37%	38%	34%	32%

Source: Data from Joyce Ivy Summer Scholar Senior Surveys, 2015–2019.

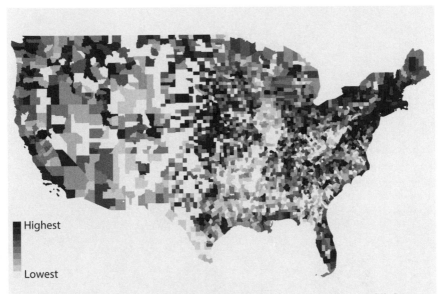

Figure 4.C. Shares of All Seventeen-Year-Olds Who Are High-Achieving, by County (Hoxby, Avery)

5

Experimenting with Teaching to Improve Student Learning Outcomes

Author Richard Light recently surveyed a group of faculty colleagues, asking simply, "What is the biggest change you have noticed in the university's culture over the past ten years?" The sample size was modest—just twenty-five professors, each of whom had been at their institution for at least a decade. Their responses are illuminating in part because there was a clear consensus: despite representing various disciplines, the faculty converged around just a few core ideas.

Seventeen respondents, more than two-thirds, immediately described a now far heavier emphasis on strengthening teaching—on working hard to figure out new and constantly more effective ways to instruct students—as the biggest change in the university's culture by far. A distant second choice, brought up by five professors, was how their university had worked remarkably hard to improve both the academic and personal advising that students receive.

The conversation that flows from collecting such simple data can often be surprisingly rich, which was what happened in this case. As an add-on to their response about noticing an increased emphasis on teaching quality, several of the respondents mentioned how they had also seen an uptick in faculty-led experimentation to truly understand effective teaching methods. Clearly this represents a major positive change both for faculty and students.

When pressed for specific examples, some of these professors seemed to enjoy listing and describing their own experiments for more effective classroom teaching. Nearly half of them had done so fairly recently, and almost all put a simple caveat on their remarks. It is that experiments for improving classroom teaching, always with the goal to enhance students' learning, must be reasonably simple to implement. They cannot be too time consuming. They should ideally be inexpensive. And the improvements in their students' learning—even if modest (as they usually are)—should be measurable and clear.

To quote one longtime faculty friend verbatim, "I of course did not come here as a professor of economics to mainly spend my time doing experiments on new ways of teaching. Yet I do spend an enormous amount of time teaching great students during my three economics classes each year. Therefore, if isn't too time consuming or too complicated to conduct research on how I can teach even more effectively, to enhance my students' class engagement and learning, of course I am happy to do that. What instructor in their right mind wouldn't be willing to try an in-class experiment—especially one that is low cost, a low time investment, and potentially high payoff—when I know I am going to invest enormous amounts of time teaching my three classes anyway?" This probably explains the enthusiasm shown by many instructors who were happy to share their new ideas, talk about what they had actually tried in their classes, and ultimately share their empirical findings about what worked or what didn't work.

A short list of examples includes:

1. *Cold calling on students*, rather than only inviting those with hands raised to speak. Does this teaching strategy strengthen what students in a class actually learn? Most faculty have clear, personal guesses. What does the evidence—collected through careful experimentation—actually show?

2. Assigning homework between classes that *requires each student to post a public response online before class*. Part of every homework assignment involves each student publicly posting and sharing a response, reaction, or question after that student does some assigned readings in advance of each class session.

Does that simple public posting strategy measurably improve students' learning? Does it help the specific student who makes a posting online? Does it help others in the same class?

3. Taking five to ten minutes of a ninety-minute class session and *inviting a pair of students to actually lead a class discussion on a pre-assigned topic*. The instructor sits quietly for those ten minutes and lets the students run the show. Of course, the two discussion leaders both know the topic in advance so they can prepare well. Do students learn more in a class with this slightly unusual structure? It certainly puts a lot of responsibility on the students. Do they feel like their expectations are being met in terms of what they signed up for during college?

4. *Conducting anonymous in-class polls of students* (perhaps using simple clicker devices) both before and after a particular class period. Students each respond to an opinion-based question—perhaps, "Do you think that the minimum wage in the U.S. should be increased?" for an economic policy class or "Is it okay to double the price of umbrellas during a rainstorm?" for an ethics course. At the end of the class period, both the pre-discussion poll and then the post-discussion poll results are shown. Students, as well as the instructor, then easily see whether many or hardly any students changed their minds or views because of what was said during their discussion. Of course, the instructor's hope is that this simple step (that takes less than one minute of class time) will push many students to focus even more sharply on the substance of their class discussions. After all, each student is being asked to share their own opinion and then can even change it as a result of others' comments. It is easy to speculate this might enhance students' engagement.

5. Particularly for classes with large enrollments, *personal communication from a professor to individual students, seeking to understand their goals and challenges*. We all know there are business or professional emails that faculty can exchange with students. In addition, there are more personal

(of course we mean "appropriately personal") emails an instructor can send to students. Does that difference between personal and business communication matter at all for enhancing students' engagement and commitment to a course? Does the difference ultimately influence how much they learn?

6. In any size class, *designing homework assignments or projects that require students to pull different concepts together across the details of different topic areas or academic subjects.* Do these types of assignments foster deeper learning? Do students dig deeper, work harder, and learn more when asked to capitalize on what they have learned across multiple subjects, rather than when they are either tested on or asked to write about one narrow or very specific idea?

Those are six quite specific examples, each of which we have actually witnessed in classrooms at strong universities around the country. We offer concrete details about three of them here. Some of these teaching strategies turned out to work remarkably well for engaging students and increasing their learning in measurable ways. The flip side is that a couple of those suggestions turn out to be well intentioned yet ultimately didn't achieve the desired results. The big point is we think any great university should constantly encourage and support its faculty to experiment with their classroom teaching. Most importantly, professors should commit (and be supported) to gather reasonably rigorous evidence and data to see if their new teaching strategies are contributing to some tangible change in student learning. Hunches are nice— we all have hunches. Concrete data are even better.

It is unrealistic to anticipate that every teaching innovation will lead to successful results. That won't happen. A strong university should encourage faculty to try new things and reward such innovative efforts *regardless* of whether a particular idea succeeds or not. Clearly it is the ongoing process of innovation and experimentation with classroom teaching that always should be rewarded. When the results of any particular new teaching plan turn out well, everyone wins. And each university should anticipate that a large fraction of new ideas won't work. If a new teaching idea were obvious or easy, it probably would have been widely adopted many years ago.

Intervention 1: A No-Cost Effort to
Reduce Anonymity in Large Classes

Joshua Goodman, now a professor at Brandeis University, tried out a near-zero-cost experiment with a class of sixty students. We will liberally, with permission, quote Professor Goodman's superb write-up of how he structured his simple experiment and what was learned.

Professor Goodman decided to try to determine whether his communication style to students in his "Regression and Causal Analysis" course made any difference to their academic performance. Goodman divided his class of sixty into three equal groups.

One group was designated to serve as the control group. They received no special intervention.

A second group received—one month into the semester course—what Professor Goodman calls an "academic email" even though each student received it personally addressed to him or to her by name. The focused email read as follows:

> Dear (Student's First Name),
>
> I'm enjoying teaching our class and would like to find out more about any specific econometric questions you might have than the large class format allows. If you're willing, would you write me back a short email describing any questions that have arisen that would be helpful for me to clarify?
>
> Sincerely, Josh

A third group received a somewhat more personal email. Goodman describes it as attempting to develop just a bit of a personal connection with some students (randomly chosen). "My hope," he noted, "was that such a connection might improve their engagement with the course and might inform my own teaching (such as choosing different examples for class)." This email read:

> Dear (Student's First Name),
>
> I'm enjoying teaching our class but would like to get to know you a bit better than the large class format allows. If you're willing, would you write me a short email describing your

personal current or budding professional interests? And your current feelings about how our course is relevant, if at all, to you personally?

Sincerely, Josh

Goodman describes the goal of this simple intervention by saying:

I thought of the more "academic treatment" as addressing specific, intellectual challenges but without explicitly addressing any issues of especially personal connection. In contrast, I thought of the more "personal treatment" as one emphasizing a personal connection between me and the students. One that conveys I am invested in their success as individuals, personally, but without addressing specific, academic challenges. After students responded to my initial email, from either group, I would always write an additional brief email in return, primarily to confirm that I had read their response.

Results

The results from Goodman's straightforward experiment are summarized in Table 5.1. In general, roughly 90 percent of students responded to his emails. A prominent difference between academic outreach versus personal outreach was the length of students' responses. The replies from students to Goodman's personal notes are on average more than twice as long as replies to his purely academic notes.

Now we get to what is usually the bottom-line question for such interventions: Did any discernible difference exist in class performance among the three, randomly selected groups? Most everyone

Table 5.1. Summary data from response to Goodman's emails

	Academic	Personal
Responded	87%	93%
Days to response	1.39	1.62
Expressed clear thanks	100%	92%
Words in response	104	216
Expressed a sense of struggle	62%	0%

Note: Results are statistically significant .05 level.

hopes for a yes, since this is such a quick and easy intervention for any professor. Yet—unfortunately—the answer is a clear no. Goodman presents data from students in all three groups in his written summary and writes in his conclusion: "If anything, the control group that received no emails at all appears to have slightly outperformed *both* treatment groups on problem sets and exams. There are no statistically significant differences, and the sample sizes are small. In short, this intervention had little positive effect on observable academic outcomes for students."

Goodman's final paragraph in his write-up is striking:

> The one constructive lesson I take from this experiment is something I had not previously fully appreciated. It is so many students' strong desire to tell faculty about their own lives and how their trajectories connect to the curriculum. I was surprised that the responses to the personal email treatment were so lengthy, detailed, and enthusiastic. That's particularly true relative to the academic responses, which often struck me as underwhelming. This suggests to me that, going forward, I will find other ways to solicit students' personal stories from them and make sure to incorporate connections to those stories into the curriculum itself. I was also struck by the gratitude students expressed upon receiving an apparently personalized invitation to communicate with a faculty member. This too suggests scope for future improvement, though I am not now certain what form such changes would take.

Intervention 2: Cold Calls and Online Posts— Do Either (or Both?) Enhance Learning?

Harvard Professor Dan Levy wanted to investigate the results of different teaching techniques in his two moderately large classes. One strategy was cold calling: a practice of choosing students somewhat at random to answer questions, rather than solely those with their hands raised. The second was the use of online web postings: requiring some or all students to post their thoughts and responses on a course web page. Levy was interested in exploring whether either (or both) of the techniques showed compelling signs they could enhance students' learning.

During one particular year, Levy taught two sections of a class called "Quantitative Analysis and Empirical Methods." Each class had approximately eighty students. He divided each class in half, for a total of four roughly equally sized groups, and implemented a different teaching technique for each group.

In one class section, half of the students were asked as part of their homework assignments to post a response online to some prompts. They were also told they were being put on a cold call list for the semester. Meanwhile, the other half of the students were put into a control group. The members of the control group were all encouraged by Levy to read before class (a pretty standard remark) but otherwise received no intervention nor change from traditional teaching.

In the other class section, Levy randomly assigned half of the students to do online postings before class (no cold calling), while the other half was assigned to the cold call list without requiring any web postings.

To offer a diagrammatic summary, Table 5.2 shows Levy's groups and the techniques he implemented.

Levy summarizes his project design: "In addition to the experiments, a qualitative study was conducted aimed at understanding students' views on how they were experiencing the web postings and cold calling." Throughout the semester, Levy met regularly with small groups of the students to ask about their perceptions. At the end of the course, students were asked to fill out a brief anonymous survey in which they indicated their predictions as to which treatment would work and why. The qualitative survey was instrumental for understanding the results of the experiments and in helping Levy draw lessons for his pedagogy.

Table 5.2. Summary data from Levy's groups

	Technique
Class 1, Group 1	Web postings AND cold calling
Class 1, Group 2	Control
Class 2, Group 3	Web postings ONLY
Class 2, Group 4	Cold calling ONLY

Brief Details of the Treatments

Treatment One—Web Postings: Students were required to post answers to three questions on the course website by 4:00 a.m. of the day of class. The three questions all were based on the readings for that day's class session. Students could see each other's postings, yet the questions were crafted in such a way that copying or cheating was close to impossible. The third question was always the same: "Please tell us what you found difficult or confusing in this reading assignment." This question, recommended by physics professor Eric Mazur, was meant to facilitate metacognitive thinking from students and to give the instructor a sense of common student difficulties. Professor Levy used this information to adjust the length of class time spent on each topic. He also shared with students the themes that emerged from the posts.

Treatment Two—Cold Calling: For each class session, Levy randomly chose one student from his cold call list of approximately forty. He typically asked that student two to three related questions, all carefully prepared. The questions tended to be factual in nature, so any student who had done the reading carefully should be able to provide a response. Levy rates this level of cold calling as "moderate" compared to many law schools and business schools across the country.

Levy carefully designed his experiments to be able to draw insights from demonstrated student performance and preparedness. He also solicited both faculty and student predictions to understand what they *thought* would happen.

His results enable us to answer two questions. The first is whether implementing cold calling and/or web postings in a course change the amount of time that students spend preparing for class. The second is whether implementing cold calling and/or web postings leads to measurable improvements in students' learning as measured by performance on exams, quizzes, and their in-class remarks.

Predictions

Dan Levy, together with his colleague Josh Bookin, conducted two surveys to compare how predictions of the effectiveness of the

Table 5.3. Predictions of results for Class 1: Views from faculty and students

	What technique was most effective at increasing . . . ?			
	Reading time		Actual learning	
	Faculty predictions	Student predictions	Faculty predictions	Student predictions
Web postings and cold calling	88%	92%	74%	57%
Encouraged reading (control)	0%	2%	0%	16%
Same	12%	6%	26%	26%

Table 5.4. Predictions of results for Class 2: Views from faculty and students

	What technique was most effective at increasing . . . ?			
	Reading time		Actual learning	
	Faculty predictions	Student predictions	Faculty predictions	Student predictions
Web postings	78%	69%	74%	66%
Cold calling	22%	20%	11%	16%
Same	0%	11%	15%	18%

treatments would relate to their study's actual findings. One survey group was composed of all the students in the two classes that participated in these two experiments. The second group included forty faculty members who attended a research seminar where Levy and Bookin presented these findings for the first time. The faculty members were asked to make their predictions after they had heard details of the interventions but before they were informed of any results. Predictions for both groups are included in Tables 5.3 and 5.4.

Results

Overall, the key findings from Levy's experiments were:

1. Both web postings and cold calling had a positive effect on the *amount of time students read before class*, but *not on sheer academic performance* (as measured by exam results).

2. When tested against each other, *neither of the two methods* (web postings and cold calling) came out on top in terms of improving *either* class preparedness or academic performance.

Levy and Bookin also solicited verbal comments from students who participated. The students' comments may offer some insights about what students thought about the two teaching techniques:

- "Postings and reading did not enhance the in-class learning; rather, they took time away from problem sets. My time is not infinite."

- "If you do the readings hastily (because there is so much to do for this course), it does not make much of a difference."

- "While the cold calling did nudge me to be more motivated to do the readings, the intense workload of the course and mandatory bi-weekly postings completely burned me out and crushed my motivation to read by the end of the course."

- "I did not like the web postings because they distracted from my focus on studying the actual material."

These students' verbatim remarks are valuable because they are so uniformly blunt. Levy worked so hard to enhance students' learning, and many students reported they found his innovations too much additional work, or requiring too much time, or both. We were surprised by Levy's findings, and we are apparently not the only ones.

In fact, it seems clear that while one part of the results was indeed quite well predicted—both by students and by faculty colleagues—the second was woefully misjudged. This reminds us of the extraordinary value of gathering some evidence, organizing an evaluation design rigorously, and sharing the results carefully with (even somewhat dubious) colleagues.

For the first class that involved the control group, as well as students engaged with both new teaching techniques, the vast majority of both groups—both students and faculty—*correctly* predicted the interventions' positive impacts on reading time (92 percent of students and 74 percent of faculty). But the vast majority of both students and faculty members *incorrectly predicted* the lack of effect on students' actual learning (only 26 percent from both groups predicted correctly).

Students and faculty were not much better at predicting the results for the second class. The majority of them thought that students' public web postings before class would increase reading time relative to cold calling, which was not supported by the evidence. In addition, only 15 percent of faculty and 18 percent of students correctly predicted that web postings and cold calling would be equivalent in terms of their impact on students' demonstrable learning outcomes.

We find the work of Levy and Bookin to be particularly powerful. They chose to investigate a commonly held assumption: that web postings and cold calling would lead to increases in students' preparedness and ultimate academic performance. Rather than simply following the "common wisdom," Levy and Bookin set out to find out what actual data would show. In this case and for their students, the common wisdom turned out to be incorrect.

This kind of systematic investigation and evaluation of new ideas for teaching is a critical piece of continuous improvement at colleges and universities. We may be pushing an open door here; we don't think we are advocating for some sort of shocking overturn of what many good colleges and universities do now. We simply remind our readers about the power of concrete, carefully gathered evidence. The goal is of course to help college teachers improve their classroom teaching in a sustained way, ultimately for the benefit of many students.

Intervention 3: Students Leading Class Discussions in Their First-Year Seminar

I (author Richard Light, writing here in first-person for simplicity) did exactly what we are advocating here in my own teaching with undergraduates. I recently conducted a simple teaching experiment that spanned two freshmen seminar classes. Analyzing results allowed me to identify areas of improvement in my own teaching, and many of my students similarly reported that the new structure allowed them to learn about themselves as well. Specifically, they better understood how to get enormous amounts of productive work accomplished and to more effectively take charge of their own learning. As a result of this teaching experimentation, I have changed certain elements of my pedagogical strategy to encourage first-year college students to engage in learning more deeply. Some of my faculty colleagues are acting upon the new insights as well.

The Class Structure

I routinely teach first-year seminars for new students. At Harvard, these are classes specifically targeted to freshmen with enrollment capped at fourteen students. The whole point is to encourage students to speak up, get some airtime in class, and develop connections both with one another and the professor. Teaching these courses is viewed as a luxury to most professors, who enjoy interacting with a small group of students—all of whom have chosen to take the class specifically because they are deeply interested in the topic. The one and only requirement for the professor is that they host all fourteen students for a meal at some time during the semester. Some faculty members invite students as a group to their apartment or home, perhaps for a light dinner or Sunday brunch. Others take their entire class for a group lunch at a restaurant near campus. This encourages conversation in a more informal setting and helps to foster the sense of community that is a core goal of freshmen seminars at many colleges.

The Teaching Experiment

I decided to try a simple teaching experiment over a two-year period in which I would teach a freshman seminar called "Tackling Tough Challenges for Modern American Higher Education." I would teach the same seminar twice, using a different teaching method each time, and then compare the outcomes of each method. I posed an identical starting point to each group of students each year:

You have just received a $150 million grant from a generous foundation. They give you this astonishing gift because they admire your creativity and your ability to think in unique ways. *Your task this semester* is to design a new liberal arts college from the ground up. Everything can be done in novel ways. You can organize the hiring of faculty, the student admissions process, the way your new college is staffed, the curricular requirements, how you hire food services employees and janitorial staff . . . anything within reason that you wish. The only rules are that you will need to balance your budget each year. And of course, you must run your new college with impeccable ethics. You will be the founding team of this new campus. Good luck.

Getting the Students Started

Since each entire seminar class consists of freshmen, most of whom have little or no experience with *any* college, I felt I had to give the students some questions—basically a set of categories—to help them get started in thinking productively.

I distributed a list of questions that anyone organizing or designing a new college would need to think about. These questions include:

- How large a campus do we want: What is our target enrollment?

- Should the college follow the traditional, four-year model? Or should it perhaps be adjusted, for example, changing the time frame to be three regular academic years plus two full summers?

- How many courses (if any) should be required? How many electives? How much flexibility should students have when choosing courses? Is independent study encouraged or even allowed?

- Should the new college create and organize traditional academic departments, such as history, chemistry, religion, English, and psychology?

- We are now in the twenty-first century. Most information is available online or in some form of digital storage. Do we want to build a library on our brand-new campus? If yes, do we want to fill it with books—just like most legacy colleges have done right now? Building and running a library is an enormous expense. Do you have better ideas to utilize modern technology?

- Shall we give admissions preferences to any particular group or subgroup of applicants? Do we care if our students are 60 percent women and 40 percent men, which is roughly what many other liberal arts colleges have right now? How do we ensure that a good number of talented students from lower-income backgrounds are admitted? How do we make sure these students feel genuinely included and welcome at our newly designed college? After all, you are not beholden to any rules or traditions that typically constrain the choices being made now by many legacy colleges.

- What two or three factors can be most useful for differentiating your newly created college, where you have practically no constraints at the outset, from other colleges? What will make you "special"? After all, you have this opportunity to start from scratch—surely you don't want to just reproduce the hundreds of existing legacy colleges that already are doing pretty well. In fact, many of them would find it nearly impossible to drastically restructure themselves after so many years of existence.

Teaching Method 1

For one semester, I taught this class by leading an active discussion among the fourteen first-year students. It was clear who was posing the key questions to the entire group (me). The students then engaged in genuinely vigorous and enjoyable discussions in our roundtable class conversations. Often some students chose to stay after class to continue the conversations. I felt good about that, yet that isn't the most important point. The key point is that I did what most professors do. I led the follow-up discussions and summarized students' consensus at the end of each week's two-and-a-half-hour class session. My only two requirements for the students were that they (a) come to class having completed their homework reading assignments thoroughly, and (b) that each student contribute by speaking in class *at least twice during each seminar session*. I am happy to report that the student participation metric was fully and easily met. Each student did indeed speak at least twice each class meeting. Even better, this simple requirement became the source of much laughter for our class all semester. The students seemed to take enormous pleasure in figuring out who had spoken how much, and sometimes one student would nominate a classmate to have their "moment in the sun to transform everyone's thinking." It was actually wonderful.

Class Ratings for Teaching Method 1

Course evaluations from students are required for all classes at Harvard. I was particularly excited to have feedback from the first semester of my teaching experiment. Each student, in order to get their course grade and my feedback on their seminar performance, had to respond to a series of both quantitative and qualitative questions about this seminar. How demanding was it? How prepared was the instructor to run a productive and well-organized class each week? How heavy was the workload? If you had a younger sibling who was just starting at this college, would you recommend this class to them highly or not so highly? Readers of this book have probably seen many of these questions before.

On a 1–5 scale where 5 is most favorable, the overall aggregate student rating for this first-year seminar was a 4.6. That is relatively high—though several seminars taught by other faculty do score higher. In any event, I was on balance happy with the outcome.

The qualitative responses turned out to be particularly helpful for giving me good ideas about how to design Seminar 2 that would use a noticeably different pedagogical format. In summary, the qualitative course evaluations featured about four of my fourteen students telling me ever so graciously, kindly, respectfully, and politely that they thought they could be far more creative in class if I as the instructor invited *them*, the students, to organize and to lead each week's discussion. Even if it were for just a small part of our two-and-a-half-hour class sessions each week.

They pointed out that because I was the one always steering the conversation, they didn't all feel a full sense of agency or urgency to "take charge of our own learning" (those words are a direct quote from one student). Of course, all the students understood that the professor ultimately is the person who organizes the entire class. Yet these students suggested they would relish the opportunity to play a major role in leading seminar discussions week to week.

As a side note—my PhD is in statistics and of course I *love* concrete, hard-nosed data and evidence. So I would have put a lot of chips on assuming the quantitative sections of these course evaluations would be especially valuable. Yet I confess it was the qualitative, judgmental, and subjective bits of feedback from students that I learned the most from and that I took most seriously. Several of those responses changed my behavior for Teaching Method 2.

Teaching Method 2

The following year I organized another first-year seminar. Again, enrollment was fourteen talented new students—all recently arrived on campus and eager to get to work. I used the same homework assignments, statements of purpose, and requirements for each student as during the previous year. In experimental terms, we "held the class curriculum constant." Students each had to do their homework readings carefully and come to class prepared to contribute and speak up in class—at least twice in each session. Same as during the prior year.

For this second seminar, again about designing a brand-new liberal arts college from scratch, the topics were similar to those from the previous year. *But here the instructional plan was different.* Now I divided the fourteen freshmen into seven pairs. Each pair received a schedule on the first day of class, informing them that they would be in charge for thirty minutes during a particular week. I suggested what their main topic of focus should be, but each pair was tasked with leading the discussion around the table.

So, to be clear, *what did NOT change?* I still ran our freshman seminar for 80 percent of our time together each week. It was entirely clear who was in charge for that 80 percent.

What DID change? For the remaining 20 percent of seminar time each week, that half hour belonged to each pair of students who were assigned to lead the discussion: a different pair each week for the first seven weeks. The student discussion leaders had near total freedom to design their half hour. Their only constraint was they needed to actually focus on leading a discussion and pose good questions to the class that focused on their assigned topic.

One Additional Adjustment in Class Structure

A few months before teaching this second year of the seminar, I had been invited to a wonderful dinner party at a friend's home. She had twelve people around the dinner table. Everyone was having a great evening chatting, and roughly halfway through the evening my host clinked her glass and said, "I want every gentleman here this evening to stand up and move two seats to your left. That way you will be around our table and now sitting between two new dinner partners—two new friends—for the rest of our time together."

Thinking this was a great change for my second teaching experiment, I adapted the idea for our class of fourteen students. Halfway through the semester, when each of the seven pairs of students had experienced the opportunity of leading one vigorous class discussion, I surprised the students by creating seven new pairs. For the second half of the semester, now they would lead discussions about the assigned topics with their *new* partners. The students seemed a bit surprised. Yet they willingly accepted this adjustment (I should add just one student pair resisted a little bit—the two discussion leaders in that duo had started dating and hoped to stay paired. I told them the firm plan was that they had to switch to a new discussion leader colleague, yet may their dating activities outside of classes prosper).

What Did Students Learn?

At the end of the semester, the students were required to fill out evaluation forms for this class just as their counterparts had done the year prior. In addition, I took the liberty of asking everyone in the class for a small additional personal favor: their anonymous responses to my own handful of questions. I focused the survey on how the new class structure had affected each student, asking specifically what features of the seminar enhanced their learning and which they believed had done the opposite.

The student evaluations generated some surprises. Most of all they had both good news and suggestions for future teaching. First, the mean rating of our class with the same instructor (me), basic syllabus, and homework readings and written assignments rose from the prior year's 4.6 to 4.9. This is actually a remarkable course rating. Clearly it is connected to the changes in course structure. After all, the instructor is the same guy.

On the course evaluations, students are asked to estimate how many hours, on average, they spent preparing for class each week. This new group of students reported that they worked roughly twice as much each week preparing for the freshman seminar as they did for each of their other three classes. They estimated four hours each week outside of the classroom for the others, while they claimed to spend an average of seven to eight hours a week for this seminar. Even allowing for a bit of exaggeration, this is an impressive result.

Putting aside the quantitative summary of Seminar 2, the anonymous qualitative responses were eye-opening.

Finding 1: Students pointed out that one reason they spent a lot of time on this class was because they knew they (together with their seminar partner) would be making two presentations. They also knew they would need to come to class each week exceptionally well prepared and ideally ready to offer some new ideas as the class designed a new college from the ground up. One student wrote, "I knew I would be at the front of the classroom with my discussion partner Jenna leading our seminar discussion in two weeks. Of course, I wanted *our* class discussion session to be successful. So I was always working extra hard to come well prepared when the other folks in our seminar were leading the discussion. I thought it is important to convey my respect and affection for my classmates by always coming well prepared to speak up in their discussion sessions. I hoped they in turn would reciprocate and do the same when it was my turn."

Finding 2: Several students (not all) wrote that they learned or polished two very specific and valuable skills because of this seminar format. One skill was—quite simply—learning how to lead a constructive group discussion. Some superb high schools prepare students to do this. Yet the vast majority of American high schools offer nothing of the sort. My fourteen students each had to think hard about a variety of key questions: How do I want to structure the time we have to lead discussions? How do I make sure I am being inclusive? How much should I as the discussion leader speak, versus inviting constructive conversation from others? How do I know when it is a good time to move on from one topic to the next?"

A second skill students brought up was learning how to work effectively *with a colleague* to achieve good outcomes when each student was required not just to lead—but to co-lead—a group discussion to get productive conversations flowing. Implementing productive discussions takes some planning. Both students in each pair had to learn good ways to work with their seminar colleague in constructive ways.

Finding 3: Many students in this second seminar format wrote in their course evaluations that they expected to use the skills they learned in this seminar to become more effective members of their classroom communities for the coming three years. I have no systematic way to know for sure whether that was indeed the case for most of the class. Yet since more than a few students brought up this idea of transferability of leadership skills to other classes, I hope they meant what they said.

Finding 4: I had anticipated, even hoped for, several of these findings so far. There was one outcome reported by the students in the second session that I simply had not thought about in advance. A large fraction of students said some iteration of, "Everyone in this class shared two commonalities: that it was our first semester here at college, and that we had an academic interest in this course topic. While I may not love every single other person in our seminar, I came to genuinely appreciate and enjoy most of my classmates. And I already sense that I have made some lifelong friendships. Because I had worked with my peers both in class and especially outside the classroom day in and day out for an entire semester, I have gotten to know many of them quite well."

Holding everything else constant, we find that the idea of giving the students some agency—putting them in charge and essentially requiring that they learn how to lead—led to a menagerie of positive outcomes that the students describe as uniquely valuable both for college and the world beyond. This illustration drives home the value of experimenting with teaching and testing new classroom ideas. I taught for many years before the idea of even trying out this genuinely modest adjustment occurred to me.

To conclude, we pose our favorite question: How much does it cost a college or university for a professor to organize and implement anything like this type of teaching experiment? We believe the precise answer—to the third decimal place—is zero. A university doesn't need to be wealthy to do this.

A Final Note

We carefully chose these three examples to emphasize a few main points. We hope they provide some sense of inspiration to test assumptions in teaching and think creatively about how to enhance students' learning. This process could be as rigorous as Dan Levy's experiment that incorporated predictions and multiple interventions, or it could be as straightforward as Josh Goodman's email test. In all cases, we recommend asking students for their feedback, and actually incorporating their recommendations as Light did. We hope that administrators will also commit to encouraging and rewarding faculty for trying innovative ways to teach, even if they do not immediately achieve desired outcomes. It is the spirit of experimentation that matters here.

Although this chapter largely focuses on what *faculty* can do to experiment with new teaching methods, there is also an important takeaway for students. It is that as undergraduates are choosing courses—typically involving attending a "shopping week" or collecting syllabi of interesting classes—we encourage them to look specifically for professors who are trying new things in their teaching. Students can ask faculty how they use course feedback to make changes year to year or inquire about how the professor plans to do things differently compared to the last time they taught the class. This can be a signal that the professor is committed to undergraduate education and will facilitate a thoughtful, exciting, and innovative classroom experience. We urge students to think about strategically incorporating such a nuance as they finalize their class schedules—they might be surprised at what they learn about the course content and also about themselves.

6

What Are Students Actually Learning? How Do We Know?

Students decide to attend college for a variety of reasons: earning a credential, honing their passions, competing in a sport, and meeting friends—just to name a few. Clearly, a principal motivator for just about every incoming student is to *learn*. Every college student wants to be able to know more or to do something better by the time they graduate. But how can campuses say definitively whether undergraduates are in fact achieving their aims?

Similarly, how does a campus know whether it is meeting *its own* goals for students' learning? Some colleges emphasize broad learning across many different fields and disciplines. Others promote specialization and require students to take far more advanced classes in at least one subject area. How can each of those two quite different kinds of campuses know when they are succeeding? It seems reasonable that colleges and universities should have at least a somewhat clear understanding of what students know when they arrive as freshmen. They should also seek to have some measure of what those same students know and are able to do when they graduate. But most campuses don't currently have in place a systematic way to do that—to measure student learning outcomes in aggregate.

We anticipate that many readers might react by thinking those campuses should just get to work and initiate an assessment program. That is an entirely constructive response. In this chapter we want to emphasize a different way of thinking about the word "assessment," which is often viewed as a synonym for "standardized testing." *Standardized testing is emphatically not at all what we propose in this chapter.* We are not advocating any sort of evaluative (at the level of an individual student) exercise. Instead, we believe that since one of the main goals of a university is to equip students with knowledge and expertise to contribute to society in some way, it seems clear any strong campus should develop reliable ways to understand how much its students are actually learning while they are at college.

Analyzing results from assessments to gauge students' learning is an interesting practice, of course. But what exactly is the value-add for a college or university? Greater than one may initially think. Having access to compelling and rigorously collected evidence from students can easily lead to faculty discussions about whether a university's current set of courses, requirements, and ways of teaching are leading to outcomes that achieve goals and make the faculty proud. Over time, these assessment findings can help to inspire and shape changes that are constructive for students.

We are not raising this point about students' learning outcomes because we have any secret suspicion that most colleges and universities are failing. Not at all. We simply welcome the views of W. Edwards Deming and Peter Drucker that any great organization should constantly push itself to improve—even when the organization is doing quite well right now. A systemic thirst for sustained improvement is—or should be—an aspiration of every great college or university.

Three Different Kinds of Assessment

Throughout this chapter, we highlight three different types of assessment. Each can be used to discover something about students' learning. One kind of assessment focuses on determining what undergraduates know at a given point, for example, as seniors are just about to leave campus. A second type asks more about demonstrable gains in learning and skills over time, essentially, the value added for students while they are at a college or university. A third kind of assessment strives to compare students' responses to questions that gauge their skill with different types of material. Each campus can decide for itself which form of assessment will best facilitate its efforts toward sustained improvement. Step one is having campus leaders and faculty members at a university begin to think of assessment as an *ally* for improving their students' overall experience.

We now turn to actual questions and formats that several colleges and universities have used. In every case, the campuses focused on understanding what students *as a collective, as an overall group*, are actually learning by being active members of the campus community. The goal is not to evaluate individual students on their performance. By better understanding the common gaps in student learning, campus-wide changes can be made in the way courses are organized, what faculty teach and how they collaborate, and how the classroom experience is structured. All of our suggestions share the common features of being actionable and zero-to-low cost.

Assessment Type 1: Understand What Students Know at Any Given Point

One way to get concrete information about what students are learning is to simply pose the question, "What do they know now?" For example, suppose a campus asks a modest-size sample of seniors at that campus—it could be as few as fifty students—a series of questions that tap into different facets of what students are (or should be) learning.

Author Richard Light recently collaborated with seven colleagues to do just that. Working individually, each interviewer spoke one-on-one with at least a dozen graduating college seniors. Each student was asked a list of fifteen questions that had been identified and shaped by faculty members. Each interview was conducted one-on-one and in-person, and neither the students nor faculty interviewers knew each other in advance. Two examples of questions that were asked:

1. Who was Sigmund Freud? You don't need to give an elaborate history nor explanation of his work—just talk intelligently for forty-five seconds about who he was, what he did, or why he is

quite well known today. In other words, can you convey you have a rough idea who he was?

2. What was the Human Genome Project? Again, you don't need to present a long exposition of every detail. Just talk for forty-five seconds or one minute to convey what the Human Genome Project was, why it is widely considered important, and how it might matter to future generations. Give a simple overview just to convey you have some rough idea what it was.

We are certain that each reader of this book can easily come up with their own questions tailored to their specific aims. Any faculty member, dean, or campus leader can develop several questions that get at core knowledge and principles they believe every undergraduate, regardless of major, should know. The two questions about Sigmund Freud and the Human Genome Project are simply illustrations—we present them here because these were the first two actual questions that Light used on several campuses. Both were suggested by faculty colleagues.

In the assessment that Light and his colleagues conducted, 94 percent of all graduating seniors were able to give a sensible, often more than minimal, response to the "Who was Sigmund Freud" question. In contrast, only 48 percent of graduating seniors were able to respond reasonably well to the Human Genome Project question. These results (and the findings from thirteen other questions that tapped into literature, politics, the arts, and science) were then shared with the entire faculty at the college. The faculty—now for the first time having some concrete data, instead of vague speculations, impressions, and occasional anecdotes—were able to discuss what, if any, curricular or teaching changes should be made in response. The entire assessment process was done for the benefit of future generations of students.

Of course, different campuses should be prepared to find noticeably different results. One campus might be thrilled that roughly half of its graduating seniors can identify and briefly discuss the Human Genome Project, while a campus down the road will be dismayed that *only* half of its seniors can discuss what most faculty at that college consider a core idea for the sciences. Either way, colleges who administer such a simple (and for many students, even fun) questionnaire now have additional information about what their students know at certain points in time. How much effort did this form of assessment take? Each of eight interviewers met with a dozen students for approximately a half hour each for a one-on-one friendly chat. The entire project took two weeks of very part-time work. That is the total effort. Not a budget buster.

Assessment Type 2: Measure Change over Time

A second way to get concrete information about what students are learning is to actually quantify the difference between what they know or can do when they first arrive on campus versus when they are about to graduate. Ideally, a campus would do this for the same set of students (longitudinally) over their approximately four-year college career. A secondary choice would be to measure (cross-sectionally) what first-year students know or can do while simultaneously gauging the same metrics for the campus's current seniors. This is an admittedly inferior option because they are not the same students, and the assessment process would not be directly measuring their individual growth over time. However, if campus leadership is interested in a shorter-term project, we can reasonably infer the comparison between freshmen and seniors offers a solid estimate of change and growth for students during their time at that college.

Example: How Much (If at All) Are Students Improving Their Writing Over Four Years At College?

Two hundred entering freshman at a particular university were asked during their first month of college which specific skill they most wanted to improve during their undergraduate experience. The researchers expected students to cite technological skills or perhaps public speaking. In fact, the students overwhelmingly (by a factor of 3.5 times more than any other) chose some variation of "I want to improve my writing." Though what students choose may differ among universities, we expect improvements in their writing to be in the top group of skills that students identify as seeking to improve. To assess whether students' writing skills really are getting stronger during their time at college, there is a simple and cost-effective strategy that has been conducted successfully at several campuses.

First, choose a sample of first-year students who are brand new to campus. A group of roughly one hundred is probably sufficient. A small college could do this with its entire incoming class. Ask the group to arrive at a specific time in a large classroom or auditorium. As each student enters the room, they take a seat at a desk with a single sheet of paper placed face down and a blue book that many colleges use for handwritten exams (an alternative would be to have students complete the exercise on a laptop). When everyone has arrived, the "proctor" (perhaps a graduate student) asks students to flip over the paper and do their best to write a compelling response to the question on the sheet within an hour. The instructions should remind students what most faculty would want to see in such an exercise: an essay that draws on evidence to support conclusions, has a clear structure and flow, and uses correct grammar and punctuation. Ideally, the question would *not* have an obvious correct answer *nor require* any in-depth background knowledge. The point is just for students to be able to write a well-organized and thoughtful essay in response to the posed question.

Students should be told that their response during this exercise will not count for any grade. It is imperative, however, that they put forth their maximum level of effort—as the college needs to know a baseline level of writing ability in order to tailor resources and instruction appropriately for the next three years and beyond. It is not only just that group of one hundred students who benefit from their hour of work, but also their peers and potentially several years of undergraduates to come. We find that nearly all students find that a compelling reason to try their best. It is actually quite heartening.

Before the students return their blue book or submit their online exercise, they should be prompted to *not* enter their name or student identification number anywhere on their response. Students should instead print the last four digits of their most permanent phone number. Then, the next time they are asked to complete the exercise (it could be at the end of their first year or during senior year—whenever the college decides to give it) they should enter once again their last four telephone digits. This serves two good purposes. First, students really do believe that this maintains anonymity, which the college has promised them. Second, this practice allows faculty to link each student's pre- and post-exams. We have *never once* had a student complain about this request. Students quickly learn to trust, absolutely correctly, that the entire process is to help the college understand how much students are improving their writing while on campus.

Collecting the Data

At one campus where Light implemented this assessment, he and other project leaders invited several outside graders to do blind grading of each paper. "Blind" in this case simply means that not only is each essay anonymous with no student's name attached, but in addition the grader did not even know whether they were grading a pre- or post-college essay. They simply gave each essay a holistic score from 1–10 that captured their clear impression of the quality of the evidence and arguments presented by the student, overall organization of the essay, and grammar. Professors of English and instructors in writing classes do this sort of grading routinely. The graders were paid an honorarium, yet the total cost of this entire project was less than $5,000. Not zero, yet certainly not millions.

Interpreting the Findings

What did a campus that actually implemented a pre- and a post-college writing assessment learn? More than they anticipated.

First, the writing instructors on this campus learned that over their four years at college, the undergraduates on average improved their writing substantially. The one hundred pre-tests had an average score of 7.2 on a 10-point scale. The post-tests showed a significant improvement; the average score was 8.9. Standard deviations were similar on both the pre- and the post-tests, at about 1.5. That means that the gain scores, overall, were highly statistically significant at the 0.01 level. We think any campus would be thrilled to find such a major improvement in a specific and important skill—in this case the ability to write well.

When the writing faculty members proudly reported these positive findings to the university leadership, they were certain the results would get a great reception. They were therefore a bit surprised when the response from deans was mixed. "Did you do separate sub-analyses to explore how our three main groups of students: the humanities majors, social science majors, and physical science majors each fared in the pre-post comparisons?" asked one dean. The writing faculty responded, "No, but we certainly can do that."

Once they went back and examined the data as the dean had suggested, results were striking. Put simply, the humanities majors gained a lot. The social science majors gained quite a bit as well. But the physical science majors, approximately one-third of the total sample? On average, they had almost no gain.

The end of this story is that at a subsequent faculty meeting, this somewhat troubling finding was discussed. With remarkably little awkwardness or disagreement, two requirements were adopted for physical science majors. Each student is now required to take one of a special group of science classes that are designated as "writing intensive." These are in no way remedial—they simply have a writing instructor connected to each class so students can get substantive feedback and reactions to the quality of their writing as well as the paper's scientific content. The second change is that a new group of writing class options were added to prompt students to write for a scientific audience. This turns out to appeal to most physical science majors, who are easily able to see the importance of (and get to practice) writing for an audience they care about. Now they are learning valuable future skills.

The campus leaders had carried out several important steps throughout this process. They gathered information from undergraduates and analyzed the data carefully—including examining different subgroups of students when appropriate. They also put a distinct emphasis on sharing findings widely with faculty. It may sometimes even be sensible to share such findings with students, if they are leading to changes in curricular requirements.

The big point is that faculty members will get some concrete and evidence-based feedback on how students' work is changing over time. Then faculty and college leaders can digest the findings and suggest useful modifications to the curriculum or campus offerings.

Assessment Type 3: Compare Students' Skills
for Solving Different Types of Problems

Faculty members at a strong university had devoted multiple meetings to discussing how to adjust and modernize their curriculum. Each had ideas based on their professional work and specific classes they taught, but the dean wanted to consider the bigger picture.

The dean asked the professors gathered in the room whether they had a sense of *what type* of problem-solving ability students were developing through their classes. Was their newly acquired knowledge broad or deep? Could they connect ideas across topic areas, or was their focus narrower?

The professors fell silent. They had midterm and final exam scores from prior classes, but there was no other substantive evaluation currently given that would be able to assess how a typical cohort of students thought about addressing problems. This seemed like a missed opportunity that the professors were eager to remedy.

The faculty members at this campus sprung to action and worked together to develop a set of seven questions. They decided that the first group of students would be asked to submit responses at two points during their time on campus: late August, before students had even set foot in the classroom, and again at the end of the academic year in April.

An Actual Assessment Design and Set of Questions

The faculty carefully designed the assessment to fit their goal of discerning what kinds of problems students were excellent at solving versus those that befuddled them. Two of the seven questions were very short and specific. "Define concept X, and when would you use concept X?" Professors noted that those questions were designed to tap into a topic introduced at a single point in one course. Each of the two questions had a clear, unarguable, correct answer.

The next two questions were noticeably broader. They were designed to test skills that were honed over a full semester, rather than during a single class period. The questions posed a problem with many potential reasonable solutions. The faculty's goal was to measure how effectively they were teaching their students to draw upon ideas that they had learned over time, yet still within a particular field or topic area.

The final three questions were intentionally the broadest of all. They presented policy problems and invited students to describe in detail how they might solve them. To do a good job responding to this last set of questions, students would have to draw upon multiple courses they had taken. For example—history, economics, philosophy, ethics, and even some statistics. Faculty members were fully aware they were asking their students to do something quite difficult. To respond successfully, each student would have to go beyond any one detail or any one class—they would need to integrate ideas across different fields and topic domains in order to come up with a constructive solution to a challenging problem.

Sample Questions

Below are three actual questions that faculty developed and used with a set of graduate school students. The findings were transformative, leading to significant changes in required classes for all students. We are confident most campuses could adapt questions with this approximate format for undergraduate purposes.

The first set includes examples of questions that test whether students have picked up a specific detail from class. They have a concrete correct answer.

- What is a randomized controlled field trial?

- What are two key advantages of trying out a new policy program, medication, or education intervention using a randomized controlled trial?

The next set asks students to synthesize multiple ideas, including ethical issues, that came up in one course all students took.

- You are the special assistant to the executive director of the World Food Programme. You learn that a certain country faces imminent, severe food shortages. These shortages could lead to widespread malnutrition or even starvation in that country. You would like to donate food supplies to that country, yet you are also aware that this is perhaps a short-term solution.

a. Describe how you would recommend dividing your total dollar resources between shipping food because people need it now, versus perhaps helping farmers and food organizations in that country to grow and produce their own food more efficiently than they do currently.

b. Whatever you chose to recommend about how to allocate the limited resources of the World Food Programme, briefly justify your choice on *ethical* grounds. Give two arguments in favor of your recommendation and why you believe it is the most ethical choice to make.

This final three-part question requires synthesizing ideas across multiple classes: political science, economics, statistics, philosophy and ethics, and demography.

- An old friend from your university days has reached out about a work challenge. Last year she took a job as a financial analyst with the Public Utilities Commission of a large state. At first her work was sophisticated but routine, helping to calculate fair selling prices for the electric utility that supplies over a million households.

  What has made your friend's job considerably *less* routine is the discovery that the chief financial officer (CFO) of the utility had been using subtle accounting tricks to deceptively overstate costs for over a decade. This meant that customers have paid at least $100 million more, in total, than they should have paid for their electricity. The utility does not dispute that it has deceived regulators and cheated customers; several employees have been fired, and the former CFO is in prison. The utility's current leadership accepts that there will have to be a substantial penalty. The question is what form it should take.

  On one side are those who think the utility should be required to pay a fine to the state government. This fine would be set to equal the total excess charges over time, plus interest (and maybe a little more, to discourage future cheating). The money received from the fine would be pooled with state taxes and other revenues to support general state spending. Others call for a very different kind of penalty focused only on electricity customers. Under this approach, electricity rates would be kept *below* the level needed to cover the utility's fair costs until the sum of the discounts cancels out the sum of the prior overcharging.

Your friend has been tasked with preparing a report on these options and has asked for your thoughts. This is all the information she has provided in her initial message to you, though you both expect this is only the start of your exchange.

Please respond to the following three questions, 3a, 3b, and 3c. Feel free to use bullet points or outline form as long as your meaning is clear.

3a. Purely on the basis of what you already know, which form of penalty—the fine or the discounts—strikes you as more appropriate? Why?

3b. What are three or four questions you will ask your friend in order to get a better-informed sense of which penalty is more appropriate? Indicate very briefly why the answer to each question might matter.

3c. What answer could your friend give to your question(s) that would cause you to *change your mind* about which form of penalty is superior, either from fine to discount or from discount to fine? Why?

Assessment Process

Similar to the writing assessment in the previous example, the faculty member or teaching assistant in charge explained to students that the assessment was in no way evaluative of each individual student.

Individual responses would be anonymous both to the faculty and graders. The faculty member in charge explained that there were two goals in having students respond to these carefully selected questions. The first was that it would enable faculty to get a sense of where students are starting from before even beginning classes for the first time. The second was to assess students' learning during their first year on campus so faculty could better tailor their future teaching strategies and possibly even the curriculum. This was in *no way* a placement test of any kind; the faculty overseer guaranteed to students that their response would stay absolutely anonymous. In fact, they were not even asked to include their names. Instead, all they had to do was note the last four digits of their phone number (or realistically, any number they wanted) on their paper and be sure to use that same number during an end of year post-test. This would allow graders to match the exams based solely on the numbers written on the exam's front cover. Students were given sixty minutes to answer all seven questions on this pre-test. We have included three of them here.

Post-tests were given at the end of April, about three weeks before the end of the academic year. The faculty decided to use precisely the same seven questions, word for word, to get the clearest possible evidence of how much learning had taken place. The chance that any student had memorized the questions or been practicing a response in preparation seemed very low. After all, students would never be informed nor recognized if they had achieved a "high score." There was widespread hope, certainly among faculty and also among most students, that the students' responses to the post-test questions would be deeper, fuller, and more comprehensive than the answers to the pre-test questions that students took before they had set foot in any class.

The students' compliance was high, though not perfect. For the pre-test, when newly arriving students were eager to get going, the response rate was 97 percent. For the post-test, it dropped to 80 percent. Not perfect, but still adequate to get a sense of how much students are actually learning.

Analyses of the Pre- and Post-Tests

Two graduate students were hired to grade each exam. The grading was done independently—the graders did not consult one another. As an extra shield against scoring bias, the graduate students didn't know whether they were grading a pre-test or a post-test. After the tests were graded, an analyst pulled insights using a simple one-letter code to be able to see whether a score was for a pre-or post-test. Each of the seven questions was graded on a simple 1–10 scale. A 10 represented a superb response, and a 1 represented a weak response.

The entire faculty of 150 were exceptionally interested in learning about the assessment findings. After all, they are the people who come in every morning and do the teaching—it would be nice to know the big takeaways about what students are (or are not) learning from their classes. Some faculty members had speculated in advance what the findings might turn up, and in some cases their predictions had been correct. In almost every case, the results were even more compelling than most faculty members expected. The main findings were:

1. Students were doing an excellent job learning precise details within specific classes. For example, the gain scores on the question about randomized controlled field trials averaged nearly two standard deviations. That is an *enormous* gain. It means that a large number of students on day one had really no idea what those words meant, nor why anyone would ever use a randomized controlled field trial. By the end of the first year, nearly every student responded with a crisp and thoughtful answer.

2. For the second group of questions, those requiring students to incorporate several concepts from a single course, gain scores dropped off noticeably compared to the first set. The average gain from pre- to post-test on these questions was approximately half a standard deviation. Though lower than the more specific questions, that is still an impressive result by traditional education standards.

3. Then the faculty learned something disappointing, though ultimately transformative. For the third set of questions—those that asked students to incorporate ideas from across several different courses they had taken—the analysis of scores turned up an average gain of 0.3 standard deviations. In other words, when it comes to pulling together elements from history, politics, economics, philosophy, ethics, demography, and statistics into a single thoughtful response, there were only modest gains in students' responses over the year. Compared to other types of learning, the faculty decided this clearly was a weak spot in the curriculum and that changes were needed.

University Response

The sharp differences in how students seemed to be learning based on these assessments led to multiple faculty discussions. For the first time, they knew where they were starting from and could identify how they hoped to improve. Two years later, three new courses were developed that will be required of all first-year students in this particular graduate program. They have been specifically designed to present information in entirely different ways. They include topics where the learning assessment found students to be a bit weaker than faculty had anticipated.

For example, a traditional economics course has been refreshed to include far more current ideas from behavioral economics. Meanwhile, data analysis classes have been converted to include far more data science and big data analysis. A critic may say, "This should have happened anyway—why did it take an assessment of students' learning to create faculty incentives to make such changes?" That is a reasonable question. Nonetheless, the point is that as a result of having some concrete, very specific data from students to look at, both university leaders and faculty members could respond to those data in a way that is very different from their having "some general impressions of what is going well and what is not going so well."

Thoughts on Designing Learning Assessments

We would like to think that many colleges and universities might benefit, each in their own way and given their own priorities, from doing some version of a student learning assessment. As a campus considers implementing a strategy—perhaps some version of the three that we have described here or maybe something completely novel—there are a handful of ideas to bear in mind:

1. ***How often should this be done?*** No one proposes these learning assessments need to be done every year. Perhaps not even every other year. Yet surely once in three to five years, campus leaders and faculty members will benefit from taking a pulse check of how students are doing in achieving learning aims. They can also work systematically to determine if curricular changes are warranted as a result.

2. ***Who should be involved?*** We find that when faculty are invited to take on key leadership roles for this process, there is often enormous buy-in from their colleagues. Clearly if campus leaders do all the planning, design, and implementation without including faculty members, it might lead to many saying, "Why don't you just hire an outside consulting firm like McKinsey and have them do what you want?" Our experience is that including faculty in planning and design of learning assessments is critical.

3. ***Details about the assessment process really do matter.*** Each campus should come up with its own good way to guarantee genuine anonymity to students, while devising a system to match pre-tests and post-tests, student by student. The example in this chapter, which is a real example from a major university, asked each student to simply write the last four digits of their telephone number on the cover of their exams. Other campuses may have different ideas, perhaps better ideas, for how to do this.

4. ***How should results be reported?*** Each campus needs to decide how it values and interprets different findings about

students' learning. Each must decide what they consider substantial learning, versus modest or hardly any gains. Some years ago, a professor named Jacob Cohen, a psychometrician at New York University, offered some rough rules of thumb that campuses might find helpful. He noted that a gain of 0.8 standard deviations or more over one year constitutes major learning. A gain of roughly 0.5 standard deviations constitutes moderate learning. And a gain of 0.2 means that students have learned a little bit yet not much. Reasonable people can disagree about these precise numbers; our view is that with many educational innovations, achieving even modest gain scores are valuable.

A Final Note

More and more strong campuses are beginning to adopt some sort of effort to answer the basic query about what their students are really learning. We observe two key changes in how campus leaders have begun to conduct such assessments and think about their findings.

One change is that campus leaders are increasingly putting faculty members at their campuses in charge of the process. This is a sharp contrast from several of the earliest efforts for campus assessment, where a president or provost simply announced, "We need to do this." Gathering and analyzing evidence about students' actual learning *clearly should be a faculty driven enterprise*. It is the faculty who create curricula. They are the ones teaching multiple classes. It is the faculty who will need to be on board if changes are called for and implemented. This management plan to give faculty a major leadership role for evaluating students' learning is relatively new for many campuses. We strongly endorse the spirit of this perspective.

A second change is that more and more presidents, provosts, and deans are coming to *learn to treasure small improvements*. When early efforts at measuring gains from new curricular ideas began to take hold, campus leaders sometimes were disappointed to find gains over a year's time of roughly 0.2 or 0.3 standard deviations. In fact, both of those numbers exceed the impact of widespread popular programs that are accepted across America. For example, the famous Head Start program for lower-income young children to improve their school readiness has shown typical gains of less than 0.2 standard deviations for children's learning over a year. Yet the Head Start program is widely agreed to be highly successful and has enormous bipartisan support.

We believe that this effort to systematically assess student learning, gather data, take that data seriously, and make corresponding changes to a curriculum or way of teaching is a way to show the utmost respect for students. Who wouldn't want to attend a college where leaders are constantly striving to make improvements? Rather than the drudgery often associated with the word "assessment," especially when it is linked to evaluative testing, we believe this can be one of the most exciting initiatives that students can be part of during their time on campus. Not only does it help shape their direct experience, but it also provides insights for years to come. As students choose a college or move through their undergraduate experience, they should feel empowered to ask questions about changes that colleges are making in response to data from students. Everyone is working toward the same goal—to make student learning the best it can possibly be—and all campus community members have a role to play in ensuring continuous campus improvement toward that aim.

7

Acting on Students' Opinions, Ideas, and Advice

Every college and university has an exceptionally powerful resource sitting right on its campus. That is, of course, the students. Each individual has chosen to enroll at that particular campus for a reason, and there is no one—not an administrator, advisor, nor faculty member—who has the same type of immediate perspective on the undergraduate experience.

One thing any university owes to its students is to learn from their experiences and focus on moving continuously toward improvement. By this, we mean *actually asking students* about their experiences—both good and disappointing—and then taking what they say seriously. When appropriate, campuses can put what they learn from undergraduates into practice; for example, adjusting policies to offer students more resources to implement their own good ideas.

In this chapter, we offer a variety of questions that colleges and universities can ask their undergraduates. We also illustrate how students' insights have on several strong campuses led to new practices, programs, and traditions. Some examples come from students' suggestions for changes in the classroom, such as how assignment feedback is conveyed. Other examples illustrate improvements to on-campus life outside of classes. These range from updates to extracurricular offerings to creating innovative ways of interacting with faculty.

The Process of Asking Students about Their Experiences

Colleges and universities that have begun to systematically explore their undergraduates' experiences generally find it both straightforward and inexpensive. Choices must be made, such as how much detail to ask students to share, how many different topics to cover, and how to gather information (online surveys, personal interview, focus groups, etc.). Once these decisions are addressed, campus leaders can mobilize interviewers and begin their efforts to gather feedback and ideas from students.

Although online surveys may be appealing, in part because they tend to be low cost and easy, they generally have a lackluster response rate and often do not provoke reactions that are sufficiently detailed. Therefore, though it is more time consuming to do one-on-one personal interviews, we find the benefits far outweigh the costs. Students can be asked by an interviewer to elaborate on their initial response. They can be prompted to clarify or expand their comments, if a gem of a great idea seems tucked into an initial reaction. The interviewers can be people already on campus, including faculty members, carefully trained (and paid) undergraduates, graduate students, or staff. This approach does not require any substantial outside investment or additional hiring.

Before interviews take place, each campus should create its own set of questions that are oriented around their specific culture and focus. A small liberal arts women's college and a large public flagship university may choose to ask quite different questions—or their lists could be rather similar. Every campus's leadership should tailor their questions around what topics they choose to emphasize. One college may ask primarily about advising experiences, while another seemingly similar college may choose to focus on topics such as students' views about inclusion and belonging.

Several great universities have implemented this relatively simple idea for years, while for others it may be a new and hopefully intriguing idea. Clearly campus leaders can learn a lot from hearing from students—in their own words—about their actual experiences, suggestions, and constructive ideas for change. The students, in turn, need to understand they have a crucial and respected role to play on campus. Their creative ideas can impact their experience and shape the college for years to come.

How Much Data Should a Campus Collect? How Many Students Is Enough to Ask?

Gathering data about the student experience can feel like a daunting task, particularly for large campuses with up to tens of thousands of undergraduates. What is an appropriate sample size? How much time does a campus need to spend collecting such information? Our response to both questions is, perhaps predictably, "The more the better." Still, any carefully gathered information is far better than none at all.

During conversations with leaders of several large public universities, Light enjoys pointing out that even a small sample can provide valuable new insights and inspiration. Interviewing even just one hundred students per year invites each of those campus community members to share their ideas and experiences. Some fraction of the interview results will not be particularly constructive (undergraduates, for example, seem to love to complain about dining options). But there will, on every campus, be another group that can provide surprisingly insightful and actionable suggestions. Their ideas can give campus leaders new perspective on the undergraduate experience. If a significant fraction of students bring up details of a negative experience in their residence hall, or if a suggestion that something should change comes up over and over, that gives leaders a jumping-off point for further investigation.

We turn to five concrete examples of when great universities have learned from students' suggestions and feedback to tangibly change the way they organize the college experience. All five are either no cost or low cost, and each can be implemented at small colleges or at the largest public universities with a few modifications.

Example 1: Helping Students Strengthen Their Writing Skills

When two hundred incoming freshmen at a medium-sized university were asked which specific skill they most wanted to improve upon during their undergraduate experience, the researchers expected students to cite technological skills or perhaps public speaking. Instead, the answer was decisive: students said that they wanted to improve their writing abilities. It may be analytic writing. It may be reportorial writing. It may be creative writing. Whatever the details, this is what students chose as their main focus for self-improvement.

Surprised by the result, interviewers dug a bit deeper and asked students a follow-up question: "So, what is stopping you from improving your writing? Why is that so difficult or challenging for you?"

The most common response from students, by far, included a single word: *revisions.* They noted that throughout high school, their teachers often returned papers with a grade and a single word: "Revise," scribbled in the margins as a piece of summary advice. "What does that even mean?" students said, frustrated. They hoped that their college professors would be able to provide much more specific feedback, host workshops, or perhaps even sit individually to help explain *how* students should think about revising.

The result of gathering such feedback on our own campus led to actual changes by faculty members. Professors who teach writing courses began to run special class sessions focused specifically on ways to revise. Others coached students on tangible ways to improve a draft, rather than the faculty just assuming that students already knew.

Here are five strategies for revising that students report they find most helpful. Each goes beyond simply asking students to change part of what they wrote.

Goal: To check the organization of an essay, ask: Does it have a clear beginning, middle, and end?

Revision strategy: Make an outline that consists of sentences, with one sentence capturing the main idea for each paragraph. Ask yourself: Is the flow clear and smooth from beginning to end? Does your essay have a clear and crisp organization?

Goal: To make an essay more personal, or to clarify your own views about a topic.

Revision strategy: Write out one thoughtful page of personal opinions about your topic. Read what you wrote to a friend or another student and ask whether it is clear. Do they now understand clearly what you believe?

Goal: To understand and respond to counterarguments.

Revision strategy: Talk to someone who has a different opinion about the topic and ask them to argue the opposite position while you argue yours.

Goal: To identify awkward phrases or words.

Revision strategy: Have someone read your essay aloud to you, slowly. See what you think.

Goal: To see if an essay's main point is clear, compelling, and focused.

Revision strategy: Have someone read the essay and quickly identify the main point and major supporting details or evidence. If your reader can't do it, you need to keep working on the essay.

Helping students to become more effective and confident writers is a widespread challenge on many campuses. This is not a secret. We believe this relatively simple example of helping students learn to revise their papers more effectively, *especially when this help is specifically what they are asking for*, conveys a measure of respect and caring for undergraduates that many colleges talk about, yet only some actually achieve. What better way to treat students with genuine respect than to ask them what a college could do more effectively, and then take what the students say seriously by putting programs into place to be helpful?

Even if only a modest fraction of undergraduates end up taking full advantage of the changes a college puts into place (such as these ideas for helping students learn to revise their written work effectively), the benefit is worth the investment. Ohio State University has thirty thousand undergraduates. Suppose only *2 percent* are interested in coming to a few workshops (offered at no charge and for no academic credit) that offer suggestions for how to become a more effective writer. Two percent seems small—yet Ohio State will be helping roughly six hundred students learn to write more effectively thanks to this practically no-cost initiative. Meanwhile, this all happens while a university is being responsive to undergraduates as they try to take charge of their own learning. An ideal outcome.

Example 2: Working Together to Develop a Speaker Series

At one Big Ten university, students were asked to comment on the quality and value of the many guest speakers—typically experts in a field or individuals with strong opinions about a particular topic—who were invited by various student groups to come to campus. In a systematic series of in-person interviews, undergraduates surprised the interviewers when one after another they characterized most of the university's on-campus events as being less impactful than they perhaps could be. The students noted that what they really wanted was some well-thought-out debate or disagreement, rather than simply having three guest speakers on a stage, all of whom agreed with one another about nearly everything.

Students commented this was especially true of politically focused guests who came to give presentations or speak in classes. One student laughed and commented,

> As soon as I heard our guest speaker begin to speak, I realized nearly every word and every view she would be sharing in the coming hour was totally predictable. And there were no other visiting speakers up on that stage to offer different views. I simply got up and left, and I am not the only one. My peers and I came to college to hear thoughtful, sometimes unpredictable, reflections and analyses with lots of evidence to back up all assertions. Far too many of our presenters here on campus seem to think their role is to lead a "pep rally"—for whatever goal they happen to favor.

This point came up in several student interviews, and campus leadership decided to pursue the point to see if they could possibly do better. They collected even more student feedback and put a plan into action the very next year. Rather than having (for example) the College Democrats invite a speaker one night and the College Republicans invite their speaker a different night, students suggested that special groups and clubs on campus should be invited to *work together to create a speaker series*. It was customary on that campus for student organizations to be given a modest sum of money to reimburse their guest speakers' travel and lodging expenses when they were invited to campus. Now, some students were simply suggesting that there be a source of funding available only to groups who cordially collaborate to bring speakers with different viewpoints to campus. This would allow students to not only hear from talented and passionate individuals, but also would model respectful and productive disagreement. The university leaders enthusiastically adopted these suggestions. They simply allocated a portion of speakers' expenses to situations where two or more student organizations collaborate to invite guests for a single evening or sometimes for a full-day symposium event.

What was the impact of responding to students' suggestions to push campus groups to collaborate? In the past three years, student attendance at these guest speaker events has more than tripled. For the first time, each student knows they will hear guests up on the stage who are (hopefully cordially) disagreeing with one another. Several undergraduates even commented they were attending more such events because they enjoyed hearing new ideas; in some cases, they had even changed their mind about something. Importantly, encouraging student groups to work together, even if just to agree on the logistics and an agenda and whom to invite, provided each with a lesson in collaboration and constructive interaction.

This simple illustration of gathering feedback from students and responding to their suggestions to collaborate when inviting guest speakers is uncontroversial. It does not cost more than the traditional method, and it broadens and deepens students' participation in activities outside of classes that can lead to real learning and even some new friendships. Clearly, the students appreciate it. They vote with their feet, so to speak, by coming out to more events and challenging themselves with new ideas.

Example 3: Showcasing Faculty Ideas

Several years ago, when undergraduates at Harvard were asked for suggestions about how to strengthen their college experience, several students highlighted an interesting point. They noted although Harvard has about one thousand professors who teach undergraduates, each student only gets to interact with about thirty-two of them over the course of eight semesters. It seemed to them a shame that with so many distinguished professors on campus who work with fascinating ideas, they only get to benefit from roughly 3 percent of them.

Two undergraduates, Derek Flanzraich and Peter Davis, decided to do something about that. They analyzed the results of a campus-wide survey asking about the most memorable and interesting faculty members that students had interacted with in their classes. From that list, they carefully chose ten professors from various fields and invited them to come to an experimental event. Each professor could choose their own topic and format. They could lecture, run a conversation, show slides, or not show slides. The only requirement was that they keep their presentation to ten minutes or less. With the exception of one professor who had a prior commitment, everyone who received a speaking invitation accepted.

Flanzraich and Davis called their new endeavor "Harvard Thinks Big: Ten Great Ideas from Ten Professors in Ten Minutes or Less." On the night of the inaugural event, no one really knew how many students would show up. There turned out to be no need to worry. Harvard's largest lecture hall, Sanders Theatre, was packed with undergraduates. More than 1,200 students showed up, and long lines snaked around the auditorium. This all was done on a busy campus for zero academic credit of any kind.

The presentations during that first event captured students' attention. Some faculty used subdued podium deliveries, while others infused their presentations with drama. A professor of organismic and evolutionary biology moved around the stage for a moment in a brief,

"pretend-drunken stumble" to illustrate the confused arc of an important genetic mutation in human evolution. A computer science professor ripped a giant telephone book in half at one point, working up
a tremendous sweat as he paced in front of the crowd of students
while discussing the magic of "making machines do your bidding."
A professor of psychology focused on why he believed the world is
choosing to act relatively slowly on climate change, and his theme
centered on how the human brain responds to threats.

When asked why he thinks this incredibly simple, basically zero-
cost activity was such a success, Flanzraich commented, "It's an effort to epitomize what's best about any university—in this case it
happens to be Harvard—and remind people why we came here in
the first place: to hear incredible professors talking about the things
that they know best, and to be inspired." Though the majority of students wouldn't have been able to take a full course with any of the
professors, more than a thousand gained exposure to the ten faculty
members' work and ideas in the span of a single evening. This program, suggested by students, is now an ongoing tradition.

This is a zero-cost venture for any college or university. If undergraduates organize this event, there are no special administrative expenses. Of course, no faculty are paid for their few minutes on stage.
Since it is quite rare for most professors to be asked to share their ideas
in this format, invitees typically respond with delight and volunteer
their time willingly. So students are happy, faculty are happy, everyone learns something, and it is no-cost practice for the campus—this
seems an idea *any* college or university could easily embrace and organize in whatever ways it sees fit.

Other campuses have, in fact, implemented similar ideas. At the
University of Pennsylvania, select faculty participate in "60 Second
Lectures" that take place between classes and have become somewhat
of a campus tradition. A podium and backdrop are set up in the
middle of the main campus thoroughfare, Locust Walk. Each speaker
presents one big idea in one minute (occasionally it's more like three
or five). When this idea was first proposed in 1999, it was considered
"slightly scandalous"; faculty were hesitant about condensing their
work into such a brief window. English professor Al Filreis—who has

since won just about every teaching award that Penn offers—agreed to take the leap and he delivered a "60 Second Lecture" called, perhaps fittingly, "The End of the Lecture as We Know It." Since then, hundreds of "60 Second Lectures" have been delivered and recorded for posterity. As with "Harvard Thinks Big," this format provides benefits to both faculty and students. Professors work hard to condense years of research and thought into a brief and engaging presentation that grabs students' attention as they rush to class. Students, in turn, get to see a new professor in action and can assess whether they wish to follow up to learn more. Because these lectures are held outside, community bystanders or visiting guests—including prospective students—may also stumble upon them. What a positive message this conveys to visitors; clearly, this is a campus that cares about big ideas. Here is a college that has put in effort to expose students to the vast faculty resources that exist.

Example 4: Questions for Seniors

Though any resulting changes won't directly impact their own college experience, undergraduate seniors on the verge of graduation often can provide extremely valuable feedback based on their collective, multiyear experience. Here—from different college campuses—are three quite different illustrations of questions asked by interviewers and the paraphrased responses from graduating seniors. The point is that gathering such feedback can lead to some tangible changes on college campuses, or—at the very least—spur further research or inquiry. Each of these questions below was developed to tap into students' perceptions of their college experiences, so that college leaders could think about how to improve it.

Question 1 for a Senior:
Now that you will be graduating next month, how would you describe the impact this college has had on your personal happiness and quality of life during your time here?

Student's Response:
By and large, a very positive impact. I met wonderful people, some of whom will be lifelong friends. Maybe best

of all, I developed confidence that I can have a positive impact on the world, and I realized I can play in the big leagues when it comes to discussing ideas. On the flip side, I increasingly began thinking how all of the college leaders here keep pushing students incredibly hard to "do something great with your life." At the beginning this was inspiring. Yet over time it began to feel like a burden. You might want to rethink this emphasis of heavily focusing on a productive career. When I graduate, I hope to help small companies in the Southeast where I grew up. Despite my commitment to doing something that felt aligned with my personal definition of success, I felt inadequate when I compared my goals to those of classmates who are going to work at McKinsey, Goldman Sachs, Google, and Microsoft. If you are asking for my suggestion to campus leaders about this point, I will simply observe that our students here focus far too much on career prestige, rather than leading a life that makes sense for each individual. I can say it bluntly. Screw accomplishment—what about happiness?

Question 2 for a Senior:
What impact would you say this college community's values had on you during your time here on campus? Any advice for campus leaders as you graduate?

Student's Response:
I came here with high expectations. But there was one very specific feature of our college that blew me away the most. We have so many students here from dramatically different backgrounds. They sit in the same room every day, and we are able to discuss many sensitive issues in an amazingly cordial and even friendly way. My goodness, we have students here on this campus whose countries are literally at war with each other. These undergrads discuss tough issues, often strongly disagreeing about a number of things and then they go and enjoy dinner together to continue their discussion. This is an amazing experience—I don't expect I will be able to reproduce it for the rest of my life. The leaders of this university really got something right when we first

arrived as new students. I remember the first two weeks especially clearly. Dean after dean, professor after professor, kept telling us we all should approach our college experience by remembering that we each had a choice. We could either bring to campus all of the outside world's anger and simply replicate that anger and intolerance here at college with our classmates. Or we could use these precious few years to discuss and debate and make friends with people we otherwise would have never possibly come to know. Those repeated speeches from deans and even from the president during the first two weeks on campus clearly were purposeful, planned, policy-oriented messages to convey something important to students. I think they worked great. I constantly wonder, if more colleges did this—and if students actually took it seriously—how might it affect the next generation?

Another Response to the Same "Question 2," Representing a Slightly Different Take:

I would say this college's values were driven home pretty hard by the deans and professors. They had a fairly big impact on me—especially during my first two years. And yes, I have some strongly felt advice for college leaders here as I graduate. Let me explain.

When I first got to college as a new first-year student, it was made clear to all of us quickly that we always should be supportive and respectful of one another. The goal clearly was to establish an atmosphere of trust in our classroom discussions so we could focus on learning. This seemed to work really well and I was grateful, at least for the first couple of years.

I returned to campus for junior year having had two summer jobs—one in business and one in government—where I saw how people behave with one another in a real-world professional setting. It was a bit jarring to see how often public disagreements arose, and I honestly wasn't sure how to respond. My classroom discussions went smoothly because everyone was on the same page about how to treat one another and constructively address differing ideas. But with no such agreements in place in real-world professional settings, I now worry about how well I am prepared for that environment. I'm not saying class formats should change. But maybe there could be an emphasis on how to react when we all graduate and enter real-world circumstances that aren't so collaborative and respectful.

Example 5: Creating Unique Skill-Development Workshops

Undergraduates learn a lot in the classroom setting. They are introduced to new ideas, different points of view, and strategies for interacting with the material. But what about the topics that are *not* part of the class curriculum? How do students learn those other "life skills" that they are expected to have when they enter their careers and adult lives? This is exactly the issue that was raised by undergraduates at several campuses where deans then decided to act upon their recommendations.

In all cases, the topics in the ten examples that follow were suggested by students—sometimes even by just a few. Administrators then invited a presenter (a faculty member, staff member, or visiting expert) to organize and lead one or two sessions on a focused topic. These sessions were completely voluntary for students. The undergraduate attendees did not receive a grade nor course credit. There was no test at the end. The sessions were simply offered for the sake of enhancing students' personal and professional development.

We begin with five examples that *emphasize writing clearly and for a variety of purposes.*

1. *The Executive Summary:* Learn which elements belong in the executive summary and which do not. Understand how to establish authority and present the topic clearly and succinctly.

2. *How to Write a Policy Memo:* Understand the expectations of decision makers who read policy memos. Learn how to write concisely to create short policy memos written for busy executives or leaders who don't have time for rambling or verbose essays.

3. *The Personal Essay* (this session was especially popular on several campuses): The personal essay is about presenting yourself. How do you use rich detail and subtlety to draw upon a particular experience that allows you to connect with others more broadly?

4. *Writing and Pitching Op-Eds and Opinion Articles:* Convey to an editor why you are the ideal commentator, why the topic is important, and why the timing is appropriate. Learn how to wisely use and present anecdotes, in contrast to using solely data and statistics, together with other kinds of details to make your argument.

5. *Personal Branding for Young Professionals:* This hands-on session will focus on refining the way you present yourself to graduate school interviewers or potential employers. Bring a personal statement to our session that you believe best represents your personal pitch. In other words, how do you wish to present yourself—to the world, to a specific future employer, to a school, or to any other organization?

A second group of suggestions comes from students at several campuses who requested some extra sessions built around *public speaking, handling difficult topics, and dealing with a potentially negative response from others.* Here are five specific examples of the voluntary sessions that were offered in response to their feedback.

6. *Introduction to Effective Public Speaking:* Become a better speaker, group participant, and discussion leader by learning how to use and balance ethos, pathos, and logos when you speak and influence in public settings.

7. *Dealing with a Hostile Audience:* Sometimes you can anticipate that your audience may not love to hear what you are going to say, or that a large fraction of your audience may simply disagree with you. Learn what to do when you are being challenged or maybe even heckled, and how to keep your listeners focused on the content of your message.

8. *How to Present Yourself Effectively during an Interview:*
Learn how to get an interview off to a good start, balance
listening versus speaking, and maintain a sense of modesty
while also clarifying your strengths. Interviewers often are
unpredictable. Their questions for you, and of course their
personalities, vary enormously. What are the several core
principles that might be helpful for presenting yourself the
way you wish to be perceived?

9. *How to Give and Receive Advice:* At school, at home, at
work, we all run into occasions where we want to offer some
advice to a friend, family member, work colleague, or fellow
student. In turn, we all know that sometimes our colleagues
and friends want to share their helpful feedback to us as well.
What are ways to make the most of opportunities to both
give and receive well-intentioned advice? If you are giving
advice and you have in mind to offer some praise and some
criticism, how might you decide which to offer first? If you
are sharing your opinion and it is clear that it is going to be
quite critical of another person, are there a few brief, introductory remarks that might help to encourage your listener
to be more receptive?

10. *Delivering Bad News:* Learn how to apply a variety of
specific techniques when you need to deliver bad news to
friends, colleagues, or to a broad audience. It is rarely a
pleasure to deliver bad news. Understand tips for thinking in
advance about handling your audience's likely response.

The overarching topics for these ten examples were suggested by
students. In every case, they were actually put into practice on at least
one campus and sometimes more than one. Some of these sessions
attracted over a hundred students, while others drew only forty to
fifty. The takeaway for us is that each campus has its own unique
needs, culture, and priorities. Students on different campuses inevitably will come up with different suggestions. Since running these
one-time, ninety-minute, outside-of-class workshops incurs little to

no cost, it seems a constructive idea for every campus to consider what workshops might be most engaging and helpful for its specific undergraduate population. We have been surprised at how much students generally appreciate them.

A Final Note

We hope it is obvious we are not urging the leaders of a college to act on *all* suggestions from *all* students. If just one in five or even one in ten ideas seems worth discussing and perhaps even worth implementing, students will feel they actually have a role in shaping their own campus experiences. Meanwhile, college leaders may get ideas that simply never occurred to them.

It seems important to keep in mind that when a student makes an observation or suggestion, it may be tempting for a campus leader to wonder if the majority of other students will like the idea or participate in the initiative. That is perhaps not the best way to think about it. Instead, leaders should consider the benefit to students who are able to learn something new because a student's feedback was taken seriously. Even if just a small fraction of the student body at a college participates in a given initiative, those students can still receive great value. Not every program has to be relevant to every student. In fact, we wouldn't expect that to happen.

This process—asking undergraduates about their experiences and for their advice and then trying to implement the most interesting or promising ideas that emerge—can mean a lot to students on a college campus. Simply by virtue of college leaders inviting their opinions and suggestions, undergraduates report they feel an enhanced sense of engagement and ownership at their college. At that point, the added bonus of unearthing some exceptional ideas from students to implement almost feels like icing on the cake.

8

Facilitating Constructive Interactions among Students from Differing Backgrounds and Experiences

Have you ever taken a campus tour of a college or university, maybe either for yourself, a child or young family member, or as part of your professional role? If so, we wager that there may have been someone in your tour group who asked the spirited young guide a variation of a very common question: "In your opinion, what is the best thing about this place?" or "What do you like most about this college?" We believe the most frequent answer—by far—is, "It's *the people.*"

In almost every case at the many great universities that we've collectively toured, the tour guide doesn't spend most of her time waxing poetic about the dining hall food or explaining how she thinks the gates to the campus are especially beautiful. She doesn't talk about the *things.* Instead, she talks about the deep friendship she has developed with her roommate from Singapore, or how all of the students in her "Urban Politics in the United States" course have varying opinions and enjoy challenging each other. She tells the enraptured tour group about walking home after class and hearing no fewer than five different languages being spoken as her peers chat with their families on the phone. Without the people, specifically, without the *students*, a college campus is just a collection of buildings.

This simple fact holds truer for colleges and universities—particularly those that are residential and at least reasonably selective—than any other institution we can think of. How many other environments bring together young adults who are from different backgrounds and economic means, hold different identities, and are interested in completely different things? In most American high schools, students tend to grow up with fellow students who come from at least roughly similar economic backgrounds, and often, similar social and religious backgrounds as well. Additionally, students generally don't have any decision-making ability in selecting that specific high school. Even later in life, students' environments are not as diverse as when they were in college. The people they work or live with tend to be somewhat similar to them, at least in terms of interests or core beliefs.

It is particularly because colleges are so different than any other environment in society that higher education leaders need to prioritize capitalizing on diversity in a respectful and productive way. For many students, these interactions are an important component of what they seek from their college experience. They *want* their values to be challenged; they *want* to be sharpened by their peers. They are excited to sit in classes where debates will erupt, where students with different views will speak up, where steel sharpens steel. These students are eager to meet peers from all over the world who grew up in circumstances that differ from their own.

There is also something special about the shared experience of being accepted to and choosing to attend, out of the thousands of colleges in the United States alone, that particular one. We see this come up time and time again in our interactions and interviews with students. These young adults assume, from their very first day, a few key things about their new campus colleagues. They assume that every undergraduate on the campus (a) works hard; (b) is very good at several things; and (c) cares about education. Otherwise, as so many students we have spoken with point out, those "other" students, of whatever race, ethnicity, socioeconomic class, or country of origin, wouldn't have been accepted. Put another way, students from entirely different backgrounds feel an almost immediate kinship and sense of goodwill toward the large majority of their fellow students. For so many of them, sharing core values with their new colleagues and friends is far more important than coming from the same neighborhood or even sharing racial or religious or ethnic group backgrounds. Such assumptions could not be made about fellow students in their local high schools, particularly those that are public and draw enrollees solely from one particular town or city.

We are aware that this way of thinking paints a perhaps overly rosy picture of American higher education. Our country's colleges and universities have complex and challenging histories that do not always inspire pride for those who call them home today. For many students, particularly those who are part of groups that have faced discriminatory admissions policies or identity-based biases once on campus, it can be understandably difficult to view college as a place where they can bring their whole selves and share their stories without fear of repercussion or bias. That being said, we maintain a strong sense of optimism that colleges and universities are incredibly well suited to be places where positive, lasting, systemic change occurs. This really is the emphasis of our book: What can campus communities do to relentlessly work toward improving the system for *all* students?

So, what does all of this mean for college leaders? In many ways, the news is good. Campuses that make a point to attract and enroll a diverse array of students, which is essentially every solid residential college or university in America, already have the most important component of capitalizing on background differences: the students themselves. If there is a particular subgroup that is underrepresented or not present at all, college leadership should make an effort to address that with the Admissions Office. Getting those students to campus is not the focus of this chapter, though we do touch upon it in other parts of this book. Instead, throughout this chapter we will suggest several practical answers to quite predictable questions. For example, how can a college structure an experience for all students to capitalize on the enormous benefit of being on campus together? What can students, especially student leaders of campus organizations, do to work together cooperatively? How should residential life and in-class time be structured to allow students to learn not just from professors, but also each other? These are not easy questions to answer, particularly considering the social dynamics and identity politics that may make students mistrustful of genuine efforts to connect. The point we want to stress here is that strong colleges in the U.S. today are increasingly well positioned for this work.

Creating a Productive Residential Life Experience

It seems obvious that diversity among students could wield its biggest impact in a college's residential life setting. Students spend a tremendous amount of their time—indeed, the overwhelming majority of it—outside of the classroom. Rather than simply being a place where they store their belongings and try to get a few hours of sleep each night, a student's residence has enormous potential for becoming a natural and hopefully comfortable place to debate new ideas. It offers a place to share unique perspectives.

Freshmen might crowd their narrow hallways as they lean against the walls, sliding a communal carton of pretzels or cookies back and forth across the floor while they debate philosophy and politics (plus more personal topics, such as what it means to build good interpersonal relationships) long into the night. A group of sophomores interested in leadership may choose to apply for housing in a residential hall that is focused on that topic. Realizing that they only have two years left, junior roommates might choose a class to take together for fun so they can study together, enjoy one another's company, and simultaneously deepen their learning. Seniors in the same residential setting rely on each other for support and encouragement during their job search or graduate school application processes.

For many students, these are the experiences that they dream about having before they even start college. These can be a key differentiator in distinguishing high school from college. So how can universities position their residential living options to offer such opportunities and potential for growth? Put differently, are there certain policies that campus leaders can put into place or encourage, that generally lead to good outcomes and enhance students' experiences? Every university and college leader we know has thought hard about these precise questions.

Building a Residential Experience Where
People Who Disagree Can Learn from Each
Other and Even Become Friends

College is often the first time when eighteen-year-old students find themselves living, usually in very close proximity, with other eighteen-year-olds. It's also not just living; it's sleeping, studying, eating, and often even sharing bathrooms. This is a dramatic adjustment from living at home with parents or guardians. It means students will be closer together, both physically and psychologically, than most of them have ever experienced before. The *psychologically* part matters a lot. A predictable result is that certain disagreements or differences in viewpoints can become magnified. College leaders (including student leaders) have a great opportunity to convey a specific message to students:

> All boundaries are permeable. One reason you are here at this superb college is to learn not only from faculty but also from your fellow students. That means you have to be willing to come together, discuss, and sometimes disagree. The key point is to always do it in good spirit and commit to maintaining a respectful dialogue. If you disagree with someone about almost anything, of course you can question their thinking, their evidence, and their assumptions. Yet you should avoid questioning their motives. If you question a fellow student's motives for presenting who they are or what they believe, this makes it very difficult to have a cordial, helpful conversation where everyone can learn something and hopefully even enjoy it.

Author Richard Light remembers an instance with one of his first-year advisees, a young woman who came to him one day years ago looking rather distraught. She told him about her assigned roommate and shared her concerns about whether they would get along. She sounded pretty unhappy. "I have certain core values that are an important part of who I am and how I see myself. There is a big problem here. I can't imagine how it can be resolved. I am philosophically pro-choice for women. I have thought about this view for years. It is an unshakable part of how I define who I am," the young woman explained. "Yet I was assigned to live with a roommate whose core value is that she is pro-life. I can't even begin to imagine how the two of us will ever get along. . . ."

Light is entirely clear that he is not a psychoanalyst. But he is comfortable sharing simple bits of advice with his students. "I fully understand and respect what you just told me," he began. "I have a suggestion for you to consider—please just give it some thought. Why don't you share your concern, tell your roommate the truth that you don't share her views, and simply agree to disagree with her on this point. Surely there are *dozens* of other topics where you can enjoy your roommate's company. It is your choice and her choice if you want to try to change each other's beliefs. I am simply saying that because you disagree on one big point, important to you as it is, that doesn't make her a bad person and you may end up enjoying her company in sixteen other dimensions."

At the beginning of spring semester, this same young woman came to see Light for her monthly academic advising appointment. When Light asked her whether she had plans for where and with whom she would live next year, the advisee responded, "Yes—my current roommate and I enjoy each other a lot, so we invited two more friends to join and the four of us will be living together in one of the residence halls." The two women had—without either of them changing their opinions or adjusting their core values—figured out that they had plenty of other beliefs and shared interests that brought them together.

This is the type of positive growth and genuine human interaction that we believe every college should strive to foster in students. By reminding them to embrace background differences rather than be put off by them—and work to unearth common ground—students may find a happier coexistence than they ever initially imagined. Often, they will even develop close unexpected friendships. This is a lesson not only for college, but for life itself. It is impossible, and highly undesirable, to avoid interacting with people whose backgrounds and ideologies differ from our own. By equipping students with the tools to reject the idea that their differences should separate them, colleges can help create a better, more tolerant citizenry.

This simple example of these two roommates is all good to write about—our recommendation to any dean would be to take one more step. It would be to share this true story, or any other similar example that comes to mind from a particular campus, with the entire incoming freshman class as they assemble at the beginning of their first year. The point of the example is obvious. It is wonderfully constructive if a dean reminds incoming students that one goal of college is not to simply replicate a student's high school experiences—similar activities, similar friends, similar sets of beliefs. The whole point is to grow, to expand perspectives, and to think in new ways. Even better, if a student is comfortable and willing, the dean might want to encourage every student to make a point to seek out others who may disagree with them about something. Spending time with a group of friends all of whom agree about most everything—why bother? You don't need the whole group. Just one person would be enough. Because that one person could speak for the entire group since everyone agrees. Each dean can craft these welcoming words to suit her or his campus culture. The main point is to say the words out loud. Don't assume the students all know this already. Many don't.

Living Together in a Residential Setting Where Others Share Your Interests

One of the other elements we inquired about during interviews with 240 students was their impression of "race-based dorms" where students from a particular racial group might opt to live together. There is overwhelmingly little support for this concept among those we interviewed—half from private colleges and universities, and half from public universities. In our recent survey, a total of 11 graduating seniors out of 120 at private campuses supported this idea. On public campuses, the support came from 28 out of 120. These are slight differences, yet the overarching takeaway is that most students do not favor "race-based" residential living arrangements.

One caveat may be important to add. The fraction of students supporting these types of residential settings is low. Yet many of these same students are entirely comfortable with "theme-based" residential living, when the theme is a substantive topic, skill, or common interest shared by a group of students. For example, it is rare to find undergraduates who oppose residential living based around "French Literature" or "STEM lab work" or "Asian History."

Many students, each in their own words, make a simple point. It is that each of us individually lives with two very different sets of variables. One set is the *uncontrollable variables* of our lives. We are born into a specific geography, perhaps into a certain religion, to parents who may be high income or low income—the point is we have no control whatsoever over the starting position of any of these categories. Students overwhelmingly feel that the way a campus organizes students' living arrangements should not simply build upon, codify, or strengthen these "uncontrollable" variables. Students don't choose their parents, where they grow up, how much money their family has, and so on. To formalize and basically design these differences into living arrangements is certainly not a way to encourage students from different backgrounds to learn from one another.

In contrast, each student brings to any campus certain *controllable variables*. Do they choose to work hard? That is up to them and entirely within their control. Do they enjoy writing and want to produce articles for a campus's student newspaper? Again, this is up to each student and entirely within their control. Same for their substantive academic interests, whether it is Italian Renaissance history, physics, or anything else. Do they enjoy participating in drama, or any number of arts-based opportunities on many campuses? Entirely up to each student to decide. There are so many controllable variables in each student's life. Most undergraduates find it an appealing idea to live alongside students who share the common interests that they themselves have chosen. This allows them to have deeper discussions and often gain new insights.

Many colleges call these living arrangements "Living and Learning Communities," or some variant of those words. We think this is terrific. Opting in to such a residential structure allows students to connect with others who share a chosen interest and can set them up well to constructively contribute to each other's learning, both inside and outside of the classroom.

Emphasizing Shared Goals in Extracurriculars

Two sophomore students at a given college sprint after a soccer ball, sweat flying from their foreheads as they hustle down the field. One swiftly sends the ball careening toward his teammate, who scores the winning goal of the match.

Fourteen students, freshmen through seniors, saunter up the stairs of the theater and take their assigned spots around the semicircle of microphones. As the soloist opens his mouth and begins to sing, the others harmonize in perfect unison beside him.

Ten students gather around a conference table at 10:00 p.m., cold brew coffee parked in front of each one. The president of the club glances over at the secretary and asks if he is ready to begin their undergraduate board meeting.

In these moments, each group of students is *focused on a common goal*: achieving the result that brought them to the field, the theater, or the meeting room that day. In a perfect world, this is arguably when any particular bias should matter the least: students should be purely focused on how they can work constructively with their fellow student who is sitting, standing, running, or singing next to them. However, we know that this is not always the case. Humans hold preconceptions and make assumptions about others. That said, we believe in the power of extracurricular activities as a catalyst for constructive sharing of experiences and gradual tearing down of whatever stereotypes students may hold. It is specifically because of the emphasis on the shared goals that this is the case.

When it comes to extracurricular activities, campus leaders have to make decisions that set students up for success in positive, constructive interactions. The answers are not always easy. We have seen many situations in which students come to a leader asking to create a new group on campus, oriented around a particular topic that is important to them. Each school has different rules about starting new organizations, and we suggest that these be reviewed to ensure that they are *as inclusive as possible* without creating confusion or resentment among students.

Campus leaders also have to make decisions about the membership of such groups, particularly for those that are identity focused. As a somewhat lighthearted example, several universities have Canada Clubs. Should membership be restricted solely to Canadian passport holders? Maybe citizens as well as those who have parents or grandparents who were born in Canada? Should it be open to anyone, even if their only connection to Canada is a love of hockey and admiration of a particular prime minister? Although many leaders may tend toward being as inclusive as possible, it could have negative ramifications for the full group if someone joins whose intentions are not pure. Maybe someone shows up to a meeting not to show appreciation for Canada, but rather to cause commotion and make fun of participating students' accents. We see various policies playing out at campuses across the country, without a clear answer about what is "best." We offer this point just to reinforce the importance of having conversations when setting extracurricular policy on a campus. Each college or university needs to consider its unique culture and student body when making these decisions.

Setting Standards for Inclusion

As we write this book, many colleges are working hard to develop robust policies built around the word *inclusion*, perhaps especially for extracurricular activities. What exactly does it mean to be inclusive? It certainly is an easy catchword, and it has become widely used. The serious question is how do presidents, deans, and student leaders actually implement this word in the most constructive way to fit a campus culture?

One way to make this idea concrete is to think about several examples. Right now, on some of America's most well-known college campuses, you can drop into the Hillel (a place of community for Jewish students) and oftentimes find some Muslim students sitting and joining their Jewish friends for dinner. Some campuses, like Oberlin College, even have formal operations (there, it takes the form of a Kosher-Halal Co-op) that practice interfaith cooperation and friendship oriented around common dietary laws.

How does this happen? Does it happen organically, all by itself? Not usually. Instead, these campuses have generally put into place some rules about inclusion and been strategic about organizational setup. Put simply, these rules—dictated sometimes by administrators but in other cases the students themselves—require that campus organizations make every effort to include any student who wishes in good faith to participate.

An example that author Richard Light has experienced firsthand involves Harvard's Kuumba Singers group ("Kuumba" is a Swahili word that means "to create"). In 1970, Black students on campus organized in the pursuit of a space that would allow them to celebrate who they were and where they came from. Many decades later, the group remains a place where *any* student is welcome.

The Kuumba Singers website heartily proclaims, "As a non-audition choir and as a community, this space is always open to all identities and their intersections. Come as you are." The result is that if a visitor comes to Harvard and takes a seat in a large, often-packed, auditorium to see a Kuumba performance, they will see dozens of students take the stage to sing music from the African diaspora, dance, and perform spoken word. These students hold a variety of identities, both visible and not visible, and it is quite clear even to the audience that everyone is welcomed and appreciated.

The week following one such performance that Light attended, he interviewed several of the African American student performers in this interracial and inclusive Kuumba Singers group. He asked each one about why they believed that the group's membership model worked so well. He encouraged them to be honest. The students each gave some version of a similar response.

To quote one student: "I care so much about this activity—it is entirely voluntary, and I love singing the songs, dancing, spending time with the other members, all of it. All of us who show up to sing share one simple goal. We want to sound great and be part of a community. I don't care about my friends' race or ethnicity; all I care about is their voice. I want all of my fellow singers to sound great, and I try to help them to do that. They do the same for me. Our goal is simple, and it unites everyone who participates."

Meanwhile at other colleges, the same inclusion idea is rejected or not yet possible. A white, Asian, or Latinx student is not really welcome to join a group like the Kuumba Singers. Instead, students try to keep groups' membership more restricted so they can have a safe place to be themselves on campus. This should signal something important to campus leaders as well. Although inclusive extracurricular groups that work as constructively as the Kuumba Singers may be a goal for many colleges, we understand that not every campus community is set up for such inclusive policies to work well. Each campus must decide what policies should govern its student organizations. This is a judgment call for thoughtful leaders on each campus, and they may come to different conclusions that change over time.

Inviting Unique Perspectives into the Classroom

Diversity in the classroom can be a sensitive subject. Faculty members can be so focused on "getting it right" that they skew toward not mentioning it at all. Background differences can be a delicate topic for many students, and most faculty simply have no wish to offend them. Students, especially underclassmen, may assume that their experiences are commonplace or that others might find their perspectives obvious or predictable. Some students tell us straightforwardly they occasionally are fearful of triggering negative reactions from their fellow students. Occasionally this could be due to others' biases or prejudices. Other times it is simply that students have different core values, so the result is students who hesitate to share views they anticipate might be controversial.

Yet if diversity—of background, thought, and ideas—is one of the key reasons that college is so important, it should be widely viewed as a disaster when students do not feel comfortable sharing their views openly about controversial topics. One of the best avenues for not just allowing but *encouraging* students to have that experience is in the classroom. It is there that they are sitting with peers who share a common interest (we assume students taking a class either are genuinely interested in the topic, or that it might be a requirement for their course of study). Yet they might otherwise not know their classmates, which is all the more reason for faculty to encourage students to speak up and to engage with some vigorous discussion. Clearly faculty members need to play a critical role here, juggling the need to welcome unusual or unpopular views from students, while simultaneously creating a tone of trust and mutual respect among those in their classrooms.

Using Teachly to Enhance Inclusion in the Classroom

One method we admire for inviting students' varying perspectives is Teachly, a tool that has been introduced with success at several universities by creators Dan Levy, Karti Subramanian, and Teddy Svoronos. Teachly allows faculty to collect information about students before they even set foot in the classroom, but also to monitor things like a professor's calling patterns and student participation. When students enroll in a given course, they are sent a link prompting them to complete a Teachly profile. Students can input information with as much detail as is desired, including interesting facts about themselves, their substantive background in the academic subject, and their goals for what they are hoping to gain from the class. This allows students to self-define their own background and short- and long-term aspirations. The instructor can then inform his or her teaching accordingly. For students who might be hesitant to speak up verbally about elements of their identity, Teachly may provide a welcome entry point.

For example, perhaps a theology professor is preparing for a class session about monotheism. He skims through the Teachly profiles to see if any students have noted that they practice any of the monotheistic religions. When he does, he notices that one of the students has not yet spoken up in class during the past four weeks. He sends that student an email to ask if she might be willing to share her experience, along with some sample questions that he would like to pose. She responds enthusiastically. "Thank you for asking! I've been a bit hesitant to speak up in class; I'm a freshman and I'm a little intimidated by some of the upperclassmen in the course," she admits. During the class session later that week, the student speaks about her firsthand experience and she helps other students in her class to get a perspective that they may not otherwise have had. This, in our opinion, showcases one of the very best parts of college: when students from all different backgrounds come together to learn and share.

Inviting and Welcoming Students' Suggestions for Class Readings

Another suggestion is inviting—or perhaps even requiring—students to comment on a course reading list, and ultimately to make suggestions about additional texts that would enhance the diversity of perspectives, as well as the diversity of authors' backgrounds. This requires students to do serious, scholarly research, instead of simply lamenting that there are too many dead, white male authors. Many students seem to have not thought about this option before coming to college—the idea that they as undergraduates could play a serious role in shaping their course reading lists. This also gives them a deeper sense of investment and interest in the course itself. They "have skin in the game," so to speak. Because they have to put in some work, their engagement in the class will almost certainly be greater.

Importantly, when faculty invite undergraduates' suggestions, those students see that the instructor is thoughtful about shaping the course to fit their interests and ensuring that multiple voices are heard through the text. This is also a great opportunity for students who may have great ideas but are a bit more hesitant or shy about speaking up in class. By suggesting a reading for the class that is meaningful to them, they can contribute to shaping the course curriculum. A professor may well feel free to invite these students to speak up since they are the ones who suggested the readings for that day.

How Much Should a Faculty Member Share about Themselves in Class?

For those for whom it is comfortable, we recommend that faculty be transparent in sharing relevant details about themselves. This may be best done during an opening class session when the professor is welcoming students to the course. Clearly, he or she holds a deep passion for the subject that was shaped by their unique background and experiences. Perhaps one professor grew up with highly religious and conservative parents but now holds a doctorate in Women's Studies. Maybe another was the only female student in her high school Chemistry Club and decided to pursue a PhD in molecular engineering after a classmate made a snide comment. A third could have grown up hearing that people who looked like him couldn't lead a business, so he worked to get an MBA and recently retired as CEO of a Fortune 500 company so he could teach at the local university.

There is a story to every advanced degree, and we encourage faculty to share that pathway with students when appropriate. Doing so serves many purposes. It immediately humanizes the professor, especially to first-year students who can often feel intimidated at first. Hearing their professor's story might give a nervous student the confidence to attend office hours to learn more. It can also encourage students to share their own stories and experiences by creating an environment where doing so is welcomed. This can enhance the class conversation—as well as establish a sense of trust—for the rest of the semester.

Don't Assume All Students from a Certain Background Share the Same Experience

Students who are the first in their families to attend college. Students of color. Students who are "at academic risk." Students from low-income backgrounds. It is human nature to sort large groups into "buckets" that make the components easier to understand. In many ways, this can be positive. More scholarships for students of a specific income level: often a good thing. Extra academic support if needed for those who may come from low-quality high schools: also a good thing. Peer support for groups that are deemed underrepresented on that campus: certainly it has potential.

Yet there is a flip side that we feel is too often ignored. Far too many campuses have not yet figured out that not all—but many—such students emphatically do not want, and in some cases strongly resent, such categorizations. Labeling first-generation college students almost immediately upon acceptance as "students at risk" (which some colleges do) or designating them as students who should all be put into some sort of special group with special needs, may indeed fit some modest fraction of such students. For those students, special categorizations can be helpful; they may even be an academic life-saver. Yet for many others, it is a poor fit. Many students in these supposedly identifiable subgroups have no wish to be classified in a college bureaucrat's checkbox list. It is not how they view themselves. It is not how they wish others to perceive them.

Many students instead prefer an entirely different sense of self-identification. When asked to describe who they are, students often respond, "I am a writer," "I am a theater buff," "I thrive in a chemistry laboratory," or "I love analyzing modern art." They then go on to note that their own self-definition has frankly little or nothing to do with being the first generation in their family to attend college, nor is it connected to the adjusted gross income of their parents. Many such students continue by indicating their disdain for being pigeonholed into a special subgroup. "I am here at college to get the full, American collegiate experience. *I* want to define which groups I am part of—not an administrator who thinks they know who I am before even meeting me."

One bit of concrete evidence: at an Ivy League campus, first-generation college students were asked if they had any interest in joining a newly formed "First-Generation College Student Union." Eleven percent enthusiastically said yes. Forty-six percent said they couldn't imagine attending such meetings. The other 43 percent said some version of, "Get that away from me." For these students, college was viewed as an equalizer; now that they were on campus, they wanted to be viewed as equal to their peers in every way. Every college leader we know talks constantly about the importance of treating each student with great respect. We couldn't agree more. What better way to treat each student with respect than to let each person choose their own way to describe or to identify themselves. Our point is that every single person on a college campus has a different lived experience. Each college should do its very best to serve each student authentically without making assumptions.

We assume it is obvious that pigeonholing students into categories that don't align with their own sense of self, and their personally chosen self-identity, has the potential to introduce frustration, ill will, and demoralization. We see this arise quite often during summer bridge programs for students who are deemed by their college to need extra academic support due to a piece of their profile: maybe test scores, the high school they attended, or first-generation status. No office aspires to offend a student when they ask them to attend a bridge program, but this messaging can easily come across as, "We admitted you, but actually we don't think you're quite smart enough to thrive alongside your classmates unless you do something about it this summer." How demoralizing to begin your undergraduate experience that way, thinking that the college you were so excited to attend now apparently doesn't believe it is clear you can succeed.

Many of the students who step onto a college campus for the first time have an extremely limited reference point; they have generally not interacted in regard to academics with those from either more or less rigorous high school settings. Really, the only point of comparison they may have is their standardized test scores, which are somewhat limited by subject. When a student enters her Introduction to Economics course, she has little concept of how well prepared she really is compared to everyone else in that room. In one sense, this is a strength: the student might be more motivated to do the reading and study on the weekends if she senses that she might be behind. But, if she is *really* behind, she might also struggle to identify the appropriate resources until it is too late to improve her grade in the class. Some colleges try to account for this by allowing students to complete their first semester under a flexible "pass/no pass" option rather than requiring letter grades. This allows students to learn what is available by way of academic support and better identify a workable study strategy. But what if students could better understand this context and learn how to seek the help that they need *when they need it*?

We suggest putting this power in the students' hands; after all, they are the ones who best understand their own background irrespective of any particular labels that college administrators might bestow. As with nearly all of our recommendations, one strategy for this is particularly low cost and not hard to implement: ask the students about their experiences before entering college. This could take the form of a mandatory incoming student survey or even a friendly one-on-one chat with the academic advisor. Yes—this takes some effort, yet the payoff can be high. Rather than just assuming that all low-income students are less prepared than their peers to succeed in a rigorous academic environment, for example, this allows students to self-report information about their high school setting, study habits, or confidence about succeeding in college classes. Offering suggestions or invitations using such information from students still allows colleges to send out information about resources or bridge programs in large, cost-effective batches. The difference is that it is a bit more tailored for the reality of a student's life rather than some uncontrollable circumstances that might not reflect their reality.

Set a Positive Tone and Stick to It

Many undergraduate students arrive to campus with relatively few preconceptions about what to expect. Many have never set foot in a college classroom, much less a residence hall, dining facility, or university library. They are impressionable, which makes *the tone that university leadership sets* all the more important.

The Welcome

Almost all colleges and universities welcome new students to campus during a period of time (ranging from a few days to a week or more) known as orientation. This is a time for students to meet each other, figure out how to navigate their new environment, choose classes, and learn about what is to come. It is also the ideal time for campus leaders to set a tone for the expectation of how students will interact with each other. These conversations can take place by different people and in different mediums, but we suggest that each college's core message should come from multiple leaders to reaffirm the commitment. A few examples:

- A president might send out a welcome email to the whole university community emphasizing her commitment to fostering a respectful and collaborative environment where all students feel comfortable being themselves and sharing what makes them unique. In addition to setting the tone, she may offer data about the racial, ethnic, political, or religious differences that exist on campus and generate positive excitement around them. In almost every case, the profile of a group of students on a college campus looks quite different from profiles of most public high schools. Students will be navigating an environment that may be very new to them. Those differences and changes should be publicly acknowledged and *celebrated*.

- During his opening address to first-year students, a dean may speak in further detail about the "controllable" versus "uncontrollable" variables that we mentioned before. "Every one of you sitting before me today has two broad sets of characteristics," he might begin. "One set are your uncontrollable factors: who your parents are, your race, your height, your family income. A second set is what you can do and accomplish and become during your precious years here at this great college: how hard you work, what goals you set, how you spend your time, how you treat your friends, how you might work at least a little bit to think beyond yourself and work to make the world around you a better place." The dean may go on to share a personal anecdote or give specific examples of when students with different backgrounds have come together in collaboration. The dean might share just one example from his own life. Immediately this helps to make it personal, rather than just saying, "These things exist."

- A freshman residential hall advisor could share success stories of people who came into the dorm not expecting to get along with their roommate (see example above with the pro-choice and pro-life young women) but who have now become lifelong friends. He may offer himself as a resource for students as they have concerns throughout the year or point them toward who they should talk to for specific things, such as roommate troubles, bias in the classroom, or interest in starting a new student organization. Students always should feel they have tools and know who to turn to for questions or support.

We are happy to report that the cost of each of these conversations is essentially zero dollars. Aside from the time that it takes to craft a message or schedule an event where students can hear it, this suggestion does not require any vast cash infusion. We wonder, having heard more than a few welcoming speeches to new students when they first arrive at different colleges, whether people sometimes forget how powerful words can be. Adapting messaging or being extremely intentional about conveying meaning doesn't seem like a "big" thing; after all, it's not necessarily creating any new initiatives nor launching a new academic department. Still, word choice can matter a lot. The college welcome is a critical opportunity for deans and other leaders to signal to new, understandably nervous first-years that there are people on campus who will be there to listen to them no matter what, and that leadership is committed to making sure that every student has a positive experience.

Sustaining the Welcome Message

Some colleges offer a terrific welcome and then forget to follow up. The initial warm welcome message should not be lost as the year progresses. Undergraduates need to see that their leadership is excited about the mix of students that are on campus and interested in helping them learn not only from textbooks and professors, but also from each other. If that message comes once and then fades into the background or periphery, students are likely to either forget it or begin to believe that the campus is not actually committed. Undergraduates should feel proud of their leadership. That starts with college leaders conveying—early and often—what their priorities are and what is being done to accomplish them.

Back Up Words with Actions (and Funding)

From the student perspective, few things are as meaningful as when an administrator states a priority and actually places funding behind it. Rather than simply "talking the talk," they are solidifying their commitment to a specific ideal. The student then feels empowered to innovate within that space and dream up new initiatives that move the dial toward achieving the environment that they want. A powerful example of that would be an emphasis on encouraging different student organizations, often with nearly diametrically opposing goals, to work together and to create constructive campus conversations.

When a group of College Republicans are meeting at any school, one student might observe to her friends, "You know, we always have speakers who share our core views. Because of that, we have the same audience at every one of our events—I can even show you on the attendance sheet. What if we partnered with the College Democrats to host a good-spirited and respectful debate?" The Republican Club considers it and ultimately decides to invite the College Democrats to work together and create an entry for the college's "Collaboration Grant." This would be a specific fund allocated to encourage different groups to work together on campus projects. The endowment could first be set up by a team of alumni who value diverse thinking by sponsoring collegial debates. The college would ideally both encourage it and help steward it through a straightforward application process.

How might this work? The heads of outreach for both the College Republicans and College Democrats meet for an hour over lunch. They agree on shared goals and outcomes for the event, as well as how a grant award would be spent. They submit their proposal to college leadership and learn a week later it has been approved. The groups then invite two relatively prominent political experts for an off-the-record debate, and event attendance is through the roof. Both clubs see a spike in their membership, and the student newspaper profiles the two students who led the planning process. They reference the grant as the catalyst for making it happen, and several additional groups submit applications later that week. Importantly, the students who helped plan the event *and* those who attended not only had their own viewpoints expanded by the content, but they also learned that such intelligent and objective discourse is important enough that the college is willing to actually put tangible resources behind it.

Meanwhile, this simple idea of two or more campus groups cooperating generates some additional side benefits. First, the leaders of the College Democrats and College Republicans may—after several planning meetings together to decide whom to invite, how to organize an event, and how to most wisely spend their grant money—realize that they enjoy working together. They certainly may form some personal friendships. That is bonus number one. Second, because the two groups with clearly different ideologies are publicly cooperating to develop a speaker's series, the benefits from this collaborating resound across the entire campus. Many other students see how Democrats and Republicans are—quite publicly and enthusiastically—working together effectively. Can this be a bad thing? We think it sends a clear signal across any campus about the benefits and pleasure of working constructively with fellow students who may disagree about something that matters to them. Yet everyone can be cordial, supportive, and friendly every step of the way, even while having some disagreements.

Actions like this contribute to an overall spirit of encouraging innovation from students on a campus. Undergraduates understand that their work can have an impact. They see firsthand that administrators are actually listening to what they have to say. This seemingly simple idea of student groups and organizations with different goals cooperating and working together can help to create a culture of continuous improvement, student engagement, and positive change for any campus.

A Final Note

Throughout this chapter, we made several suggestions for how colleges can generate their own good ideas to enhance interactions between students from varying backgrounds or identities, whatever they may be. Award-winning author and historian Tara Westover points to this as a key element of being educated: "Part of the way that I would define education was getting access to other points of view," she notes. We love her perspective here, particularly since she was once the type of student that others might have held a strong and immediate bias against (her father opposed public education, so she was seventeen before she set foot in her first classroom). Getting an education isn't just about winning arguments.

When college alumni are asked what they remember as their best moments at their college, they sometimes describe in remarkable detail moments where they learned to hear opinions that differed from their own. Sometimes hearing such views—especially for the first time—surprised them. Alumni also point to how many of their best memories often involve moments in which they learned how to make informed arguments, and how to converse civilly with people they seemed to have nothing in common with on the surface. Events like these really are what make a college campus special. It is each student's interactions with people who are different that broaden horizons, shape perspectives, and clarify ideas. One of our favorite quotes comes from that pro-choice student who learned how to build a great friendship with her pro-life roommate: "Our discussions didn't lead me to change *what* I believe. But for the first time after our many discussions I really understand and can explain *why* I believe what I believe." We consider this to be college at its very best.

9

Building Opportunities for Lifelong Learning and Engagement

Each spring, colleges and universities send out enthusiastic letters to the group of new students that their admissions teams have chosen to admit. A typical letter proclaims something along the lines of, "We are pleased to inform you that you have been accepted to the four-year program leading to a bachelor's degree at our wonderful college. We hope you choose to join us." Now imagine an expanded sentence in that same admissions letter with an additional clause: "We are also admitting you to a seventy-year journey—built around your college community—for the rest of your life." Do most college graduates remember such a line in their own acceptance letters? Maybe. Would they say that their alma mater has actually delivered on that promise? Perhaps, but probably not.

It is not that university leaders don't *want* to provide students with lifelong learning experiences. In Drew Faust's final year as president of Harvard, she shared with several colleagues that her highest priority was to initiate a systematic, serious, rigorous, and substantial program of lifelong learning for Harvard graduates. Yale's dean of social sciences, Bryan Garsten, has commented that building a platform of lifelong learning is the leading goal of his deanship.

As one looks across the enormous variety of different colleges and universities across America, it is hard to find examples of those that are managing lifelong learning effectively. There is no clear model or "best practices" checklist to follow but rather still a lot of questions.

How can such a venture be organized? Who will pay for it? Would it be a mix of on-campus and online learning for graduates of a university? How would the teaching work? Would it be primarily an academic, social, or networking venture? No clear answers have emerged.

Our view is most college leaders' time and energy are consumed by what appear on the surface to be more time sensitive issues. As they grapple with declining enrollment, skyrocketing costs, and a growing public skepticism of higher education, lifelong learning has unintentionally but understandably fallen into the category of "nice to have but not essential." It is not difficult to imagine that if your graduation rates are crawling along below the national average, you probably are not spending much time thinking about whether alumni are participating in webinars or attending Alaskan cruises together.

We would like to present our optimistic point of view: many universities have *already started* on the path to lifelong learning, whether it is intentional or not. For the most part, the infrastructure and actors are already in place; the work is just not yet being conducted through the specific lens of lifelong learning. The question we seek to answer in this chapter is how to build upon those existing frameworks to really catalyze students' engagement *both* during their time on campus as well as years after their graduation caps have been catapulted into the air.

We believe that thinking in this way will address the longstanding dilemma of what to do about lifelong learning. For another bit of optimism, we suggest how a robust lifelong learning strategy may very well also be one of the most valuable tools for combating the more proximate challenges related to enrollment, costs, and mistrust. When implemented in a way that addresses specific campus needs, the components of a lifelong learning strategy can be some of the most powerful tools available to campus leaders.

A Small but Important Shift: "Lifelong Learning" to "Lifelong Engagement"

Word choice can matter. Our view is that the goal for colleges and universities is not only lifelong learning for its students and alumni—really it is to promote graduates' sense of lifelong *engagement* with their college or university. Why might this matter? In our eyes, the word "engagement" differs slightly from the word "learning" in at least one important way—engagement implies a commitment, or at least the possibility, of an alumnus giving something back. Once students graduate, their relationship to the campus doesn't diminish but rather adapts to their new circumstances. A wonderful form of engagement might be a graduate who volunteers to mentor a current undergraduate or a fellow alumnus. This hopefully conveys our wish to connect older alumni who are delighted to teach with younger or future alumni who are eager to learn, by facilitating a series of enjoyable and productive human relationships.

But don't extension schools and continuing education programs already do this? Actually, no—this isn't exactly what we mean. These programs, many of which are highly regarded and of excellent quality, offer both alumni and others the chance to take classes outside of a traditional four-year experience. They offer a certain kind of lifelong learning that can be excellent—yet we view such programs as just a piece of what is possible. The personal connections we are emphasizing in this chapter are different from what is included in these continuing education or lifelong learning programs.

A Useful Analogy

Several years after graduating from college, author Allison Jegla was interviewing to become part of a work and international travel program called Remote Year. "If accepted to the cohort, what are your unique strengths and skills that you would be able to share with the Remote Year community?" the interviewer queried. Jegla paused; she hadn't really thought much about that. Instead, she was focused on the prospect of participating in such a once-in-a-lifetime experience. She was transfixed by the excitement of living abroad and meeting new people. Feeling a bit selfish, Jegla realized that she had been focused inward: on what *her* experience would look like and what *she* would gain.

Sound somewhat familiar? This thought process mirrors that of many entering college freshmen. Like Jegla interviewing for the

Remote Year program, they are excited about the prospects that await them. They are eager to live in a new place, make new friends, and enrich their minds through the study of new academic disciplines. Few stop to think about their responsibility to the campus community of which they are now becoming a part.

While Jegla was participating in Remote Year, her interviewer's question kept coming to mind again and again. She felt somewhat embarrassed that it had taken an interviewer to actually ask the question. Perhaps as a result, she was constantly on the lookout for ways to add value to her community, whether that be helping raise money for a social impact partner, contributing professional expertise to cohort-mates, or doing informational interviews with prospective Remote Year participants. Importantly, that level of engagement remained just as strong for years after Jegla's program formally ended. She still champions Remote Year to anyone who will listen and travels frequently with former program participants. When she first moved to Massachusetts, the first thing she did was look up the Boston-based set of Remote Year alumni—who soon became her strongest social group.

As she was being interviewed, Jegla represented an incoming college freshman: excited about the prospect of a life-changing opportunity but not thinking much about her active participation with other members during or after the experience. As she ended Remote Year, her actions represented our vision for a successful "lifelong engagement" platform in the higher education setting: one in which students contribute to and celebrate their alma mater by engaging with the community for the rest of their lives.

By subtly setting an *expectation* that participants would not only physically be part of the community but actually, *tangibly* enhance it, the interviewer had shifted Jegla's point of view for the entire experience. It cost $0 and about thirty seconds for him to ask the one question, but it had an immeasurable effect on Jegla's behavior for years to come.

Somewhat counterintuitively, we suggest that the process of lifelong engagement needs to begin at the *start* of a student's experience, rather than as an add-on once they graduate. First-year students should be primed to both give and take from their college or university *both* during their on-campus experience and then for the rest of their lives. How does one set this expectation? We can offer several suggestions, ranging from simple nuances in messaging to larger-scale event creation. At the core, we urge college leaders to capitalize on the resources they already have rather than trying to start building a lifelong learning program from scratch. This should be less overwhelming, more effective, and probably a lot less expensive, too.

Suggestion 1: Mobilize Alumni Interviewers before Students Even Apply

Our alma mater, the University of Pennsylvania, consistently interviews more prospective undergraduates than any other university in the world. During any given year, approximately forty thousand interviews are conducted by tens of thousands of alumni who specifically block off time on their calendar to share their Penn experience. Depending on the interviewer, this generally takes one to five hours of an alum's time, once per year. What about those—and there are many—who seek to be involved beyond that commitment?

For those institutions that utilize alumni interviewing—which we recognize may only be a subset of mostly well-resourced and liberal arts colleges—the structure and management (the most time-consuming parts) have already been built. Engaging a cohort of alumni interviewers—even if just a small subsection—could prove beneficial in connecting with students before they apply. One example is training alumni interviewers to give short presentations overviewing the institution and then request that they speak in high schools near where they currently reside. This serves not only to make a connection between students and the community member, but it also reduces the need for admissions representatives to invest their time and resources visiting that school. This can prove particularly useful in areas that are typically more difficult to reach.

The message this sends to prospective applicants is, "Wow—clearly this college or university made a positive impact on this person if they are still willing to dedicate their time to talking about it even years after graduating. Perhaps I should seriously check out whether it might be the right fit for me." By engaging with students before they even apply, alumni interviewers are modeling the type of experience that students can expect to have as undergraduates. We believe it is important to put forth this messaging before an online application is ever started, because it sets the tone for what the institution prioritizes: engaged students who remain connected by sharing their positive experiences. Although campus missions may differ, we think it would be challenging to find many colleges that are *not* interested in attracting that type of student.

Suggestion 2: Weave Lifelong Learning into the Admissions Process

Similar to Jegla's experience during her Remote Year interview, the way one communicates to applicants can make a big difference in the way they perceive their responsibility to the institution. It can even convince them to attend. We invite readers to imagine themselves as a college applicant. Would you rather spend your time and financial resources within a finite two- or four-year time frame? Or, conversely, would you prefer to embark upon an experience that will endure for the rest of your life? Thinking about a student's overall college experience and return on investment, the answer seems fairly clear to us.

Fortunately, colleges and universities have already built the necessary communication channels and platforms; we are not suggesting any expensive or time-consuming structural changes. Rather, consider tweaking language and touchpoints to be more focused on the postgraduate experience. Ask applicants to provide a short-answer response detailing how they might contribute to campus after graduation. Prompt alumni interviewers to ask students about how they would engage in lifelong learning and encourage them to share with applicants why they find it important and rewarding to interview for their alma mater. When accepted students arrive on campus for yield events, host panels with engaged alumni who can speak not only about their on-campus experience *but also* about the longer-term sense of community and opportunities that await students after graduation.

When students receive this messaging early—before they even set foot in their first college classroom—it can serve the dual purpose of encouraging them to attend the institution and setting expectations around their responsibility as an engaged community member while on campus and beyond. We cannot resist pointing out that, again, the cost to a college to implement these suggestions is zero or near zero.

Suggestion 3: Proactively Strengthen Regional Alumni Clubs through Engagement with Current Undergraduates

Alumni clubs. Frankly, many undergraduates probably don't even know what they do or how to join. As a result, alumni clubs often have inconsistent degrees of involvement within their membership; graduates don't always find their way to those in their geographic region. Similar to alumni interviewing, though, we see huge potential for lifelong engagement using these alumni clubs as a platform. The infrastructure, which is almost always the most difficult part, has in most cases already been established. Now, the challenge is how to make them maximally effective. We see this as a two-part process.

Step one is to introduce *current undergraduates* to the concept of alumni clubs—answering questions like "What are they?" "How does one get involved?" and "Are there ways to connect with members now?" Some colleges try to do this before students arrive on campus, connecting incoming freshmen with alumni clubs during "Meet and Greet" events hosted over the summer. Unfortunately, not all new students are able to attend, and the quality of the experience can vary significantly based on the club's resources and members. Instead of this one-off introduction, we suggest focusing on how to make alumni clubs part of the campus culture. Low-cost examples include arranging alumni club panels for those who happen to be visiting campus, special regional events for when students return home for winter break, or social media posts explaining the benefits of alumni club membership. Depending on interest and alumni availability, consider matching incoming students with alumni volunteer mentors that supplement the rest of their advising team. If availability allows, it may be particularly helpful for the mentor to be a member of the regional club where the student attended high school. This would allow new students to build an immediate relationship with someone who knows their geographic context. The key here is to not make it a chore for either the current students or alumni; it should be something they feel excited to be a part of and that both groups believe will pay dividends. As they near graduation, the first action that students should want to complete is signing up for the alumni club in whatever region they will be living in following commencement.

Step two involves elevating the experience of *alumni club members* themselves. Graduating students should be excited to join the alumni clubs, but it is also important that their vision actually plays out in a high-quality manner. Otherwise, they may join for a year and then decide that it simply isn't worth their time. This essentially defeats the whole purpose.

To really lean into the idea of lifelong engagement, we suggest that clubs be encouraged to host events that remind alumni of the best parts of their on-campus academic experience. Planning programming in response to a simple survey might be the most straightforward way to do this. Perhaps respondents report that they really enjoyed the smaller discussion groups during college. Clubs could consider structuring in-person or virtual meetings that focus on open dialogue around books, movies, or podcasts. Some alumni may indicate that the most enriching part of college was, for them, talking about topical issues such as cybersecurity, race relations, or healthcare or education reform. The club could invite professors from the college or other experts in those fields to partake in a group presentation or debate. We have seen situations where alumni share that they especially loved always being introduced to new ideas. The alumni club could host a showcase where members each speak for three to five minutes about anything that is of interest to them, inviting their peers to get in touch after the session.

An even lower-touch method could be asking alumni to fill out a sheet with two columns: subjects they could teach, and those that they would like to learn. Perhaps one alum has always wanted to learn more about improving his strategies for investing in the stock market but isn't sure where to start. In his day job, he is a real estate agent. He may be a perfect match for someone who is well versed in brokerage strategy and now wants to learn more about how to choose an investment property. In any case, offerings through the alumni club should be responsive to what its members actually want to learn about with their fellow alumni. Special perks—such as priority access to Alumni Weekend activities, if applicable, or complimentary tickets to local sporting events or shows—could be a good incentive if awarded to particularly engaged alumni club members.

Once they do reach a threshold number of members, alumni clubs can be powerful social and professional resources. Imagine this scenario: Eric attended college in Miami and, upon graduating, moved to Raleigh for a new job. After four years, his boss asks if he might be interested in transferring to the new office the company is opening in San Diego. They intend to start hiring additional support shortly after he would arrive, but they want a few trusted employees to lay the groundwork. Eric has always secretly harbored a desire to live on the West Coast, but he's a little hesitant—he doesn't know anyone in San Diego specifically and is a bit worried about being lonely when he arrives. That evening, he calls his college roommate, Sam—who is still a close friend—for advice. "You know, I didn't know a soul when I first moved to Pittsburgh, but we have a robust alumni club here. I go to events several times a month and have met friends— and those friends' friends—just by being a member of the club," Sam explains.

Encouraged, Eric investigates the college's alumni club in San Diego and feels optimistic about his ability to get involved with it and with the larger community. He walks into his boss's office the next day and says with a grin, "So when should I start packing my luggage?" Six months after Eric moves to San Diego, he recruits a new employee for his company. Theresa is a recent graduate of his university whom Eric first met at a TED Talk discussion group sponsored by the alumni club. Theresa dives right into her new role and impresses the other employees in the office with her enthusiasm and work ethic. Prompted by a request from Alumni Relations, the club president asks Eric and Theresa to record a three-minute video showcasing how they met and began working together. The college publishes the video on its website and through social media channels as a testament to the value of lifelong engagement. Suddenly, current undergraduates see a tangible benefit that they may receive as part of active alumni club membership.

Suggestion 4: Utilize Geographic Networks, Consortia, and Conferences

Stephanie was a high school senior who had been accepted to two excellent schools. Her contenders were near equals in terms of academic and extracurricular offerings, prestige, and cost. However, one of the schools was part of a consortium with four other institutions in the area. She recalled that her childhood neighbor, now an adult, attended that college. He agreed to chat with her on the phone. "You know, it really felt like having five schools for the price of one," he explained. "As an undergraduate, I conducted laboratory research at one of the other schools in the consortium, which is renowned for its excellent science facilities. Next month, I'm speaking on a panel at a conference with alumni from two of the other universities." Stephanie couldn't get this factor out of her mind; it seemed almost too good to be true. Five schools for the price of one? "Where do I sign up?" she thought.

When thinking about the resources that a college has available to offer its alumni, college leaders' options don't necessarily have to be limited to their own institution. Instead, they might think about building upon existing relationships with institutions that are geographically nearby. Some colleges will already be part of established multi-campus relationships (for example, consortia that allow undergraduates to take classes and participate in activities across colleges). Alumni clubs can be encouraged by their colleges to host joint events. Perhaps the institutions can even incentivize such collaboration by helping with speakers, event space, or financial resources.

It may also be helpful for university leaders to model collaborative behavior by working together publicly. By publishing joint papers or developing formalized cross-university partnerships, administrators establish a sort of alliance with other institutions, signaling to students that a relationship has already been formed. By establishing partnerships that are visible to undergraduates while they are still on campus, it will make the idea of attending events or networking with graduates from different but related schools more natural.

Suggestion 5: If Applicable, Capitalize on Athletic Prowess

Walk through the gates of a college stadium on game day: What do you see? If you are affiliated with one of America's powerhouse athletic institutions, the scene in front of you is likely pretty festive. Students roam around decked out in the vibrant hues of their school colors, faces painted and singing verses of the fight song. Only a fraction are current undergraduates. The others are alumni or even otherwise unaffiliated members of the community that call the school their own. People have purchased flights and taken days off from work to attend the game. Alumni friends have booked Airbnbs so they can spend the weekend together. It is their chance to cheer for their school, relive some of their happiest days, and spend time with people who were by their side during a critical part of the process of becoming an adult.

If these alumni are a key part of the lifelong learning demographic that colleges hope to target, the hardest part of the process—*getting their attention*—is complete. Alumni are never so fully steeped in school spirit and pride as when they arrive back at campus for a game, clad in sweatshirts emblazoned with the school's name and crest.

Alumni come back to a campus on game day to have *fun* and *connect*. They may not want on that festive athletic weekend to sit through a presentation about the value of mentoring a young student or engaging in online classes as an alumnus. If anything, they want to actually *meet* that student or *take* that class.

How can colleges and universities create such opportunities? One strategy would be allocating several on-campus rooms for this purpose, perhaps roughly divided by industry "bucket" (e.g., business, medicine, engineering, education, miscellaneous). Ask alumni to give brief, one-minute presentations about their career and encourage undergraduates (or even fellow alumni) to go up and ask one-on-one questions afterward. We have witnessed alumni in this scenario who appreciate the opportunity to share their experiences and to meet and network with potential new professional connections.

Simultaneously, undergraduates are grateful to hear about even a smattering of the various career options that exist. Best of all, this entire set of opportunities can be offered at one time, in one place, and at no charge.

Most schools give out teaching awards for professors whom undergraduate students consistently rate highly. Perhaps an important athletic weekend presents the opportunity to allow that professor to give a half-hour lecture—open only to undergraduate students and alumni—purely to help those who wish to learn something new. Maybe everyone who sits in on that lecture is then invited to join a future virtual session or a topic-based online group to stay engaged with the professor and each other.

The exact structure of an event will vary by college or university, based on the goal that each seeks to achieve. The big point is that the unique opportunity to have undergraduates and alumni co-located at the same time should not be squandered. In fact, such events have the potential to be motivators for alumni to return to campus for the following year. With fresh and engaging programming, this can be done without a massive investment of time or money.

Suggestion 6: Drive Home the Shared Experience

Students come to a college or university from across the country and, for many institutions, from around the world. Aside from having completed the application for admission, there is no single factor that is common to every incoming student. Their high schools were set up differently. Their living situations and backgrounds are each unique. Even their familiarity with college may vary. Despite these immense differences and although their rationale for doing so may each be distinct, *every single student on campus* made a decision to attend *that specific* college or university. This one element can be the catalyst for launching a lifelong engagement program.

Authors Light and Jegla both attended the University of Pennsylvania, separated by about fifty years. Upon our first meeting as academic advisor and advisee, we knew little else about each other but discovered this fact within about three minutes of sitting down to do quick introductions. Instantly, we had a common language. Though much had changed during the many years between our on-campus experiences, we could still talk about the specific programs that each of us had attended and reminisce about residence halls and classroom buildings. We also immediately knew something about the type of rigorous academic experience that we had shared and about the setting that each of us had prioritized. It was an excellent jumping-off point for a rich discussion that followed.

This shared language takes years to build but only minutes to pay off. It can create an instant bond and camaraderie among people who otherwise may perceive themselves to be dissimilar. We believe these connections are a cornerstone of a high-quality lifelong engagement system. There are so many ways that people can continue to learn after graduating college: they can take online classes through platforms like Coursera, join neighborhood discussion-based book clubs, or become members of interest-based clubs or organizations. There is little, though, that rivals the magnitude of connection between those who have completed a multiyear degree program while living on a college campus.

So, what can a university do with this information? Our suggestion is to remind students of the power of that shared language and how the college's name on top of their diploma provides them with an instant connection to graduates who are living all over the world. In this spirit, one feature of a good lifelong engagement platform is for a college to understand the information that would allow people to connect and then provide this material to them readily.

As a recent example, the department chair of Jegla's academic program from college sent an email asking alumni to submit a brief response about what they are currently doing for work or graduate school. By what seemed to be an error, one person must have hit "reply all" and emailed the entire listserv (containing thousands of alumni) with his current plans. *People loved it.* After about fifty more emails came through that way, the department chair finally respectfully asked people to send updates only to her. That didn't stop them. Email after email continued to flood Jegla's inbox, and she read them all. "It is so great to see what everyone is up to—thanks to everyone who keeps replying all!" several of the emails exclaimed. One alumnus even noted that he had found someone (through the email responses) who would be starting residency at the same hospital that year. They had started chatting on their own, and now they would each have a friend when they moved to a new city to begin the program. What started out as a complete accident served to connect people, and it renewed Jegla's pride in her major and her university.

Of course, not everyone appreciates this kind of contact. We understand that for some people, receiving incessant email messages can be obnoxious. Again, we urge each college and university to make an effort to better understand what would be helpful for alumni to continue to learn and grow from each other—especially across class years—and to develop effective platforms that provide such opportunities.

Suggestion 7: Make It Fun

Princeton University is known for many impressive things, not least of which is its passionate and active alumni community. Legend has it that its Alumni Reunion Weekend accounts for the second-largest beer purchase in the United States, after the Indianapolis 500 automobile race. Year after year, thousands of alumni flock to New Jersey to reconnect with old friends and meet graduates from across class years. They partake in "The P-rade," a procession of classes led by the eldest members of the Princeton community. Graduating seniors, clad in matching class jackets of their own design, march behind alumni and are officially welcomed to the Alumni Association at the end of the parade. Neither co-author of this book attended Princeton for any part of our studies. Yet we both have immense respect for the power of its community. Above all else, Princeton has seemed to have truly succeeded in making its programming *fun*. It may then come as no surprise that Princeton also consistently leads the nation in the percentage of its graduates that participate in alumni giving.

Professionalism, rigor, work ethic, and intellectualism—those are words associated with great colleges and universities. But "fun"? Not so much.

In the serious world of academia, we believe that fun is currently an underestimated piece of the puzzle. Particularly for lifelong engagement, which is fully optional, students won't participate if it's not enjoyable. Lifelong learning should never feel like an obligation; alumni shouldn't see it as a chore. Instead, maintaining a tie with their alma mater should feel like an extension of the college experience and an additional perk of having been invited to attend and graduate from that campus.

Infusing fun into the equation doesn't necessarily require a massive (or massively expensive) weekend event of the sort Princeton throws for its alumni. Fun can and should be a component of marketing materials, event design, and decisions about tone. For this work, we suggest strategic hiring or the inclusion of creative undergraduate interns on programmatic planning teams. Leadership should set "fun" as an actual stated goal to work toward. Throughout preparation, staff should periodically ask themselves and each other questions such as, "Would I be envious of someone who got to participate in this if I could not?" Or "Does this event reflect the many serious aspects of our college in terms of demanding the highest quality work, yet without being boring?"

Anyone participating in lifelong engagement with their alma mater should perceive such activity with a sense of pride, invigoration, and fulfillment. Rather than create a culture of attending events sporadically, well-planned alumni events can energize graduates of all ages around real, sustained engagement and learning opportunities.

Key Principles to Consider

In the spirit of respecting that each college or university has its own unique culture and traditions, lifelong engagement can look entirely different at different campuses. That is probably a good thing. Nonetheless, we can share several core principles that emerge from our own thinking, as well as from conversations with deans who are working hard to create appealing and impactful lifelong learning opportunities.

1. *Building lasting, personal relationships—starting with current undergraduates.* We believe that a key to students' lifelong engagement is getting started while they are still on a

college campus. At any university, a twenty-one-year-old under-graduate expresses an interest to that campus's Office of Lifelong Engagement to work with an alumnus who has certain skills—perhaps, for example, in entrepreneurship. The college connects her with an alum, perhaps who shares her major, and they begin a mentor–mentee relationship built around sharing new ideas and ways of thinking that are focused on real-world experiences.

Of course, the key is how this simple, two-person con-nection can serve as an additional tie that binds both the alum and the undergraduate even more strongly to their mutual college for years to come. Several years later, the undergraduate—who attributes some part of her success to the early connection with an alumnus—feels encouraged to do the same and to pay it forward for a next generation of her beloved campus. The more such paired relationships a college can build, the stronger the lifelong engagement model be-comes for any college or university.

2. *Expand the idea of pairing an undergraduate with an older, successful alumni mentor to create small ongoing working groups of mentors and mentees.* A college may want to begin its efforts by focusing on connecting pairs of people, such as a current undergraduate and an older graduate with shared interests. A natural expansion of this concept might be creating circles of mentors and mentees where the group becomes three to four students meeting with three to four mentors, where all members share a broad yet common interest. Often the topics may be unusual, and that just might be the most valuable time for a college to create such small mentoring groups to enhance lifelong engagement both for current alumni and for current students. In one such ongoing group, the broad topic is "Museum Management—Creating New Models of Museums to Appeal to New Audiences." How many colleges currently offer formal coursework about this topic? We think not so many. This is a simple example, and of course there could be hundreds more.

3. *Consider sharing mentees across several campuses to expand lifelong engagement.* We see no reason to restrict lifelong mentoring or pairing or engagement opportunities solely to a single campus. As colleges increasingly begin to collaborate and cooperate, especially colleges that are geographically close to one another, staff who run lifelong engagement programs may find it a wise option to work collaboratively with other colleges when connecting current students with alumni.

One example we can point to is how Wellesley College (a top-notch liberal arts college), Babson College (a renowned business college), and Olin College of Engineering (consistently rated in the very top echelon of engineering schools)—which practically share parking lots because they are located so close together—have increasingly encouraged undergraduates to cross-register at all three campuses. The engineering student at Olin who wants experience in sociology or history is warmly encouraged to take classes, fully for credit, at Wellesley College. The Wellesley College student who wants to sharpen her skills in business, which so many traditional liberal arts colleges simply don't offer, is warmly invited to take classes for credit at Babson College. We see no reason a similar collaboration could not or should not be developed for lifelong engagement purposes. We anticipate that, for most alumni, having access to other alumni resources from three colleges for the price of one is a winning proposition.

4. *Foster lifelong engagement connections that appeal to current undergraduates.* Creating simple, appealing, and low-cost opportunities for current students at any college to seize the opportunity to make productive connections with successful alumni should not be difficult. Surely there are many options. Here is one that two colleges have actually implemented with great success: create just once each semester a particularly nice group dinner. Invite five successful alumni, each of whom has had a different career path. Students will hear from them about the particular skills or classes that have helped them to

succeed, or what they wish they would have taken more advantage of while on campus.

Current undergraduates should be encouraged to follow up with whichever speaker on whatever topic appeals to them. The students might simply want to have a brief chat. Or they might inquire about a summer internship, paid or unpaid. They might even ask for a bit of early mentoring. The point is obvious—this is a simple way to begin to make connections, especially for those students who are interested. How nice for any college to feature several prominent younger alumni, perhaps even recent graduates, who all represent clear success stories to model for current undergraduates. A key result of such evenings seems to be a strong sense of shared pride about the opportunities and privileges of attending a particular college or university.

How to Know If Lifelong Engagement Is Happening

When most people think of lifelong learning in higher education, the elements that come to mind are fairly easy to measure. Alumni-only international trips? Count the participants. Course offerings for graduates? Track registrations and number of classes each year. Much of what we have heard of universities doing in the name of lifelong learning are such individual, one-off events. However, what we're calling for is creating a culture of sustained engagement that involves both undergraduates and potentially the entire pool of living alumni. It's a lot of people involved in a deeper way than ever before, which makes the metrics slightly more complex.

We believe that the core of lifelong engagement is *the development of relationships*: between prospective and current undergraduate students and alumni, alumni and fellow alumni, and alumni and the school itself. When these players interact, information can be shared and perspectives shaped. Although it could be argued that one alumnus in a vacuum technically could be engaged in a process of lifelong learning, we believe that the highest quality and most lasting examples of lifelong engagement are those that involve exchanges between people. These are the data that we recommend trying to understand; namely, how are these interactions forming, what is their strength, and how long do they last?

The specific information that a college or university chooses to collect and track in a database will vary based on factors that are unique to the institution, but we urge leaders to consider (and showcase) these sustained relationships. Document the percentage of current graduates who have gotten to know an alumnus as a result of a campus program or record the number of alumni relationships between members of different classes that have lasted more than five years. Calculate the percentage of alumni who say that they have learned something through the university after graduating, or determine the number of alumni interviewers who are involved in more than just interviewing prospective students. Then, *publicize* that information. We do not mean for this to be a boasting tactic; rather, it sets a tone for students that this type of engagement is something that the institution considers to be of high value.

Examples of Success

Are these suggestions for lifelong engagement a bit "pie in the sky"? We don't think so. The best testament to our strong optimism comes from scattered examples and success stories from various colleges and universities. We find substantial variation among these still relatively early efforts from many universities. One theme so far is that business schools, for whatever reason, seem to be taking the lead with lifelong engagement programs so far. We see no reason that undergraduate colleges could not create their own imaginative new efforts.

An Example from Wellesley College

One liberal arts college is already off to a great start. In 2020, the Wellesley College Career Education office joined forces with the Alumnae Association to launch a new initiative in response to the COVID-19 pandemic. The program, called Hive 2020, has the goal of supporting students and alumnae both on and off campus. To do so, Wellesley built upon its existing alumnae network, which is arguably the strongest system of women in the world. Alumnae can create internship projects centered around meaningful work experiences; for example, marketing and design, scientific research, startups, and publishing. Alumnae or project overseers provide support and mentorship to students, who also earn a non-academic credit on their transcripts. These opportunities have been available to undergraduates both during winter break and over the summer.

Additionally, Wellesley's Senior Support Network matches alumnae—either one-on-one or as part of a mentorship pod—with members of the current undergraduate senior class. In their groups, students can discuss everything from job search and interviewing tips to finding postgraduate housing. Through these programs, which have proven hugely popular at Wellesley, undergraduates have multiple touchpoint opportunities with alumnae. Just as importantly, alumnae are constantly engaged with their alma mater. It may take a few years to learn how well these programs are succeeding—the point is that Wellesley College has done an admirable job in starting the lifelong engagement process and getting an ambitious project up and running.

An Example from the University of Pennsylvania

An example from a graduate school illustrates how, in principle, any college can connect alumni and current students to literally change lives and create bonds with the university for years to come.

Doris Huang was an MBA student at the University of Pennsylvania's Wharton School. One evening, Wharton sponsored a dinner featuring a successful alumnus—Dave Marberger—exactly as we suggested earlier in this chapter. Marberger was thirteen years older than Doris and happened to be senior vice president at Godiva Chocolates. This was a brand Doris had not only heard of, but that she had actually shopped over some years. As he was leaving, Marberger offered his business card to any student who might want to follow up with any questions.

Doris used the card and sent Marberger a simple, cordial thank you note. He responded with a short message that included a comment that he remembered her sharp and incisive questions. He also invited her to send him her résumé. She did. He replied by asking if she might be interested in an internship at Godiva. It caught Doris off guard, but in a wonderful way.

Doris did indeed spend a summer working as an intern at Godiva. She did not work directly for Marberger, yet the proud Penn alum made a point to meet with Doris once a week. He made sure she got introductions to the right people so she could fully learn about and understand Godiva's business. He even introduced young Doris to the CEO. Doris later describes Marberger as "a terrific champion."

The bottom line is that Penn's dinner for current students, featuring a successful alumnus, changed Doris's life trajectory. Godiva offered Doris a good job at the organization, and she worked with her mentor to actually design the position description to align with her long-term goals of running her own company (which, years later, she is now doing). One dinner landed Doris a perfect mentor and also a slightly unexpected career path.

We do not anticipate this will happen for every student who attends a dinner with successful alumni. We do believe this happy example illustrates the good that can come from a relatively straightforward university effort to figure out and create multiple ways to enhance lifelong engagement—both for its current students and alumni.

A Final Note

When you began reading this chapter, you perhaps wondered whether we might help you to think about how to build a system in which alumni continue to engage with their alma mater for years after graduation. Yes, lifelong learning or lifelong engagement primarily involves alumni, but the messaging starts *much* earlier: during a student's years on campus and maybe even a bit before. Reaching students during their undergraduate experience is critical; it is quite overly optimistic to expect that alumni will simply stumble upon lifelong engagement opportunities on their own. The expectation has to be set that lifelong learning and lifelong engagement is something that the college considers to be of high importance. This messaging begins before students even apply.

There are many, many ways that high-quality and fun lifelong engagement experiences can be crafted, and we encourage campus leaders to deeply consider their specific target population before making such decisions. Then, utilize existing infrastructure—with advising, alumni interviewing, alumni clubs, and on-campus events—to incorporate these elements in a systematic and highly public way. The playing field is wide open for campuses to create innovative lifelong engagement programs. We believe campuses that do it well will be able to execute their plans with very little financial investment. Doing so will pay dividends, primarily because not many campuses handle lifelong learning well (yet).

Students are increasingly looking for undergraduate campuses that give them a maximum return on investment. This means a traditional four-year experience may soon not be enough. As virtual learning becomes more commonplace, graduates may be more open to and enthusiastic about engaging with remote opportunities to continue to develop both personally and professionally. When prospective undergraduates are deciding between universities, evidence of a robust lifelong learning platform could very well be the difference maker in shaping where any student chooses to enroll.

Alumni who are happy with their college experience are likely to be more engaged with their alma mater. How do you begin to create happier alumni? Make them happy college students. Enhancing the experience of current students is a process of continuous improvement. We hope that some suggestions in this chapter help colleges to start this process.

10

Inspiring Students to
Think Globally

Today's generation of college students have grown up in an age of information. With just one click of a button, they are able to view a livestream from India or share an Instagram photo posted by someone in Haiti. Unlike millennials, Generation Z grew up knowing how to do this. It is in some ways a part of their DNA. Make any argument you want for the negative influence of technology and social media, but this access to information is undeniable and powerful. Gone are the days when students had to wait for something to be published in textbooks or to be reported on during the evening news to be able to learn more about it. Now, they can do so in almost real time.

The effect of this access is robust enough for a doctoral dissertation or probably even a series of books, but here we seek to generalize. From our standpoint, conditions are ripe for students to become well-informed global citizens—perhaps more so than at any other point in our nation's history. With thoughtful and well-planned guidance, they can learn how to sift through information and use it to make informed arguments and decisions that catalyze positive change far beyond their own communities and even their own countries.

The technology is there, and perhaps more importantly, students are generally primed to take advantage of it. Young people care about the world, and higher education needs to be ready with the tools to help them make their impact. This core belief, *that students really do care about the world beyond their specific context*, is what guides this chapter. We offer ideas for inspiring them to use their studies in an immediate and productive way, engage with their peers to create lasting change, and develop the skills and perspective to be the constructive global citizens and thinkers of tomorrow.

Throughout this chapter, we offer specific suggestions—some that have already been implemented on a few campuses and others that have proven successful in settings outside of higher education—for helping students to cultivate a sense of global-mindedness.

Celebrate the Language Requirement

Nearly every college or university has a world language requirement, and students generally fall into one of three categories with regard to it. Some are able to waive the requirement based on their achievement in high school, and they decide to take other types of classes instead. Others continue learning a language that they have previously been exposed to, perhaps in high school or as part of past international travel. The third group has experience with a particular language but decides instead to delve into one that is completely new. The world language part of their class schedule is, for many students, little more than a passing thought. They may ask a friend about what language they're taking over a meal in the dining hall or shout, "Sorry—can't chat, I'm late for French!" as they dash to class.

Students rarely pause to consider *why* their peers have chosen to learn a particular language, and we see this as a missed opportunity. Almost every student has a story to tell. Are they continuing Spanish because it was the only class offered at their high school? Whatever the interpretation, that gives us more insight into a student's background. Are they starting Gujarati to be able to converse with their grandparents who live in India? Maybe that's a jumping-off point for a connection with a fellow student. Is another student engaged in African studies and wants to be able to converse in at least one African language? Great, that's excellent insight into why they are sitting in the Introduction to Swahili classroom. The background stories behind students' courses of study are as numerous as the students themselves. Why not invite undergraduates to talk about those elements?

We see this as an excellent icebreaker activity for small-group meetings of incoming students during Orientation week or even during accepted student programming before they arrive at college. We have never seen this simple suggestion implemented at a college. It is something that every student can participate in, even if they have little or no exposure to a world language so far (in this case, consider asking, "What language would you choose to learn if you could pick any?").

The cost of opening up these sorts of conversations is zero. Yet simple questions can help students to form connections with their peers or even introduce them to a completely new language or way of thinking. It also expands their perspective beyond the often-limited view of high schools, which typically are constrained in what languages they can provide. Maybe a certain student only had three options for language learning in their high school, but heard a peer speaking about their study of something completely new. That student may be inspired to think more deeply about how they view world language and develop a plan for how they hope to utilize their proficiency.

For those of us who value the study of international cultures, it is also striking how few language classes at universities actually make a serious effort to incorporate deeper cultural components into the language classes themselves. College leaders may assume that by virtue of being enrolled in a language class, students are also learning something more about the history, political situation, art, and social elements of a given country or region. However, when we ask students how much they are genuinely learning about culture in their language classes, the vast majority report that there is in fact no serious emphasis.

Assuming that colleges and universities do believe that additional cultural components should be part of a student's language learning journey while on campus, leaders can assess how to do so in a way that is aligned with faculty resources. Language classes could in principle serve as a wonderful entry point for introducing students to novel and different cultures in a broad variety of countries. In order to do this well, language instructors will need to figure out their preferred way to implement this idea, and the best answer may vary quite a lot from instructor to instructor and college to college. It seems to us that step one is for most colleges to not pretend they are doing it now, when they, in fact, are not.

Invite International Perspective into the Classroom

The classroom is one of the most obvious places for students to be exposed to international ideas and perspectives. We see two primary ways for inviting such perspectives into the classroom, with a goal of reminding students that there are multiple ways to do things, and that the system they are used to is not necessarily the best or most efficient.

The first is to take advantage, respectfully and as is appropriate, of those who already have international experience upon which to draw. Perhaps an economics course has reached a module about taxation. The professor has planned a class session that provides students with an overview of the difference between the U.S., German, and Canadian systems. She knows that there is a student originally from Berlin in the course, so she takes him aside before class to ask if he might be willing to share his perspective on how the German tax system impacts the way people work and behave on a daily basis. Proud to share more about his country, the student happily agrees. The teaching assistant for the course recalls that he has a graduate school colleague who is from Vancouver. He asks if she might be available to attend the course, and she agrees as well. The result is that all students in the class not only hear the facts of how the countries' taxation systems are built—they also learn directly from their peers' firsthand experiences. Ideally, they become able to compare and contrast some of the different policies that exist and determine why each one functions effectively or not.

Learning across Disciplines

When a university decides to build classes that promote global thinking into the curriculum, usually the main goal is to do exactly what those words suggest: teach undergraduates to think about other countries and cultures that differ from their own. At the same time, we are struck at how easy—yet also how rare—it is for universities to use such topics as a scaffold for other ancillary benefits. One illustration is how thinking globally can push students to draw from and expand upon very broad sets of information to synthesize ideas across multiple disciplines.

Classes in economics can do a great job teaching students how to think about ideas in economics. Classes in history similarly can do great for helping students to put events into historical context. Same for classes in politics, political theory, and sociology. We find it a rare class that can draw on big ideas from *all* of these individual disciplines to help students learn to understand the world in clearer ways.

By posing questions rooted in global thinking in a way that encourages students to draw on multiple academic disciplines, it becomes possible for faculty to do something that few discipline-based classes offer. These professors are able to push students to disentangle multiple competing explanations for how or why an observed feature can vary among different countries, cultures, or ways of living. We believe simply taking seriously the goal to help students to learn about thinking globally—to better understand a complex and interconnected world—can change students' lives and prompt them to think in new ways. We offer specific examples that have been used at two excellent universities.

Example 1: University of Virginia Challenges Students to Compare Differential Growth among Nations

During a recent class at the University of Virginia, a professor asked his students a relatively straightforward question. The primary goal was to encourage students to call upon multiple disciplines to think about a highly nuanced topic:

From 1960 to 2020, the gross domestic product (GDP) per capita in India grew from $82 per person to $2,200 per person. During those same years, the GDP in Pakistan grew much more slowly: from a starting figure of $83 per person to $1,150 in 2020. This is a fairly dramatic difference in growth rates where even slightly faster growth can offer more opportunities for more citizens. What key factors might explain this difference? The countries are geographically contiguous. Both achieved political independence at almost exactly the same time. Can the noticeable difference in growth rates be explained by religion? By culture? By differences in their education systems from K-12? By differences in how their universities are organized? By the role of their two somewhat different government structures? By the role played by women?

Students at UVA found this precise question incredibly challenging. They were right to think so. Developing a thoughtful response requires a serious student to bring in many factors from across multiple disciplines—economics, politics, culture, anthropology, sociology, history, and others. Most of the students grappling with this question concluded there is no *single* factor to explain the difference in growth rates. The virtue of this example is that a group of students was pushed to really dig in and learn about both of these countries (their history, culture, religion, governance, and education system), as well as their relationship to each other. The students worked on learning how to juggle multiple factors and make complicated trade-offs to understand differences between the two nations and reach some overall conclusions. They found this challenging but rewarding. We consider it an admirable way to teach students how to synthesize large bodies of evidence.

Example 2: A Unique Instructional Method at the University of Pennsylvania

In one of the required classes for the health and societies major at the University of Pennsylvania, students are asked to consider multiple perspectives during a real-world simulation involving international challenges. For the first half of a semester-long course, each member of the sixty-person class is assigned one specific country and tasked with becoming an expert to the best of their ability. They consult census documents, watch online interviews with the nation's leadership, speak with peers who may have lived there, and read as much as they can about everything from its political system to its geography to its racial and ethnic makeup.

During the second part of the semester, students work together in groups of eight to ten. Each member of the team serves as a sort of ambassador for the country that they were originally assigned, but now they represent just one member of a broader geographic region. For example, if a student was first asked to learn as much as they could about Indonesia, they are then placed into the Southeast Asia group during the second half of the semester. Together, the students work together toward the goal of the project: creating a plan to address a health challenge of the entire region. Each person therefore must learn to balance advocating for his or her specific country, while also making certain compromises for the good of the region as a whole.

Within the structure of the small teams, each member is assigned a specific role. The project manager oversees all efforts and keeps the team on track. Researchers pull together relevant data that are then used by writers to craft a plan document. Presenters and Q&A experts speak about the team's proposal during a final full-class session that is staged as a meeting of the World Health Organization. As with the University of Virginia example, students in this class also have to draw from multiple disciplines and sort through a vast amount of information to arrive at their creative conclusions. Participants also get a chance to experience how they might be part of a group structure later in life—for some, that might even include *actually* presenting to the World Health Organization. Exercises like this not only prepare students for the world ahead and make classes themselves more interesting; they also serve to ignite students' interest and competency in topics of international importance.

Reimagine Options for Study Abroad

Some students dream of their eventual study abroad experience, even while they're still in high school. They inquire about opportunities during their college tours and, as the guide is responding, get lost in daydreams of lazy days splayed out on a blanket in Paris's Luxembourg Garden, eating baguette and drinking French wine. They fantasize about continuing their studies of Japanese while immersed in one of the world's great capital cities, dining on sushi in Tokyo and creating friendships to last a lifetime. Some listen to their parents reminisce about their own study abroad experiences, recalling stories of a semester living with Italian host families who taught them how to make authentic *cacio e pepe*. These somewhat romantic visions of study abroad inspire and excite students, who are eager to dive into college and take full advantage of all there is to offer.

Then, they actually get to campus. They realize that coursework is more rigorous than they imagined. They become involved in various student groups. Relationships develop, and housing plans are made well into the future. Soon, the student begins thinking, "I worked so hard to be accepted to this selective college. Why would I want to spend a semester away from my friends, my classes, and my extracurricular involvements?"

At many of America's great colleges and universities, a surprisingly small percentage of students engage in the traditional, semester-long study abroad experience. The title of a 2003 Harvard Crimson article put it bluntly: "Leaving vs. Leading." The article gets at the heart of the question: Do you want to leave and have this study abroad experience, or do you instead wish to have a leadership role with the student groups that you have dedicated yourself to so far in college? Beyond that, there is the classic FOMO ("fear of missing out")— think of all the concerts, parties, guest speakers, and football games a student would have to miss. For many, the challenges of making these trade-offs means an international academic experience gets pushed to the back burner.

Traditional study abroad can also be a logistical nightmare for students. Finding housing that will let them end their lease midway through the year or start in January rather than August is not always easy. They also may not be able to live with the friends they had anticipated. Or students might be forced to find strangers in similar situations to split rent. Then, each student has to contend with the intricacies of actually having to study somewhere completely new. For someone without extensive travel experience or who has lived in the U.S. for their whole life, this can be either immensely exciting or absolutely petrifying. It is easy to see why some students might simply decide, "This is not for me right now."

We have discussed this study abroad topic with more than a few Student Services and Student Affairs professionals at several colleges. Most of them consider such opportunities to be a "no brainer." We respectfully disagree. We enthusiastically support the idea of instilling in students an appreciation for different cultures. We think it is a superb idea to set them on a path to acquire an international perspective throughout their lives. The trick, though, is to help each student figure out what will work best for their specific situation and motivations. Traditional study abroad programs are a particularly clear example of "one size fits all" not being appropriate for many students. Timing of when to go abroad, choice of place, and purpose of spending time abroad (work, absorb culture, sit in a different university and take classes, sit in libraries and do archival research) really does matter.

We absolutely cannot and should not steer students away from exploring the world simply because they deem it inconvenient; we need to find new ways to help them fit it into their lives, whether during their time at college or at a future point.

Different Options for International Experience While in College

To be clear, we *strongly* support the broad concept of study abroad. Our suggestions emphasize the great value of devoting resources to making sure students understand their many options. We encourage every academic advisor or peer advisor to have this conversation with a student, getting at the heart of their hesitations (if any) around traditional study abroad and trying to unearth alternative options. We also suggest that colleges hold international experience events, bringing back alumni or upperclassmen who have engaged in various programs abroad to help current students understand the pros and cons. International experience is valuable, memorable, and almost always enjoyable. But it also has to work for students and their specific goals.

The options for obtaining international exposure and experience can be broadly organized into at least four main categories, some of which may not be initially obvious to students.

The first option is the traditional model: literally spending a semester studying abroad, living there and taking classes. This is what most students immediately think of when they hear the words "study abroad." This type of experience is typically organized by a student's home campus, so class credits transfer and they are able to graduate in the time that they had anticipated.

A second category is to spend a semester or full year away from campus, either directly following high school (a gap year) or during college itself (a leave of absence, if allowed). During that time, the student is generally not taking classes but rather traveling from place to place or working at an actual job or internship. This extends a student's time until graduation by a semester or a year. The benefit is that it still allows them to spend a full four years on their home college campus.

A third option for gaining international experience is to utilize times when classes are not in session. Summer in particular may be a great option due to the longer length, typically for as much as three full months. Yet for many students, the shorter winter or spring breaks at their home college may provide ample opportunity for exploration. Students can take classes, complete internships, travel, live with friends or family, or participate in external programs. Particularly in circumstances where students have to arrange this themselves—as opposed to signing up for an existing program—they gain valuable knowledge about navigating the country. If able to secure a job or internship, undergraduates are sometimes able to pay their own living expenses for the time they are abroad.

A fourth category requires developing a certain infrastructure on the part of the college but can be highly engaging and memorable for students who are able to participate. A subset of campuses offer hybrid classes, during which students learn about a particular topic—for example, the comparative political systems of Germany and Italy— while sitting in their home campus classroom. Then, the class travels together for a short amount of time to actually visit those places, meet with political or civic leaders, and see their learning come to life. These types of experiences are especially visible in graduate school programs, though many colleges are thinking about offering them for under-graduates as well.

We are not suggesting that a single correct answer exists here for every student. In fact, that is the whole point. We *do* urge that universities should emphasize these options and creative choices to all students. Any student considering studying abroad who truly thinks hard and strategically decides when to go, where to go and for how long, and how to spend their time when they arrive is far more likely to have a terrific and fulfilling experience than a student who simply says, "I hear good things about the study abroad experience, so I guess I'll participate."

One solid piece of research done at an Ivy League college found that 66 percent of undergraduates who spent one term studying abroad found it overall an eye-opening experience. The other 34 percent were far less enthusiastic. More than a few described their semester abroad as a waste of time or money, and a disappointment. They viewed it with regret. Roughly half of these students wished their home campus had helped them see the tradeoffs more clearly and to think strategically about how to choose among their various options.

Borrow from Existing Effective Models

In encouraging a sense of global-mindedness for students, one model from which colleges and universities can draw is set forth by the Global Citizen organization. At its core, Global Citizen is quite simple: it is an international platform for engaged citizens. Since 2011, they have tracked over 25 million actions taken to support a number of causes, such as health, education, and the environment. Activists are motivated to record their work in order to earn prizes, such as concert tickets and sports passes. Arguably the most recognized event is the organization's Global Citizen Festival, during which some of the best and most famous music artists and human rights advocates perform and speak. One way to attend is to *earn* your spot. Global Citizen treats activism as a currency of choice, encouraging individuals to take action in order to join the crowd.

Connecting students with Global Citizen itself is one option for college leaders, though we recommend taking it one step further by actually replicating parts of the program. Students could compete throughout the semester or year to record their work in serving a community beyond their own. Those who reach a certain threshold can be invited to an event in recognition of their efforts, perhaps to hear an acclaimed social impact speaker or see an artist perform. Again, this type of program will take time and money to execute, but it is a potentially valuable way to unite the campus while also teaching students to make global action a sustained habit.

Link Funding with Communicated Priorities

In several chapters of this book, we reference the concept of signaling to students that a particular topic is a priority through the intentional allocation of funding. The concept of equipping students with a global mindset is no different. We want to be clear: we aren't necessarily implying that colleges and universities should set aside hundreds of thousands or millions of dollars—not even close. Depending on the activity (and, of course, the school itself) an investment in global projects can be as little as a few thousand dollars. The important thing is to get students thinking about such topics and working together to develop—and potentially even implement—practical solutions.

Each college has a chance to be wonderfully creative in how they create funding opportunities. For example, a college could specify a challenge for students to create ways to make the world a better place. University leaders or professors could outline a number of specific requirements, perhaps that a program has to involve at least three countries outside of the United States, must be focused on one of the United Nations Sustainable Development Goals (SDGs), or that the proposed budget must be less than $10,000 USD. Then, students could have as much leeway as possible to innovate and explore. This invites students to be creative and to work collaboratively in groups.

One team creates a plan for a conference with speakers from a variety of countries who all have different perspectives on how to achieve the SDGs. A second group develops an internship exchange program for students in three countries within South America. A panel of judges evaluates each proposal, and the winning one or two might receive funding from the college to move toward implementation.

The budget for this sort of thing doesn't have to come directly from a college's bank account. If there ever were a prime opportunity for an advancement office to identify just one or a few generous donors who care, this could be it. An ideal supporter may be an individual or a company that has already publicly committed to advancing international goals. Perhaps a student alumni group, specifically an advisory board or class council, may be eager to raise funds to support a new venture. When executed well, this can be an opportunity to provide not only a new program for current students, but also to reengage alumni in a new, exciting venture that reignites their pride in and engagement with their alma mater.

How Can a University Know Whether It Is Succeeding?

Ask the leaders of any college or university how well they think their institution is doing in terms of helping their students learn to think in global terms; some will respond and say they think overall they are quite successful. Our view is that they may well be correct. The basic question is—with the absence of any concrete data—how can campus leaders have any real sense of whether their students are truly thinking globally?

Author Richard Light grappled with this challenge several years ago and shared the dilemma with his undergraduate research assistants. One student responded with an idea that was elegant in its simplicity. Why not just ask students a few well-chosen questions? Students' simple answers can tell us a lot about how they think and what they think. While not a perfect measure, these quite straightforward data would at least allow colleges to understand at a high level how their students are thinking about certain issues.

Several colleges actually tried this idea out. Three different campuses each chose a random sample of eighty seniors and invited them to a brief interview a few months before graduation. Interviews were done one-on-one and in-person by several different interviewers on each campus. It was made clear to students that this exercise was in no way a test of their individual knowledge or skills. Students understood their responses would inform their university about what answers graduating seniors offer when asked certain questions. All campuses achieved a high response rate thanks to personal invitations and multiple follow-up efforts.

Here are examples of questions that were asked, and the actual responses that were collected across the three campuses.

Question 1: "Think of all people who have lived anywhere—in *any* country—in roughly the past 100 years. Name the three people who come to mind who you believe have had the biggest positive impact on the world. Then just say in two or three sentences why you are including each person on your short list. This is not a test. There are no correct answers. Clearly different students will choose different people. We simply want to see how you respond to this broad question."

Responses:

At University 1, the top five selections were Barack Obama, Bill Clinton, George W. Bush, Sam Walton, and Bill Gates.

At University 2, the top five selections were Franklin Delano Roosevelt, Ronald Reagan, Gandhi, Eleanor Roosevelt, and Wilbur and Orville Wright.

At University 3, the top eight selections were Gandhi, Franklin Delano Roosevelt, Ronald Reagan, Nelson Mandela, Martin Luther King Jr., Winston Churchill, Margaret Thatcher, and Anwar el-Sadat.

Given each university's relatively large sample size of eighty undergraduates, these results can help shed light on how students are thinking at a high level. It might be a fun exercise to imagine whether the presidents of each of the three institutions could identify their own campus based on these results. It is fairly clear that most observers would quickly see a clear difference between the campuses. The third campus especially stands out, with students' responses conveying that its seniors think in more global terms than the other two.

Question 2: "You are graduating from our university in about a month. Name three books that you believe every college graduate should have read by the time they leave campus."

Responses:

Student 1: Thomas Hobbes: *Leviathan*. William Shakespeare: *Hamlet*. Aphra Bain: *Oroonoko*.

Student 2: Gabriel García Márquez: *One Hundred Years of Solitude*. Jane Addams: *Twenty Years at Hull-House*. Ernest Hemingway: *The Sun Also Rises*.

Student 3: Aleksandr Solzhenitsyn: *The Gulag Archipelago*. Thomas Hobbes: *Leviathan*. Antoine de Saint-Exupéry: *The Little Prince*.

Student 4: Niccolò Machiavelli: *The Prince*. Ursula Le Guin: *The Dispossessed*. Laura Z. Hobson: *Gentleman's Agreement*.

Student 5: Plato: *Republic*. Leo Tolstoy: *War and Peace*. Milan Kundera: *The Unbearable Lightness of Being*.

Why might this question be appealing? First, most college leaders would simply find it fascinating—and insightful—to get a sense of what books their students consider especially valuable and important to have read. Second, if a majority of students actually have trouble thinking of the titles of three books, then a college knows that it has some work to do. We include this question here particularly as it relates to the theme of thinking globally. Analysts can easily see how often a group of graduating seniors includes one or more books written by authors who are not from the United States. It doesn't seem far-fetched to anticipate that on a campus where global-mindedness is encouraged and embedded into students' lives, they will at least occasionally choose authors who are not American. The example of actual responses given above from just one college—which we consider to be quite impressive—drives this home. Clearly a significant fraction, actually more than half, of these five sets of three books have authors who are from outside the U.S. It would be hard to argue that this college is failing its students when it comes to thinking globally.

Taking It One Step Further

Interviewers at any college can sometimes learn even more by prompting students to expand upon their simple list of names or titles. Each student who was interviewed was asked to add just a few sentences to explain why a person or book they chose earned a spot on their list.

Light fondly remembers being the interviewer during one memorable exchange with a graduating senior, a young woman who named Margaret Thatcher as one of the three people who she believed had provided extraordinary positive benefit to the world. When Light asked her to expand upon her response, she could hardly be stopped. "Thatcher saved the United Kingdom. She essentially changed the way that British infrastructure was run," she began. The senior then went on to speak about the specific political situation in the United Kingdom in the 1970s and how Thatcher worked to denationalize state-run industries and move toward privatization. The student spoke passionately about the leadership that Thatcher had shown in developing relationships with the pope and Ronald Reagan that ultimately helped dissolve the Soviet Union. The impressive point is how it quickly became clear that the young woman hadn't just picked the name "Margaret Thatcher" out of a hat; she actually knew what she was talking about and could explain her choice in detail. Whether a reader agrees or disagrees with the particular choice isn't at all the point. Any college leader should hope that many of their students would be able to speak thoughtfully and knowledgeably about both people and challenges beyond their own country.

The takeaway from these two simple examples is that they can serve as a useful exercise for any college or university to get a handle on how well it actually is doing in helping its students learn to think in reasonably global terms. Notice that a university does not need to spend much—if any—money to get some answers. Just ask students a series of carefully chosen questions. The kinds of questions seem almost limitless. The insights that all members of a campus community then can get from the students' responses may help them to understand how globally their students are thinking. The difference between having hunches about how students think, versus having even high-level actual evidence from what students actually say, can have a big impact on leaders' ability to make productive decisions about course curricula or areas of emphasis.

A Final Note: Global Thinking on Campus

During alumni interviews for our alma mater last year, one memorable applicant explained his primary interest in biology. He spoke with gusto about his lab work and described his fascination with medicine, explaining how he had shadowed doctors at his local hospital. Then, he said something pretty remarkable. "But I also want to minor or potentially double major in international relations," he declared. He went on to speak about how important he believes it is to understand different cultures and how countries each make decisions, particularly in today's ever increasingly connected world. "Yes, I want to be a doctor—but I also want to be able to talk about issues that affect people hundreds or thousands of miles away from where I practice. I want to be a responsible citizen." These are the students that give us hope; they are the ones we had in mind when writing this chapter.

Some students will choose to devote a significant portion of their time at college, or even their lives, to global understanding and action. Others may opt to take a simple action here and there to better understand their fellow humans, particularly those who speak a different native language or whose passport cover is emblazoned with a different design. The world will almost undoubtedly continue to globalize, and we anticipate that future generations of prospective college students will be increasingly interested in the issues that affect their communities and also those a world away. Higher education has a big role to play in that evolution, and we are optimistic that both college leaders and students themselves will rise to the challenge.

A Success Story in Detail: Small World Coffee Hour—Promoting Global-Mindedness at the University of Minnesota

In 1991, administrators at the University of Minnesota were alerted to a hateful attack against an international student. "Go Back to Where You Came From," a sign jeered.

Campus leaders evaluated the possible courses of action. Though publicly denouncing the xenophobic message was one option, it didn't feel like enough. They decided to do something to foster the development of a globally minded community of students through authentic connection with their peers from around the world. This way, something negative could serve as a launching point for increasing interconnectedness, cultural curiosity, and understanding.

With that, the first iteration of Small World Coffee Hour (SWCH) was born.

SWCH Program Structure

Today, the Small World Coffee Hour program at the University of Minnesota is student-led with support from the International Student and Scholar Services office. Members plan and host regular events—each oriented around a different country and topic—that inspire students to connect with peers and learn about different cultures. Events always include a traditional food item from the featured country, importantly not as "bait" to get students to attend, but rather as an accessible way to connect with students and make them feel at ease. After all, as program advisor Alex Cleberg points out, "Many people's first experience with cultural difference comes in the form of food."

There are two student teams that produce SWCH events: Program Leadership (including a treasurer, marketing specialist, social media lead, supply chain manager, and data analyst) and

Project Managers (each of whom "owns" an event and oversees all planning and execution). Project managers collaborate with other student groups before planned events to set themes and identify countries of focus, and they meet several times during the day of an event to make sure everything is set up properly. As event participants arrive, each is asked to fill out a name tag that includes their answer to questions such as, "How many jobs have you had?" "What is your favorite festival?" and "What is your favorite musical genre?" These name tags have been a hallmark of SWCH for nearly twenty years. As the programs evolved, leaders have emphasized their importance in inviting students to engage in comfortable conversation that ultimately contributes to drawing out unique cultural awareness.

As students mix and mingle, SWCH leaders assigned the role of "social butterflies" proactively engage students who may be attending by themselves or who seem a bit timid. SWCH understands that introducing oneself to strangers (or, in the words of the SWCH team, "potential friends") is done differently between cultures and carries different levels of anxiety depending on one's personality and experience. The SWCH social butterflies chat with isolated students to identify an interest of theirs and then introduce them to other students based on that element.

Next, project managers give short presentations introducing attendees to the theme of the event. The presentations are short (three slides maximum) and always conclude with an interactive activity such as a dance, quiz, or demonstration of a childhood game from the country. Participants then navigate to topic tables, each featuring either an artifact (something students can experience sensorially) or an activity (a game, quiz, or challenge). Sometimes topic tables feature traditional garments that can be worn. Cleberg recalls hearing a student say, "Seeing my new friends, or what I call my family, here in Minnesota wear traditional Sri Lankan clothes made me feel even more connected to myself. Seeing that was like a bridge between my Minnesotan self and my Sri Lankan self." As social media became prominent and selfies more popular, Alex became concerned that taking photos with the garments would be interpreted as cultural appropriation. As a proactive measure, SWCH instilled a philosophy that this practice was an invitation, not an appropriation. An invitation is wearing traditional clothes at the request of someone who has the cultural authority to do so.

As students engage with the topic tables, they gather tickets that allow them to enter the line and collect a small plate of food. Although there is a modest budget (between $500 to $1,000 per event) to the food during each session, SWCH student leaders have made an effort to reduce costs by soliciting donations from local vendors. They established a successful partnership with an Australian entrepreneur who owned a coffee shop, and they also collaborated with a couple from Honduras who agreed to donate coffee from their shop. In that way, not only are they reducing the cost for the event, but students are also helping to promote and publicize a local business. Between coffee, food, and supplies, the SWCH team strives to involve the community as much as possible, particularly those who are immigrants themselves.

Since the SWCH programming is funded by the student services fee, each event is open to the entire undergraduate body, graduate students, professors, and alumni. On average, the program serves two thousand participants per year, about three hundred of which are unique attendees.

"Mash-Ups"

In recent years, Small World Coffee Hour has introduced a unique idea to encourage student cooperation: something that advisor Alex Cleberg refers to as "mash-ups." Project managers choose two student groups that on the surface seem to have little, if anything in common. The clubs are asked to collaborate with each other and the SWCH leadership teams to produce an event that showcases the common ground between them. This is also an ingenious way to engage with students who may not have otherwise naturally sought out an SWCH event. Because each event is publicized by both groups and involves something that is at least tangentially of interest to the students within it, participation in the event is expanded beyond an international audience or students who already consider themselves to be globally minded.

One example sought to involve students from two clubs that superficially would seem to have nothing at all in common: the EDM (electronic dance music) Club and the Russian Speaking Society. Club leaders were asked to collaborate on a SWCH event, somehow finding the common ground between their two interests. Amazingly, they did. The overlap was a Russian subculture associated with hardbass and Gopnik culture. Each of the groups had something to contribute to the conversation based on their interests or experiences, even though members may never have interacted before.

Communicating with Others

A 2019 University of Minnesota graduate and former SWCH presentation manager remembers interviewing for an electrical engineering job as he wrapped up his undergraduate experience. "Interviewers would be looking for three main things," he recalls. "A degree, research and internships, and leadership. As they scrolled down my résumé, they would see a section where I have Small World Coffee Hour and would ask to hear more about it." In his explanation, the student highlighted the leadership—specifically communication—skills that he learned through participating in SWCH. One specific example stands out.

"We were having a Malaysian night, and as the coordinator I had to speak with the Malaysian group and get the information about what they needed for their event," he recalls. "I then communicated that information to our supply chain manager who was from Russia. I also had to speak with our promoter, who was from India. I am from Oman, and all of this communication is going on in the United States."

The student's interviewers explained that in a work environment he would be interacting with people from different majors and backgrounds, and that his communication skills were exactly what they were looking for in their incoming employees. Today, the graduate works in project management for a technology consulting company where he continues to use the skills that he developed through Small World Coffee Hour.

Owning Leadership

Rada Kolarova was first introduced to Small World Coffee Hour when she volunteered at an event alongside her mother, who was a graduate student and SWCH member at the University of Minnesota while Rada was in high school. When Rada was accepted to college herself, she applied to SWCH before even arriving on campus so that she could dive right in during her first semester. Her tenure as a SWCH participant and leader would later be known fondly as "the Rada years," and she won the President's Student Leadership and Service Award in recognition of her impact on the campus.

During a recent conversation, Rada spoke about the way that SWCH helped her to own her ability as a leader. She mentioned how advisor Alex Cleberg was instrumental in this: he would say to students, "Okay, your role is 'analyst.' What recommendations are you proposing based on the data?" Students were expected to contribute to the team specifically based on their particular role, and in doing so they gained confidence in their own abilities. When Rada ascended to a position of power within SWCH, she had to learn how to be comfortable with being a recognized source of authority.

Participating in Small World Coffee Hour also helped Rada understand more about what she was seeking in a full-time professional role. "SWCH set the standard for being intrinsically motivated toward the mission of my organization. The feeling of working for an organization that I'm proud of and that supports values that I care about—I definitely felt that I was chasing that after college. It helped build up that gut instinct of knowing whether I was in the right role." She also learned how much she enjoys training other people and the value that her naturally extroverted personality can bring in daily interactions. These lessons have informed Rada's work post-graduation and prompted her to be persistent in finding a role where she could capitalize on her interests and character traits.

Program Outcomes and Metrics

After each Small World Coffee Hour event, the Program Leadership team debriefs and captures written reflections on how each component was executed on a shared Google Sheet, which helps carry forward lessons learned for future teams and events. Each leader gives reflections based on their specific position; for example, the analyst reports trends in attendance by specific class year and major, and the social media manager shares reports of online engagement. They also carefully track total participants, percentage of international participants, and projected versus actual event costs. Student participants are also surveyed at the end of each semester. In the five semester reports that we analyzed, 67.3 percent (316/469) of respondents indicated that they made at least one new friend from a different culture through their participation in SWCH events. In addition, 71.3 percent (253/355) reported that their participation at least moderately encouraged them to seek out and partake in a global experience (e.g., learning abroad, internship abroad, vacation or work in another country).

Selected student responses on the impact of the program:

- "SWCH helped me in having new friends, and from them I have learned a lot more about their language and culture."

- "SWCH events have been some of the best Fridays of college for me. I have gone to many during my four years here at the U, and I meet someone new every single time. One event this fall even helped me reconnect with a friend I made during freshman year. She and I have hung out several times since and are now in regular contact. Thank you!"

- "I have made friends that come from around the world who have showed me aspects of their culture that I never knew existed."

- "Through this event, I was able to discuss some interesting topics with people from different countries. They are always different from what I think. It made me learn to see the world from many angles."

Looking Ahead

As other colleges and universities consider possibly implementing programming that mirrors Small World Coffee Hour, a key element that Rada Kolarova mentioned during our conversation is the important of consistency. When she was a part of SWCH, students initially had to apply for grants to cover event costs— which took time away from planning and introduced a great deal of uncertainty about calendaring and sustainability. After Rada and her colleagues secured dedicated funding directly from the university, they could focus exclusively on making events as high quality as possible rather than worrying about how they would pay for them. Funding consistency also allowed for regular events that students could rely on and plan for in advance.

Small World Coffee Hour at the University of Minnesota was built in response to an unacceptable event on campus that university leaders chose to confront by expanding opportunities for students' understanding and growth. We encourage other colleges and universities to be creative in adapting the core model for their own campus needs, bearing in mind the central idea of bringing students together to create something of mutual benefit. The University of Minnesota initiative has proven clear benefits, particularly as a return on a relatively small budget. It seems reasonable that any campus, regardless of its size or financial health, could implement a similar student-run initiative.

11

Bringing It All Together

Suggestions for Getting Started

This book offers many action steps for colleges and universities to initiate, or in many cases to continue, their ongoing quest for sustained improvement. We want to stress the overarching theme or key idea or unifying principle that can help any reader to bring our many suggestions together.

Our unifying theme is that the suggestions in this book will be *most productive when different constituencies and groups on a campus are willing, able, and indeed incentivized, to work collaboratively*. Each group of people on any campus is, after all, committed to the common goal of enhancing their undergraduates' experience at their college. Some colleges and universities already are quite good at building on this collegial culture and commitment. Other universities are perhaps more balkanized. Especially at large universities, it may not come so easily to have different constituencies working together. We make no judgments here about why some campuses practically radiate more of a collaborative spirit than others. Each university has its unique culture and history. We simply urge all universities, regardless of their starting point, to work toward as much productive collaboration as possible among their various constituent groups.

We therefore conclude this book with a series of concrete suggestions about how any university can enhance its level of innovation while maximizing its on-campus collegiality. Our hope is campuses can begin to organize their efforts toward building a collaborative culture so that such efforts generate an even greater good for students than the sum of what any individual or small group on campus working separately could produce. This "culture building" can be hard. It takes real effort. The good part is it should be one step forward for a broad group of colleges and universities: private and public, rich and nowhere close to rich, selective or unselective. We believe this principle of finding evidence-based ways to help students improve their learning and overall experiences, at any college or university, is a widely shared goal.

Embedding Innovation into Ongoing University Activity: Getting Started

We hope various suggestions throughout this book's chapters are appealing to readers. We hope also that many readers can begin—even with some modification—to implement them. An obvious question is "Where to start?" This is often the heart of the question that Light is asked during his various campus visits. Both college leaders and faculty are eager to hear some basic principles and ideas about how to maximize their chances for success. Of course each university needs to adapt such principles to their own campus cultures, histories, and norms. A large enrollment public university may choose to begin very differently than a small, all-women's college. Yet even with these differences, each college or university needs to figure out how to begin. We conclude this book by offering our recommendations for how to get up and running.

1. Choose and Organize Projects That Can Lead to Real Policy Change

Often the questions facing a university can be exciting to discuss and to explore. Yet answering some fascinating questions—even with data in hand—sometimes generates zero findings that have specific, policy implications for students, faculty, staff, and for the university's leadership. Other questions are equally fascinating, yet they are different—finding answers to this second group of questions *could* lead to useful policy implications for enhancing student success. In other words, answering certain questions may not lead to any change on university campuses, while generating evidence-based answers to other questions can actually lead to concrete change.

We strongly urge readers to emphasize efforts that have policy implications. What exactly do we mean by this? We urge identifying questions that, upon conducting research and collecting evidence, can lead to students or faculty or staff at a college doing something *differently and more effectively. Next week, next month, or next year.* It is crucial to keep our eye on the main goal: a college or university wants to learn how it can do something better. Or learn to organize an activity more effectively. Always for the benefit of students. In other words, sometimes we will want to change something. An innovative idea or finding that seems "interesting" yet has zero implications for anyone changing anything they do, is not our goal.

To illustrate: an example of a question with little or no policy implication is "How well do students at our college write?" We think most readers might find this a fascinating question, and would love to know the answer at any college. So suppose twenty professors and staff invest a thousand hours exploring this question. After extensive hard work and data gathering, they finally come up with solid evidence that, "on average, our students write pretty well. . . ." Then what? That finding has zero policy implications. It does not suggest anyone should change any kind of teaching or studying or how writing homework is assigned, nor change any other sort of behavior. It doesn't lead to any improvement by anyone. It doesn't help students do their work more effectively. It doesn't help faculty members teach more effectively. We acknowledge "How well do our students write?" is an interesting question to ask, and the answer may well be worth knowing. Yet the big point is that posing such questions don't lead to college improvement. They don't offer specific steps for anyone to help students do something better. These questions are not "policy questions." They are simply "interesting."

In contrast, suppose we slightly rephrase that question about students' writing to become "Why do some students improve their writing dramatically while at college, while other students do not?"

Exploring that issue leads to a host of valuable follow-up questions that can actually influence policy. What are the differences (if any) between what those two groups of students are experiencing in their classrooms? When the two groups of students actually sit to write, what are they doing differently? What if anything are their writing instructors or other instructors doing differently? How can we increase the number of students in the group that improves, while decreasing the number of students in the stagnant group? Finding answers to questions such as these clearly can help more students to succeed, to do well, to improve their writing.

Findings from a project such as this one could lead faculty to adjust their teaching (e.g., teach students different strategies for revising their work more effectively). Or they might lead to students studying, practicing, and developing their writing outside of their classes in different ways. Findings might help students learn how to use feedback and comments from others on their writing more effectively than they do now. The goal is to emphasize turning up findings that can help everyone at a university—from leaders to faculty to individual students—to each do their jobs more effectively and enjoyably.

2. Begin by Choosing Projects That Are Likely to Succeed. Develop Momentum. Don't Begin with the Most Complicated Questions

For colleges where embedding a culture of continuous improvement is not already underway, developing campus-wide support for trying out new ideas—for exploring new questions—should be high priority. Beginning with complex and long-term initiatives or projects, where outcomes may not be known for several years, probably is not the ideal place to begin. Rather, suppose you start by choosing a relatively simple project that will yield results fairly quickly. Ideally, select a project to begin where—if you get useful results—then stakeholders at your university will react by saying, "Some of these new ideas and results are good. They are straightforward. These results may even be helpful to me in my work. . . . I see how this entire process of emphasizing data gathering and experimentation can be helpful."

To illustrate, consider two very different research questions. The first is a sustained, multi-faculty exploration of the important and complex question "How well are we doing with helping our students to develop their critical thinking skills?" The second is "Do our first-year students have an adult on campus to contact for support—or for information or just to let them know—in case of an emergency back home?" Which of these two options, both worthy, would be a better target for a campus just beginning to implement ideas like the ones we describe in this book?

We have a strong preference for starting with the second research question—making sure every first-year student at a college or university has a specific adult (or two or three), whom they would feel comfortable contacting (and know how to reach) in a time of need. Why is this, seemingly simple, faculty question appealing? First, the basic inquiry about students' well-being is an important issue. So getting an answer would be likely to garner widespread support across many campus groups. It is also the type of project where a dean, working together with a small group of faculty, staff, and undergraduates, can generally get a fairly quick answer. The dean can learn what the situation is right now and do it reasonably quickly (can nearly all of our first-year students immediately think of and name an adult on campus they would call? The answer is either yes or no.).

Third, if improvements need to be made because too many first-year students simply don't have or cannot identify such a person now, this finding can lead to a policy change that can be implemented fairly quickly. If such a project is started in September, it should be possible to have specific results, and even to implement specific changes and improvements, by midyear or spring. We do not have here a complex, hard to understand, multiyear investigation. It is a short exploration of an important question about the well-being of many students at a university. Starting with such projects is a helpful way to build university-wide support for innovative data collection. It can be a good way to begin trying new ideas, and making evidence-based improvements.

In contrast, the first research question about critical thinking is much more nuanced. It is an important question. Yet it would take much longer—perhaps even several years—to investigate thoroughly and rigorously. Though very much a worthwhile question, it may not offer the most effective place for a campus to begin. Instead, such elaborate explorations could take place in year two, or year three, of a university's effort to try new ideas. The bottom line is that we strongly recommend beginning with simpler challenges to improve the quality of students' experiences. Coming up with helpful results quickly, sharing the results widely on campus, and then putting improved policies into place to widespread student acclaim, seems a constructive first step for building broad university support toward a longer-term series of initiatives, experiments, and innovations.

3. Treasure Small Gains and Small Improvements for Your Campus

It is rare for educational innovations at any level, including at universities, to immediately transform everything. Suppose a university finds that women are not pursuing the physical sciences in large numbers, and the leadership and faculty want to increase those numbers. If in year one the fraction of women pursuing physical sciences is 25 percent, and then by trying an innovative advising or teaching format that fraction rises ONLY to 27 percent next year and to 30 percent the year after, some critics may say, "That gain is so small, it doesn't really matter. . . ." We disagree. Think of making small gains year after year as a rough analogy to thinking about compound interest of just 2 or 3 percent annually. In any one year, the changes may not amount to much. Yet over a period of time, the positive effects become too great to ignore.

4. Consider Starting with a Small-Scale Pilot Project

If you want to assess how much your students' quantitative reasoning skills are improving during their first year at your university, you certainly don't need to begin by collecting a baseline on day one from four thousand newly arriving first-year students. Nor is it necessary to assess that number at the end of spring during their first year. The time and effort expenditure for that sort of data collection would be immense. Rather, it may be preferable to instead get careful samples from only fifty or one hundred students. That will enable you to refine your questions or prompts for the following year's students. This can become the first step in a process of steady learning.

Then the following year you can increase the sample size to two hundred or three hundred. To be clear, you probably *never* need to get every single student to participate in such a data collection project. Samples of one hundred students will convey all the main points. Author Richard Light leads these projects at Harvard. The focus nearly always is on trying to identify important, reasonably large effects. Light's work rarely uses samples of more than one hundred students. That is less than 2 percent of the entire undergraduate student population at his university. Yet speaking as a statistician, Light can report it is a solid sample size.

5. Don't Get Too Caught Up in the Details

When implementing a new initiative or idea, it can be tempting to try to engineer every bit of the process. Though it is indeed wise to be detail oriented, we urge leaders to keep your eye on the big goal. Suppose for example you want to explore men's satisfaction with their undergraduate advising experience at your college and to compare those results to women's satisfaction. Does it really matter whether 80.9 vs. 81.6 percent of men report they are quite happy with advising? All you need to know is the ballpark. The ballpark clearly is around 80 percent. Suppose women report 65 percent satisfaction. Would it change anything if the honest-to-goodness correct answer is either 64 percent or 66 percent rather than the 65 percent our modest-size sample turns up? Most of the time it doesn't. The big finding from these modest sample sizes would nonetheless be compelling to most anyone: men are overall more satisfied than women with their advising experience at this college. This provides fodder for further discussion and thoughtful development of an intervention to change something, whatever it takes to help more women students feel they are getting good advising. Importantly, gathering such data with modest-size samples allows campus leaders to *start somewhere*.

6. Build a "Coalition of the Willing"

We have urged readers to engage faculty members with this work. In fact, invite faculty to take a lead role. Yet, do you need *all* faculty to participate, in order to get started? Certainly not. For example, suppose at a college with a faculty of 500, only a small fraction—maybe 5 or 6 percent—choose to participate in early efforts to press ahead with a certain innovation or to explore new way of doing almost anything. This is wonderful! Let's celebrate that thirty faculty have become engaged and are innovating. In fact, if the results achieved by the "only 30" faculty are impressive and positive, each of those 30 people has ten friends and colleagues on campus. So in the second year, you may well have 80 to 100 or more faculty participating. Then in the third year, it could become 150 to 300 as even more professors see a new idea working well for their colleagues, and so they happily choose to voluntarily adopt it. Why wouldn't they? Most faculty take enormous pride in their teaching and engagement with students. They would love for their teaching and their work with students to be successful as possible. Don't let the hesitancy or resistance or lack of interest from some faculty members hold back those who are enthusiastic. Even a small- to modest-size group of volunteers can begin to design and try implementing productive innovations, whether for advising, or for teaching, or for creating outside-of-class activities to enhance students' experiences.

7. Encourage Faculty to Lead Some Innovations and Initiatives

Ensuring that faculty members assume a central leadership role in the implementation of new ideas can become the difference between success or failure. Directives from campus leaders can be wonderfully helpful to offer some guidelines for new initiatives, yet it will be difficult to sustain lasting change without substantial faculty buy-in. One such experience especially stands out in Light's memory. Several years ago, he invited a distinguished professor of psychology to participate in a small group that would design and assess the value of a new, innovative effort for teaching social sciences. The professor seemed enthusiastic (that he was Light's longtime friend didn't hurt), and his immediate response to Light's invitation to participate was, "It all depends on who will be in charge of our work and who designs it and leads it. In other words, who will set our agenda?"

Light was taken aback and responded by saying, "YOU will of course be in charge. YOU will set the agenda. You as a professor, working with several faculty colleagues, plus with some advising staff and even some students, will be in charge and will shape what we do. . . . Why do you ask this question?" The psychology professor laughed and responded, "Then count me in. If I am in charge, I am happy to assume this new activity will be worth my time. If these new projects all will be a wish list from our president or provost, I love them both, yet you need to remember I didn't become a professor here at our wonderful university to be the president's research assistant."

8. Clarify How Your University Defines "Student Success"

There is no single definition of success for all students. For some, it is simply achieving a high GPA and landing a high-paying job. For others, it is building relationships and perhaps even meeting their life partner. For a different group, it is engaging in academic or extracurricular exploration that wasn't possible in high school. And for still others, it can be meeting new people from around the world and gaining exposure to new perspectives and ways of thinking.

It is critical for faculty members to remember that their goal is not to just clone themselves. At most colleges, fewer than 5 percent of students even consider becoming college faculty members. So the goal of faculty should be to prepare students for life, for work, for productive citizenship. The goal should not be to prepare most of their students to become professors—just like themselves. Designing and trying out various ideas and innovations targeted to prepare students for their constantly changing varieties of work after graduation, and for being productive citizens more broadly, is a goal worth keeping in mind. At most colleges and universities, the goal is not to have professors working to train younger versions of themselves. It is to help students achieve a far broader variety of goals.

9. Involve Students in as Many Efforts as Possible

In this book we offer many actionable suggestions for a college to try and to implement. The more that any college can involve students in the process, the more likely an innovation is to succeed. Many examples in our book illustrate this simple idea. Students play a major role in Small World Coffee Hour. New programs we describe in this book (Skill Development Workshops; Ten Big Ideas, Ten Professors, Ten Minutes Each) were either suggested by students or developed by students. Students can describe their actual experiences, they can help to formulate good questions to ask their fellow students for gathering data, and students are almost always delighted to be asked to do either of these.

10. Ensure That Senior Administrative Leadership Provides Support and Encouragement

Most innovative ideas don't just spring up on their own. Often it is college leaders who can guide an entire campus community to the starting blocks. These are leaders who can inspire, motivate, and sometimes even offer incentives to faculty and students to try new ideas and put new ways of doing things into action. The difference between a pretty good leader and a great leader is that the latter will ideally get the process of innovation up and running. An outstanding campus leader will embed an innovative spirit into many of the day-to-day operations of a university.

11. Have a Plan for Disseminating Positive and Helpful Findings

As campuses implement new ideas, they will inevitably learn along the way what works well and what does not. Suppose a new way of teaching one introductory science class leads to measurably improved student learning, more time spent on science outside of the classroom or lab, and deeper engagement with the field. Perhaps it also leads to far more students choosing to sign up for advanced classes on that topic. This appears to be great news. Should the university strive to keep that finding a secret? Of course not. Each campus should have a plan in place for sharing success stories. If the breakthrough in great teaching comes from one or two physics professors, one would like to think that other faculty members—maybe in physics, or science more broadly, or maybe even across other academic disciplines— would appreciate being informed and learning about new and successful initiatives. Each professor can then decide for themself whether a new way to successfully engage large classrooms of students in physics classes might also be useful for classes in history or economics or philosophy. This information exchange can happen at faculty meetings, or through a campus or student newspaper, or in conference settings. The big point is to share positive news widely. Sometimes small, positive breakthroughs in one department or for one student activity can have widespread and positive ripple effects far more broadly than just within one university.

A Final Note

We conclude on a personal note. We hope the many suggestions and examples across all the chapters motivate each individual at any college or university to value collaborative campus efforts for building a culture of continuous improvement. Authors Light and Jegla each attended the same great university, separated by many years. Some efforts to develop innovations in teaching, and for student advising, were already part of the day-to-day life of the university's leadership, faculty members, staff, and even in the lives of many students, when each of us were undergraduates. For Light, that was a long time ago. For Jegla, it was not so long ago. What brought us together to write this book, since we represent two different generations, is the sense that even our beloved alma mater, which has been a leader for years, and does so many things so well, has not yet perfected all the suggestions in this book. Our takeaway insight is that while many of America's great universities have done a good job with innovation and experimentation, and nearly all are loaded with goodwill, a large number might wish to initiate even more widespread efforts to try new ways of doing things.

For both authors, our visits to so many other universities are almost always wonderfully positive. At the same time, they often turn up enormous potential for improving students' experiences based on rigorous, evidence-based explorations. We hope this book encourages many others connected with a college or university to initiate this sort of work and to make a difference. This is true for readers regardless of your precise "role" at a college or university. We believe this spirit applies whether someone comes as a faculty member to work every day at any one of America's enormously diverse colleges and universities, or as an employee in one of many staff categories. Certainly, this spirit of making a difference for your university applies even to each student. Even the newest first-year student has an opportunity, from their early days on campus, to play a role in shaping the environment of their broader campus community for years to come.

We invite each reader to give some thought to how they can make a positive difference—to think about how they can work, whether as an individual or collaboratively, to make the undergraduate experience even better. When new ideas are tried on a campus, rigorously assessed, and the evidence is compelling that they work well, students on that campus win big. Even better, when other colleges and universities learn about such successes and begin to adopt and adapt such new ideas for enhancing student success, the payoff for literally millions of students can be profound.

REFERENCES

Chapter 1

Bhidé, Amar. *The Origin and Evolution of New Businesses*. Oxford, UK: Oxford University Press, 2003.

"Column: UC's Harsh Response to a Student Strike Shows It's a Business More Than a University." *Los Angeles Times*, March 6, 2020. https://www.latimes.com/business/story/2020-03-06/uc-grad-student-strike.

Drucker, Peter. Quoted in Shep Hyken, "Drucker Said 'Culture Eats Strategy For Breakfast' and Enterprise Rent-A-Car Proves It." *Forbes*, December 5, 2015. https://www.forbes.com/sites/shephyken/2015/12/05/drucker-said-culture-eats-strategy-for-breakfast-and-enterprise-rent-a-car-proves-it/?sh=239edb062749.

Ellis, Lindsay. "How UT-Austin's Bold Plan for Reinvention Went Belly Up." *Chronicle of Higher Education*, July 23, 2020. https://www.chronicle.com/article/how-ut-austins-bold-plan-for-reinvention-went-belly-up/?cid=gen_sign_in.

Ferrell, Jason Don. "The Effectiveness of Synchronous Massive Online Courses at the University of Texas at Austin." TexasScholarWorks. December 1, 2017. https://repositories.lib.utexas.edu/handle/2152/63820.

"How a Math Class Sparked Students' Engagement in Their Community." *Chronicle of Higher Education*, May 2, 2019. https://www.chronicle.com/newsletter/teaching/2019-05-02?cid2=gen_login_refresh&cid=gen_sign_in.

"Meet Swarthmore." Swarthmore College. October 19, 2020. https://www.swarthmore.edu/meet-swarthmore.

Patel, Vimal. "Grad Students and UC-Santa Cruz Chancellor Say Strike Will Have Lasting Impact on Higher Ed. They Disagree on What That Will Be." *Chronicle of Higher Education*, July 23, 2020. https://www.chronicle.com/article/grad-students-and-uc-santa-cruz-chancellor-say-strike-will-have-lasting-impact-on-higher-ed-they-disagree-on-what-that-will-be/.

"Statistician Lynne Steuerle Schofield '99 Receives National Teaching Award." Swarthmore College. News & Events. July 11, 2019. https://www.swarthmore.edu/news-events/statistician-lynne-steuerle-schofield-99-receives-national-teaching-award.

"University Offers First-Ever Synchronous Massive Online Course." University of Texas at Austin. UT News. August 26, 2013. https://news.utexas.edu/2013/08/26/university-offers-first-ever-synchronous-massive-online-course/.

Chapter 2

Robinson, Darryl. "I Went to Some of D.C.'s Best Schools. I Was Still Unprepared for College." *Washington Post*, April 13, 2012. https://www.washingtonpost.com/opinions/i-went-to-one-of-dcs-best-high-schools-i-was-still-unprepared-for-college/2012/04/13/gIQAqQQAFT_story.html.

Chapter 3

"From the Dean of Students: Get Out of Your Comfort Zone." University of Colorado Boulder. CU Boulder Today. September 26, 2017. https://www.colorado.edu/today/2017/09/26/dean-students-get-out-your-comfort-zone.

"Office of the President." Ithaca College. https://www.ithaca.edu/office-president.

Wang, Lucy. "Comping Harvard." *Harvard Crimson*, November 2, 2017. Accessed March 14, 2021. https://www.thecrimson.com/article/2017/11/2/comping-harvard/.

Chapter 4

Carr, P. J., and M. Kefalas. *Hollowing Out the Middle: The Rural Brain Drain and What It Means for America.* Boston: Beacon Press, 2009.

Chingos, Matthew. "Can We Fix Undermatching in Higher Ed? Would It Matter If We Did?" Brookings. January 15, 2014. https://www.brookings.edu/research/can-we-fix-undermatching-in-higher-ed-would-it-matter-if-we-did/.

Crozier, McKinsey. "The Rural Class." *Yale Daily News*, February 14, 2020. https://yaledailynews.com/blog/2020/02/14/crozier-the-rural-class/.

Gettinger, Aaron. "One Reason Rural Students Don't Go to College: Colleges Don't Go to Them." NPR.org. March 6, 2019. https://www.npr.org/2019/03/06/697098684/one-reason-rural-students-dont-go-to-college-colleges-don-t-go-to-them.

Giancola, Jennifer, and Richard Kahlenberg. "True Merit: Ensuring Our Brightest Students Have Access to Our Best Colleges and Universities." Jack Kent Cooke Foundation. January 2016. https://www.jkcf.org/research

/true-merit-ensuring-our-brightest-students-have-access-to-our-best
-colleges-and-universities/.

Gross, Bethany, and Alice Opalka. "Too Many Schools Leave Learning to Chance during the Pandemic." Center on Reinventing Public Education. Seattle, WA: University of Washington Bothell, 2020.

Harris, Adam. "When Disadvantaged Students Overlook Elite Colleges." *The Atlantic*, April 18, 2018. https://www.theatlantic.com/education/archive /2018/04/when-disadvantaged-students-overlook-elite-colleges/558371/.

Hillman, Nicholas, and Taylor Weichman. *Education Deserts: The Continued Significance of "Place" in the Twenty-First Century*. In *Viewpoints: Voices from the Field*. Washington, DC: American Council on Education. 2016.

Hoxby, Caroline, and Christopher Avery. "The Missing 'One-Offs': The Hidden Supply of High-Achieving, Low-Income Students." Brookings Papers on Economic Activity (pdf), pp. 14, 20, 41. Spring 2013. https://www .brookings.edu/wp-content/uploads/2016/07/2013a_hoxby.pdf.

"Percentage of Persons Ages 18–29 Enrolled in Colleges or Universities, by Age Group, 4-Category Local, and Sex." National Center for Education Statistics. 2015. https://nces.ed.gov/surveys/ruraled/tables/b.3.b.-1.asp.

"Urban-Rural Ambassadors Summer Institute." Eastern Oregon University. Spring 2021. https://www.eou.edu/urban-rural/.

Chapter 5

Goodman, Joshua. "Low-Cost Interventions to Reduce Anonymity in Large Classes." Harvard Kennedy School. Prepared for SLATE Working Paper Series. SLATE: Strengthening Learning and Teaching Excellence. June 25, 2014. https://projects.iq.harvard.edu/files/hks-slate-gallery/files /goodman_-_low-cost_interventions_to_reduce_anonymity_in_large _classes_final.pdf.

Levy, Dan, and Joshua Bookin. "Cold Calling and Web Postings: Do They Improve Students' Preparation and Learning?" Harvard Kennedy School. Prepared for SLATE Working Paper Series. SLATE: Strengthening Learning and Teaching Excellence. May 31, 2020. https://projects.iq.harvard .edu/files/hks-slate-gallery/files/cold_calling_and_web_postings_paper _for_slate_working_paper_series_fv_final.pdf.

Chapter 6

Light, Richard J. "An Actual Design and Set of Questions." "MPP Core: How Much Are Our Students Learning?" Results for the Harvard Kennedy School faculty from the SLATE Assessment of Students' Learning project. Academic year 2012.

Light, Richard J. "Report of the Harvard Assessment Seminars: Explorations in Teaching and Learning." Second Report. Published by Harvard University. Updated January 2019.

Sommers, Nancy. "How Much Are Students Improving Their Writing?" Report on writing improvement of Harvard undergraduates. Prepared for the Derek Bok Center for Teaching and Learning. Harvard University. Fall 2016.

Chapter 7

"All Boundaries Are Permeable." Quote from Dean of Students Archie Epps, Harvard College. In Richard J. Light, "Making the Most of College: Students Speak Their Minds," Chapter 7. Cambridge, MA: Harvard University Press. 2004.

Angelo, Thomas. Prepared for Report of the Harvard Assessment Seminars. Second Report. Cambridge, MA: Harvard University Press. Updated January 2019.

Bushey, Barbara. Prepared for Report of the Harvard Assessment Seminars. Second Report. Cambridge, MA: Harvard University Press. Updated January 2019.

"Escape from the Lecture Hall." *Pennsylvania Gazette*, May 3, 2013. https://thepenngazette.com/escape-from-the-lecture-hall/.

Shea, Christopher. "Harvard Thinks Big." *Wall Street Journal*, February 23, 2011. https://www.wsj.com/articles/BL-IMB-1878.

Walsh, Colleen. "Harvard Thinks Big." *Harvard Gazette*, July 26, 2019. https://news.harvard.edu/gazette/story/2010/02/harvard-thinks-big/.

Chapter 8

The Kuumba Singers of Harvard College. https://kuumbasingers.org/.

Sysadmin. "Other Co-Operatives in Oberlin." Oberlin Student Cooperative Association. May 11, 2016. http://osca.wilder.oberlin.edu/coops/oberlin.

Takavarasha, Matthew. "Tara Westover on Being 'Educated.'" *Emory Wheel*, October 2, 2019. https://emorywheel.com/tara-westover-on-being-educated/#:~:text=Another%20byproduct%20of%20Westover's%20idiosyncratic,%2C%20brainwashed%2C%E2%80%9D%20she%20said.

"Teachly: A Research Project." Harvard Initiative for Learning and Teaching (HILT). Accessed March 14, 2021. https://hilt.harvard.edu/funding-opportunities/previously-awarded-projects/projects/teachly-a-research-project/.

Chapter 9

"10 Colleges Where the Most Alumni Donate." *U.S. News & World Report.* Accessed March 14, 2021. https://www.usnews.com/education/best-colleges /the-short-list-college/articles/universities-where-the-most-alumni -donate.

"Hive Internships Projects." Wellesley College. https://www.wellesley.edu /careereducation/hiveinternshipprojects.

Chapter 10

"Leaving vs. Leading: Debating Study Abroad." *Harvard Crimson*, December 1, 2003. Accessed March 14, 2021. https://www.thecrimson.com/article /2003/12/1/leaving-vs-leading-debating-study-abroad/.

INDEX